November 2002 (revised)

FISH CONSUMPTION AND ENVIRONMENTAL JUSTICE

A Report developed from the National Environmental Justice Advisory Council Meeting of December 3-6, 2001

A Federal Advisory Committee to the U.S. Environmental Protection Agency

PREFACE

"[L]et everybody know that this environment belongs to all of us, and when you contaminate the water and contaminate the fish, you are contaminating all of us.

I tell you, I don't know if you know anything about Isaiah. Isaiah was a great prophet you know, and he said, "I have played, I have taught, and I have preached, and I wonder if anybody is listening." So I want to know if anybody is listening, and if you are listening I want to know what are you going to do about it?"

Remarks of Daisy Carter, Project AWAKE
Member of the NEJAC Fish Consumption Work Group
and its Air and Water Subcommittee

December 4, 2001
Meeting of the National Environmental Justice Advisory Council
Seattle, Washington

ACKNOWLEDGMENTS

The NEJAC acknowledges, with deep appreciation, the Fish Consumption Work Group and the NEJAC Report consultant, Catherine O'Neill, Associate Professor, Seattle University School of Law, for their outstanding contributions in developing this broad public policy issue report.

DISCLAIMER

This Report and recommendations have been written as part of the activities of the National Environmental Justice Advisory Council, a public advisory committee providing independent advice and recommendations on the issue of environmental justice to the Administrator and other officials of the United States Environmental Protection Agency (EPA).

This report has not been reviewed for approval by the EPA, and hence, its contents and recommendations do not necessarily represent the views and the policies of the Agency, nor of other agencies in the Executive Branch of the federal government.

INTERPRETIVE NOTES

The National Environmental Justice Advisory Council (NEJAC) is a federal advisory committee to the United States Environmental Protection Agency (EPA). This Report, therefore, focuses on those environmental justice issues raised by compromised aquatic ecosystems that EPA is empowered to address. That is to say, it examines, in the main, efforts that might be undertaken by EPA, as opposed to other agencies (whether federal, state, or tribal), and it focuses on sources of contamination and depletion within the United States, as opposed to global sources. This focus is not meant to suggest that NEJAC believes that the efforts of these other agencies and the contributions of these other sources are not important aspects of understanding and addressing compromised aquatic ecosystems; rather, it reflects NEJAC's role as a federal advisory committee to EPA.

This Report also examines the issues assuming a backdrop of the current state of the law. For example, in Chapter Two it discusses prevention, reduction, cleanup and restoration in light of existing environmental laws, and in Chapter Four it discusses the particular legal and political status of American Indian tribes and Alaska Native villages, given current interpretations of this status and the current enumeration of federally-recognized tribes. Again, this assumption is not meant to suggest that NEJAC supports in every respect these current enactments or interpretations; rather, it reflects a pragmatic choice, governed in part by considerations of scope.

Throughout, this Report discusses the impact of contaminated and depleted aquatic ecosystems on communities of color, low-income communities, tribes, and other indigenous peoples; Chapter Four, however, is devoted to those issues raised by the fact of American Indian tribes' and Alaska Native villages' unique status as sovereign governments. Thus, while the environmental justice issues posed by compromised aquatic ecosystems will often be common to each of these groups and their members, the NEJAC believes that separate treatment is warranted for tribes in their governmental capacity.

This Report uses the phrase "communities of color, low-income communities, tribes, and other indigenous peoples" in an effort to capture, in shorthand form, all of the various groups and subgroups that are affected by environmental injustice stemming from compromised aquatic ecosystems. It is meant to include all people of color, low-income people, American Indians, Alaska Natives, Native Hawaiians and other Pacific Islanders, and other indigenous people located within the jurisdictional boundaries of the United States. In an effort to avoid cumbersome repetition of this phrase, the Report also substitutes the phrases "affected communities and tribes" and "affected groups;" these shorter phrases are meant to be similarly inclusive.

Finally, this Report intends to address itself to the contamination and depletion of aquatic ecosystems and all of their components, including fish, shellfish, marine invertebrates, aquatic plants, and wildlife. This Report often refers simply to "fish" or "aquatic resources" or to some other shorthand term, but should be understood in each instance to refer to aquatic ecosystems and all of their components (unless the context suggests otherwise).

 **NATIONAL ENVIRONMENTAL JUSTICE ADVISORY COUNCIL**

November 19, 2002

Administrator Christine Todd Whitman
U.S. Environmental Protection Agency
1200 Pennsylvania Avenue, NW
Washington, DC 20004

Dear Administrator Whitman,

Please find attached a copy of the report entitled "**National Environmental Justice Advisory Council Fish Consumption and Environmental Justice,** *November 2002.*"

EPA, through its Office of Environmental Justice, requested the National Environmental Justice Advisory Council (NEJAC) in its meeting of December 3-6, 2001 to provide advice and recommendations on how EPA could improve the quality, quantity, and integrity of our Nation's aquatic ecosystems in order to protect the health and safety of people consuming or using fish, aquatic plants, and wildlife.

This report reflects the advice and recommendations that resulted from pre-meeting preparation, on-site discussions, public comments and subsequent analysis. Individuals and organizations with varied backgrounds and interests offered comments, suggestions and recommendations on how EPA should address fish consumption issues.

This report proposes six overarching consensus recommendations to the EPA as follows:

(1)   Require states, territories, and authorized tribes to consider specific uses, including the use of the waterbody or waterbody segment for subsistence fishing, when designating uses for a waterbody, and to set water quality criteria that support the specific designated use; *provided* that where human health criteria are established based upon consumption of toxic chemicals that bioaccumulate in fish, regulators should employ appropriate human fish consumption rates and bioaccumulation factors, including cultural practices (*e.g.*, species, fish parts used, and manner of cooking and preparation) of tribes and other indigenous and environmental justice communities using the waterbody; *provided further* that EPA should encourage and provide financial and technical support for states, territories, and authorized tribes to control effectively all sources, including both point sources and nonpoint sources, to achieve the criteria;

(2)   Work expeditiously to prevent and reduce the generation and release of those contaminants to the Nation's waters and air that pose the greatest risk of harm to human health and aquatic resources, including but not limited to persistent bioaccumulative toxics (PBTs) (*e.g.*, mercury, dioxins, and polychlorinated biphenyls (PCBs)) and other toxic chemicals, and to clean up and restore aquatic ecosystems contaminated by pollutants;

(3) Protect the health of populations with high exposure to hazards from contaminated fish, aquatic organisms and plants, and wildlife, including communities of color, low income communities, tribes, and other indigenous peoples, by making full use of authorities under the federal environmental laws and accounting for the cultural, traditional, religious, historical , economic, and legal contexts in which these affected groups consume and use aquatic and terrestrial resources;

(4) Ensure that fish and other aquatic organism consumption advisories are used by regulators as a short-term, temporary strategy for informing those who consume and use fish, aquatic organisms and plants, and wildlife of risks while water quality standards are being attained and while prioritizing and pursuing the cleanup of contamination by appropriate parties; agencies must evaluate and address such risks; and require risk-producers to prevent, reduce, and clean up contamination of waters and aquatic ecosystems;

(5) Because many American Indian and Alaska Native (AI/AN) communities are particularly prone to environmental harm due to their dependence on subsistence fishing, hunting, and gathering, conduct environmental research, fish consumption surveys, and monitoring, in consultation with federally recognized tribes and with the involvement of concerned tribal organizations, to determine the effects on, and ways to mitigate adverse effects on the health of AI/AN communities resulting from contaminated water sources and/or the food chain; and

(6) Consistent with the 1988 *EPA Indian Policy for the Administration of Environmental Programs on Indian Reservations*, the federal trust responsibility to federally recognized tribes, and federal policies recognizing tribal sovereignty and promoting self-determination and self-sufficiency, provide equitable funding and technical support for tribal programs to protect AI/AN communities and tribal resources from harm caused by contaminated water and aquatic resources and, until tribes are able to assume responsibility for such programs, implement and require compliance with the federal environmental laws within Indian country; *provided* that, in consultation with tribes, EPA should promptly develop effective and appropriate regulatory strategies for setting, implementing, and attaining water quality standards within Indian country; and *provided further* that, EPA should work with Alaska Native villages to address the special circumstances that exist in Alaska and to protect the health of Alaska Natives from environmental threats associated with their extensive subsistence lifeways.

The NEJAC is pleased to present this report to you for your review, consideration, response and action. In addition, the NEJAC appreciates any assistance you can provide in processing the recommendations in this report through the Office of Water with consultation as appropriate with the American Indian Environmental Office and the Office of Environmental Justice.

Sincerely,

/s/   /s/

Peggy Shepard   Jana Walker
Chair   Vice Chair

A Federal Advisory Committee to the U.S. Environmental Protection Agency

TABLE OF CONTENTS

FISH CONSUMPTION AND ENVIRONMENTAL JUSTICE
NATIONAL ENVIRONMENTAL JUSTICE ADVISORY COUNCIL (NEJAC)

Summary

This Report has been compiled after deliberation during the December, 2001 meeting of the National Environmental Justice Advisory Council (NEJAC) regarding the following overarching policy question:

> **How should EPA improve the quality, quantity, and integrity of our Nation's aquatic ecosystems in order to protect the health and safety of people consuming or using fish, aquatic plants, and wildlife?**

This Report works to identify and discuss the particular issues that this question raises when   as is often the case   those affected by contaminated and depleted aquatic ecosystems are communities of color, low-income communities, American Indian tribes/Alaskan Native villages and their members, and other indigenous peoples.

This report proposes six overarching consensus recommendations to the EPA as follows:[1]

(1) Require states, territories, and authorized tribes to consider specific uses, including the use of the waterbody or waterbody segment for subsistence fishing, when designating uses for a waterbody, and to set water quality criteria that support the specific designated use; *provided* that where human health criteria are established based upon consumption of toxic chemicals that bioaccumulate in fish, regulators should employ appropriate human fish consumption rates and bioaccumulation factors, including cultural practices (*e.g.*, species, fish parts used, and manner of cooking and preparation) of tribes and other indigenous and environmental justice communities using the waterbody; *provided further* that EPA should encourage and provide financial and technical support for states, territories, and authorized tribes to control effectively all sources, including both point sources and nonpoint sources, to achieve the criteria;

(2) Work expeditiously to prevent and reduce the generation and release of those contaminants to the Nation's waters and air that pose the greatest risk of harm to human health and aquatic resources, including but not limited to persistent bioaccumulative toxics (PBTs) (*e.g.*, mercury, dioxins, and polychlorinated biphenyls (PCBs)) and other toxic chemicals, and to clean up and restore aquatic ecosystems contaminated by pollutants;

---

[1]NEJAC Executive Council member Kenneth J. Warren joins in support of the Report's six Consensus Recommendations and the Report's depiction of fish consumption impacts to communities and tribes. He believes, however, that the Report should provide a more focused and well-grounded substantiation for these recommendations.

(3) Protect the health of populations with high exposure to hazards from contaminated fish, aquatic organisms and plants, and wildlife, including communities of color, low income communities, tribes, and other indigenous peoples, by making full use of authorities under the federal environmental laws and accounting for the cultural, traditional, religious, historical, economic, and legal contexts in which these affected groups consume and use aquatic and terrestrial resources;

(4) Ensure that fish and other aquatic organism consumption advisories are used by regulators as a short-term, temporary strategy for informing those who consume and use fish, aquatic organisms and plants, and wildlife of risks while water quality standards are being attained and while prioritizing and pursuing the cleanup of contamination by appropriate parties; agencies must evaluate and address such risks; and require risk-producers to prevent, reduce, and clean up contamination of waters and aquatic ecosystems;

(5) Because many American Indian and Alaska Native (AI/AN) communities are particularly prone to environmental harm due to their dependence on subsistence fishing, hunting, and gathering, conduct environmental research, fish consumption surveys, and monitoring, in consultation with federally recognized tribes and with the involvement of concerned tribal organizations, to determine the effects on, and ways to mitigate adverse effects on the health of AI/AN communities resulting from contaminated water sources and/or the food chain; and

(6) Consistent with the 1988 *EPA Indian Policy for the Administration of Environmental Programs on Indian Reservations*, the federal trust responsibility to federally recognized tribes, and federal policies recognizing tribal sovereignty and promoting self-determination and self-sufficiency, provide equitable funding and technical support for tribal programs to protect AI/AN communities and tribal resources from harm caused by contaminated water and aquatic resources and, until tribes are able to assume responsibility for such programs, implement and require compliance with the federal environmental laws within Indian country; *provided* that, in consultation with tribes, EPA should promptly develop effective and appropriate regulatory strategies for setting, implementing, and attaining water quality standards within Indian country; and *provided further* that, EPA should work with Alaska Native villages to address the special circumstances that exist in Alaska and to protect the health of Alaska Natives from environmental threats associated with their extensive subsistence lifeways.

The Report is organized into five chapters. An initial chapter provides background. The four succeeding chapters each address a more focused policy question and the issues it raises. These chapters are outlined below:

Background

This chapter explores the importance of having healthy aquatic ecosystems to address issues of environmental justice. It provides background on the perspectives of the various individuals, communities, tribes, and peoples affected by those aquatic ecosystems which are contaminated and depleted. This chapter begins with the observation that communities of color, low-income communities, tribes, and other indigenous peoples *depend* on healthy aquatic ecosystems and the fish, aquatic plants, and wildlife that these ecosystems support. While there are important differences among these various affected groups, their members generally depend on the fish, aquatic plants, and wildlife to a greater extent and in different ways than does the general population. These resources are consumed and used to meet nutritional and economic needs. For some groups, they are also consumed or used for cultural, traditional, or religious purposes. For members of these groups, the conventional understandings of the "health benefits" or "economic benefits" of catching, harvesting, preparing, and eating fish, aquatic plants, and wildlife do not adequately capture the significant value these practices have in their lives and the life of their culture. The harms caused by degradation of aquatic habitats and depletion of fisheries, moreover, do not only affect the present generation. They take their toll on future generations and on the transfer of knowledge from one generation to the next (e.g., ecological knowledge, customs and traditions surrounding harvest, preparation and consumption of aquatic resources).

Many of the rivers, streams, bayous, bays, lakes, wetlands, and estuaries that support these resources on which communities and tribes depend have become contaminated and depleted. Contamination is causing the communities' and tribes' everyday practices   their ways of living to serve as a source of exposure to a host of substances toxic to humans and other living things. The depletion of aquatic environments and resources also threatens these groups' subsistence, economic, cultural, traditional, and religious practices. Aquatic ecosystems are contaminated with mercury, PCBs, dioxins, DDT and other pesticides, lead and other metals, sediments, fecal coliform and other bacterial and viral contaminants   in short, a host of toxins, most of which are particularly troubling because they *persist* in the environment for great lengths of time and because they *bioaccumulate* in the tissues of fish, aquatic plants, and wildlife, existing in greater quantities higher up the food chain.

For many communities of color, low-income communities, tribes, and other indigenous peoples, there are no real alternatives to eating and using fish, aquatic plants, and wildlife. For many members of these groups it is entirely impractical to "switch" to "substitutes" when the fish and other resources on which they rely have become contaminated. There are numerous and often insurmountable obstacles to seeking alternatives (e.g., fishing "elsewhere," throwing back "undesirable" species of fish, adopting different preparation methods, or substituting beef, chicken or tofu). For some, not fishing and not eating fish are unimaginable for cultural, traditional, or religious reasons. For the fishing peoples of the Pacific Northwest, for example, fish and fishing are necessary for survival as a people   they are vital as a matter of cultural flourishing and self-determination.

When health and environmental agencies respond to contamination and its impacts, they typically employ one or both of two general strategies: *risk avoidance*, whereby risk-bearers are encouraged or required to change the practices that expose them to contamination (e.g., through fish consumption advisories, directed to those who eat fish) or *risk reduction*, whereby risk-producers are required to cleanup, reduce, or prevent contamination (e.g., through water quality standards, applied to industrial sources that discharge contaminants into surrounding waters). In either event, agencies rely on assumptions about fish consumption rates, practices, and needs that reflect the circumstances of the general population, but often are not reflective enough of the circumstances of affected communities and tribes. Agencies' approaches to risk assessment, risk management, and risk communication similarly fall short of taking into account that affected groups consume and use fish, aquatic plants, and wildlife in different cultural, traditional, religious, historical, economic, and legal contexts than the "average American." These observations have policy implications that are taken up in the remaining chapters.

Chapter One: Research Methods and Risk Assessment Approaches

Chapter One focuses on the tools that agencies use to define, evaluate, and respond to the adverse health impacts from contaminated aquatic environments. It examines the research methods that agencies use to obtain information about the lives, practices, and circumstances of affected communities and tribes. It also examines the risk assessment approaches that agencies employ to evaluate and address these health impacts.

This chapter begins by noting that agencies typically focus on "adverse impacts to human health" that tend to focus narrowly on individuals and physiological harms. Some affected groups, by contrast, may view the harms from contamination more broadly: they are not only physiological, but psychological, social, and cultural; which may not only impact an individual, but a group overall.

This chapter then devotes considerable discussion to differences in various groups' circumstances of exposure. It documents the marked differences in how much fish is eaten (measured by fish consumption rates) between the general population and higher-consuming "subpopulations" such as communities of color, low-income communities, tribes, and other indigenous peoples. It canvases agencies' standard assumptions about the fish, shellfish, plant, and wildlife species that people consume and use; the parts of these species they use; and the preparation methods they employ. It points out that these assumptions often do not reflect the practices among the various affected groups. It observes the different cultural, traditional, religious, historical, economic, and legal contexts in which many affected groups consume and use aquatic resources. It takes up the issues of aggregate or multiple exposures and cumulative risks, noting that whereas agencies' current methods proceed as if humans were exposed to a single contaminant at a time, humans are actually often exposed to multiple contaminants at a time or in succession, and often by more than one route and pathway of exposure. This is especially likely to be the case for many members of communities of color, low-income communities, tribes, and other indigenous peoples. Each of the considerations raised here contributes to the observation that agencies currently underestimate the extent to which members of these groups are exposed to environmental contaminants. The result is that standards set or advisories issued based on these estimates will not be sufficiently protective of these affected groups.

This chapter next considers the different susceptibilities and "co-risk" factors that may characterize affected groups and their members, noting again that these differences are unlikely to be accounted for by current agency approaches.

This chapter then explores suppression effects and their implications. A suppression effect occurs when a fish consumption rate for a given subpopulation reflects a current level of consumption that is artificially diminished from an appropriate baseline level of consumption for that subpopulation. The more robust baseline level of consumption is "suppressed," inasmuch as is does not get captured by the fish consumption rate. Suppression effects may arise as a result of contaminated aquatic ecosystems, depleted aquatic ecosystems and fisheries, or both. When agencies set environmental standards using a fish consumption rate based upon an artificially diminished consumption level, they may set in motion a downward spiral whereby the resulting standards permit further contamination and/or depletion of the fish and aquatic resources. This chapter discusses the policy implications of suppression effects.

This chapter then addresses research methods relevant to risk assessment, risk management, and risk communication. Much of the preceding discussion is brought to bear, as it underscores the fact that it will often be crucial to the relevance, accuracy, and acceptability of research in these areas that the affected community or tribe be central to the process throughout. This is not only a matter of community access or tribal consultation, but, importantly, a matter of scientific defensibility. There are currently sizeable gaps in the data and methods that EPA and other agencies use to assess, manage, and communicate risk, and it is often the case that these gaps can only be filled by community- and tribally-based research. As the large literature on "participatory research" documents, affected communities and tribes have expertise that is simply not going to be able to be replicated by non-member researchers. Notably, it will be important to ensure that this community participation and tribal consultation is adequately funded and supported technically. This chapter also discusses the need for research that seeks not only to describe affected groups' exposure, but also to connect exposure to sources of contaminants in aquatic environments.

Finally, this chapter examines efforts to refine current risk assessment methods in order to address issues raised by these methods for communities of color, low-income communities, tribes, and other indigenous peoples, and discusses efforts to reevaluate the use of current risk assessment approaches in light of alternative approaches, particularly those that focus on prevention and precaution.

Chapter Two: Using Existing Legal Authorities

Chapter Two discusses agencies' risk reduction efforts, that is, strategies that look to risk-producers to prevent or reduce contamination in the first place, and to cleanup and restore those environments that are already contaminated. It examines the legal authorities that might be invoked more effectively to sustain healthy aquatic ecosystems and to protect the health and safety of people consuming or using fish, aquatic plants, and wildlife.

This chapter begins by providing background on the contaminants of greatest concern, not only from the perspectives of health and environmental agencies, but also from the perspective of affected groups and their members. Chief among the contaminants of concern are mercury, PCBs, dioxins, DDT, and chlordane. In addition to these five contaminants, at least eight others are a source of concern, given that they are highly *toxic*; they are *persistent* once released into the environment; and they *bioaccumulate* in the tissues of fish and wildlife. These eight are: aldrin, dieldrin, endrin, heptachlor, hexachlorobenzene, mirex, toxaphene, and furans. Finally, a host of other contaminants are troubling here, including: lead and other metals; numerous other pesticides; fecal coliform, marine biotoxins and various other bacterial and viral contaminants; sediment and silt loadings; and numerous others. This chapter outlines briefly the health effects of each of the major contaminants of concern, as well as its sources in the environment.

This chapter discusses how EPA might better prevent and reduce contamination in the first place, focusing primarily on efforts under the Clean Water Act (CWA) and secondarily on efforts under other legal authorities, such as the Clean Air Act (CAA). It then turns its discussion to how EPA might better clean up and restore those aquatic ecosystems that are already contaminated. Again, it looks first to the authority provided by the Clean Water Act, and then discusses other legal authorities, such as "Superfund," the Comprehensive Environmental Response, Compensation, and Liability Act (CERCLA).

Chapter Three: Fish Consumption Advisories

Chapter Three discusses agencies' risk avoidance strategies, focusing on fish and wildlife consumption advisories in particular and on risk communication in general. It asks what role fish consumption advisories should play in efforts to protect more effectively the health and safety of people consuming or using these resources. It considers how agencies can identify, acknowledge, and meet the real needs of those who are affected — how they can work to make affected groups whole once the fish, aquatic plants, and wildlife on which they depend have already become contaminated.

The chapter first takes up the question of the advisories' proper role. Drawing on the observations presented above about the impracticality and/or unimaginability of reducing fish consumption or of altering practices connected with catching, harvesting, preparing and eating fish, this chapter notes that the answer to the question of fish consumption advisories' role will likely be different for different communities or tribes. Importantly, it should be for the affected group to determine what will be appropriate from its perspective. Tribes' particular political and legal status as sovereign nations must also be taken into account here, as tribes will be in the position, in their governmental capacities, of deciding for themselves what role fish consumption advisories should play in their environmental protection efforts.

This chapter next explores fish consumption advisories' "effectiveness." It discusses briefly the potential differences in how "effective" might be defined by various agencies and by various affected communities and tribes. It reviews the current state of research regarding how those to whom advisories are directed respond to this information, observing that the available evidence suggests that low-income, people of color, those with limited English proficiency, and those with relatively little formal education are less likely to be aware of advisories.

In light of this evidence, and in view of current EPA efforts to this end, this chapter then devotes considerable attention to the matter of improving the effectiveness of risk communication and fish consumption advisories. As a general matter, it observes that if risk communication is truly to be a "two-way street"   if *communication* is actually to occur, - affected groups must be involved as partners or co-managers at every point in the risk communication process. All of the elements of effective advisories   including "audience identification," "needs assessment," message content, media choice, implementation, and evaluation   will fall into place if agencies and affected communities or tribes consider together the questions and answers. In general, EPA and other agencies should work to reconceptualize risk communication approaches from large-scale, abstract, one-time efforts to develop and disseminate various communication "products" (e.g., developing and posting fish advisory signs) to local, contextually-supported, ongoing efforts to establish and maintain relationships with a particular affected community or tribe.

More specifically, it will be important for EPA and other agencies to recognize the diverse contexts, interests, and needs that characterize the various affected groups   including, but not limited to groups with limited English proficiency; groups with limited or no literacy; low-income communities; immigrant and refugee communities; African American communities; various Asian and Pacific Islander communities and subcommunities (e.g., Mien, Lao, Khmu, and Thadium communities within the larger Laotian community in West Contra County, CA); various Hispanic communities and subcommunities (e.g., Carribean-American communities in the Greenpoint/Williamsburg area of Brooklyn, NY); various Native Americans, Native Hawaiians, and Alaska Natives (including members of tribes and villages, members of non-federally recognized tribes, and urban Native people).

"Affected groups" also refers to subgroups within these larger groups, including but not limited to nursing infants; children; pregnant women and women of childbearing age; elders; traditionalists versus modernists in terms of practices surrounding fish consumption; and subgroups defined by geographical region. Affected group involvement in aiding identification and understanding of the diverse contexts, interests, and needs of these various groups will, perhaps unsurprisingly, be essential. The content of the message and the media selected need to be effective and appropriate from the perspective of the affected group, and this chapter examines several specific considerations to this end. Implementation efforts, too, must be effective and appropriate from the perspective of those affected, who will be particularly well-positioned to take the lead in implementing an advisory and outreach strategy that has been developed by and for their group. Evaluation will also be most usefully conducted together with members of the affected group, whose ability to help define and measure "success" will again often be unparalleled.

Additionally, this chapter observes that capacity-building or capacity-augmentation is in and of itself and environmental justice issue, for both communities and tribes. Involvement by those affected at each point in the risk communication process would go far toward enabling them to shape the process so that it is not only relevant and appropriate, but also useful and empowering from the perspective of the community or tribe.

Finally, this chapter notes that here again, as in the context of research in general, financial and technical support will be crucial to enabling communities and tribes fully to be involved.

Chapter Four: American Indian Tribes and Alaskan Native Villages

Chapter Four addresses issues unique to American Indian tribes, Alaskan Native villages, and their members. Although tribes and their members share many of the concerns discussed in the preceding chapters, tribes' political and legal status is unique among affected groups and so warrants separate treatment. Tribes are governmental entities, recognized as possessing broad inherent authority over their members, territories, and resources. As sovereigns, federally recognized tribes have a government-to-government relationship with the federal government and its agencies, including the EPA. Tribes' unique legal status includes a trust responsibility on the part of the federal government. For many tribes, it also includes treaty rights. Other laws and executive commitments, too, shape the legal obligations owed to American Indian tribes and Alaska Native tribes and their members.

This chapter describes the EPA's Indian Policy for the Administration of Environmental Programs on Indian Reservations; tribes' efforts to assume responsibilities for administering environmental programs on their reservations under various federal environmental laws   notably, the Safe Drinking Water Act, the Clean Water Act, the Clean Air Act, and CERCLA; and tribes' work as co-managers of cleanup and restoration efforts and/or as Natural Resource Damage Trustees. In these and other roles, tribes will have environmental justice concerns of a different and complex nature.

The chapter then outlines the ways in which the political and legal status of Alaska Native villages has been interpreted to be both similar to and different from the status of tribes in the forty-eight contiguous states, and notes briefly some of the circumstances unique to Alaska Natives that are likely to raise particular concerns for this group.

Finally, this chapter outlines the particular circumstances of tribes and their members with respect to susceptibilities and co-risk factors; these have implications, as discussed more generally in Chapter One, for agencies' risk assessment, risk management, and risk communication approaches.

FISH CONSUMPTION AND ENVIRONMENTAL JUSTICE

BACKGROUND CHAPTER

The National Environmental Justice Advisory Council (NEJAC) is a federal advisory committee of the U.S. Environmental Protection Agency (EPA). Under its charter, the NEJAC's mission is to provide advice and recommendations to the EPA Administrator on matters related to environmental justice. In July, 2000, EPA requested that NEJAC address issues raised by the relationship between fish consumption, water quality, and environmental justice. This issue was the focus of the NEJAC's December 3-6, 2001 meeting in Seattle, Washington.

This Report focuses on the following question:

How should EPA improve the quality, quantity, and integrity of our Nation's aquatic ecosystems in order to protect the health and safety of people consuming or using fish, aquatic plants, and wildlife?

This chapter provides background necessary to address adequately the above policy question. This chapter seeks to explain why contaminated and depleted aquatic ecosystems are an environmental justice issue. Importantly, this chapter seeks to present the dimensions of the problem from the perspectives of the various individuals, communities, tribes, and other peoples affected.

This chapter begins in Part A by gathering the accounts of a number of different people who suffer the ill effects of contaminated and depleted aquatic ecosystems. Although these stories do not catalogue exhaustively the harms felt by all of those who are affected, it is hoped that, taken together, they will provide a sense of the breadth and enormity of the impacts on communities of color, low-income communities, tribes, and other indigenous peoples. And it is hoped that, in their diversity, they will provide a sense of the differing dimensions of the ill effects for these different affected groups. This chapter begins with these accounts because they are properly the starting point for any discussion of environmental justice policy: they present the *real* stories   the stories told from the perspectives of those on the ground, and not as they need to be told to fit into the bins and categories created by environmental laws and regulations. These accounts should *frame* the discussion   rather than be merely "inputs" into a discussion already framed in someone else's terms.

In order to speak to government agencies that work within the boundaries of environmental laws and regulations, however, it seems useful to work to "translate" these stories so that their relevance to agencies' efforts can be appreciated. NEJAC's attempt at translation will often mean breaking things down and naming their component parts in ways that are more likely to be understood by agencies, given agencies' current categories, programs, and approaches. So, for example, in seeking to convey the importance of salmon in his life, a member of the Fourteen

Confederated Tribes and Bands of the Yakama Nation may invoke terms and concepts familiar to agencies such as "nutrition," "health," "economy," "resource," "subsistence," "culture," and "treaty-protected;" he may refer to laws and programs that separately address the "air," "water quality," "water quantity," and "sediments" that together are home to the salmon.

This attempt at translation may entail loss, however: it may fail fully to capture the multiple and interrelated dimensions of what is at stake; or it may risk misunderstanding or *mis*translation Yet an attempt at translation may be necessary for those affected to convey their recommendations to agency decision makers. Nonetheless, it is crucial that agencies also work to *hear* the stories in their original, whole form and to consider what these stories have to teach them how they might serve to reframe agencies' approaches altogether. It is important that agencies strive to reduce the gulf that must be bridged by translation and so to minimize the loss that accompanies translation. With these considerations in mind, the remainder of this Report looks to discuss the issues in the terms used by environmental agencies and in environmental laws and regulations, while at the same time referring often to the words of those affected as touchstones for deliberation.

Part B of this chapter then raises the question that is examined in the remainder of this Report, regarding the policy implications of the accounts set forth in Part A.

A. DIVERSE IMPACTS, MULTIPLE DIMENSIONS: THE ACCOUNTS OF ENVIRONMENTAL INJUSTICE

1. Communities of Color, Low-Income Communities, Tribes, and Other Indigenous Peoples Depend on Fish,[2] Aquatic Plants, and Wildlife

Put simply, communities of color, low-income communities, tribes, and other indigenous peoples *depend* on healthy aquatic ecosystems and the fish, aquatic plants, and wildlife that these ecosystems support. While there are important differences among the various affected communities of color, low-income communities, tribes, and other indigenous peoples, members of these groups depend on fish, aquatic plants, and wildlife to a greater extent and in different ways than does the general population.

---

[2]The term "fish," here and throughout this Report, is meant to include shellfish and marine invertebrates, unless the particular context suggests otherwise. Please see the Interpretive Notes at the outset of this Report for elaboration.

Fish are a healthful source of dietary protein and other nutrients for humans.[3] Fish are relatively low in fat, and are a good source of selenium. Fish, aquatic plants, and wildlife are major dietary staples for some individuals, and those who subsist chiefly or solely on fish, aquatic plants, and wildlife are more likely to be people of color, low-income individuals, tribal members, or other indigenous people. Thus, for example, a recent survey revealed that whereas 60% of "non-white" (primarily African-American) fishers on the Detroit River fished there to meet their needs for food or for a combination of food and recreation, only 21.7% of white fishers indicated that they fished for reasons combining food and recreation, and none indicated that they fished only to meet their needs for food.[4] In Alaska, "[a]mong Yupiks of Gambell, over one-half of their protein, iron, vitamin B-12, and omega-3 fatty acids come from subsistence foods."[5]

Fish, aquatic plants, and wildlife are important food sources for economic reasons: it generally costs less to purchase many kinds of fish than it costs to purchase other sources of animal protein,[6] and if someone can fish, gather, harvest, or hunt nearby, he or she can bypass altogether the need to get to a store and to purchase food. For some of these fishers, fishing provides not only food for their own consumption and consumption by relatives and neighbors, but also an important source of income and livelihood. As Delbert Frank, Sr., Warm Springs, explains:

> *I used to fish at Celilo falls before The Dalles Dam was built. We used to be able to fish all year long. We caught lots of different kinds of fish spring chinook, summer chinook, bluebacks, fall chinook, steelhead, and coho. When the fish were coming in good, I could catch one ton of salmon a day. And, it didn't take a lot of fancy gear or expensive boats to fish. For the cost of one or two balls of twine, about 6 to 12 dollars, I could make the fishing gear necessary for me to catch enough fish to supply my family and many others for a whole year.*[7]

---

[3]See, e.g., Yvonne Smith and Laura Berg, *Ancient Tradition, Modern Reality: Is There a Future for a Salmon-Based Culture?*, 1 Wana Chinook Tymoo 14 (1998); Renate D. Kimbrough, *Consumption of Fish: Benefits and Perceived Risk*, 33 Journal of Toxicology & Environmental Health 82-83 (1991).

[4]Patrick C. West, *Race and the Incidence of Environmental Hazards: A Time for Discourse* "Invitation to Poison? Detroit Minorities and Toxic Fish Consumption from the Detroit River"96, 98 (Bunyan Bryant and Paul Mohai, eds. 1992).

[5]Elizabeth D. Nobmann, *Nutritional Benefits of Subsistence Foods* (1997) available at www.nativeknowledge.org/db/files/aboutnt2.htm.

[6]See, e.g., Kimbrough, *supra* at 83.

[7]**Columbia River Inter-Tribal Fish Commission,** *Celilo Falls***, available at www.critfc.org/text/CELILO.HTM.**

A low-income African-American fisher on the Detroit River observes:

> *I catch to eat fish. I catch a lot of fish and bring a lot home to eat. Bring home Perch and Bass. I eat more because I like fish and it is easier to feed a family because of money.*[8]

For some groups, fish, aquatic plants, and wildlife are consumed or used for cultural, traditional, or religious purposes as well. For members of these groups, conventional dominant society understandings of the "health benefits" or "economic benefits" of catching, harvesting, preparing, and eating fish, aquatic plants and wildlife do not adequately capture the place of these practices in their lives and the life of their culture. Cultural, traditional, and religious understandings will, of course, differ among various groups; the following excerpts provide but a few accounts. Winona LaDuke, Mississippi Band of Anishinaabeg, explains:

> *There are many wild rice lakes on the White Earth reservation in northern Minnesota; my community, the Anishinaabeg, calls the rice* Manoomin, *or a gift from the Creator.*
>
> *Every year, half our people harvest the wild rice, the fortunate ones generating a large chunk of their income from it. But wild rice is not just about money and food. It's about feeding the soul.*[9]

Similarly, Horace Axtell, Nez Perce, explains:

> *According to our religion, everything is based on nature. Anything that grows or lives, like plants and animals, is part of our religion. The most important element we have in our religion is water. At all of the Nez Perce ceremonial feasts the people drink water before and after they eat. The water is a purification of our bodies before we accept the gifts from the Creator. After the feast we drink water to purify all the food we have consumed. The next most important element in our religion is the fish because fish comes from water. It doesn't matter what kind of fish. If we have suckers or eels or steelhead or salmon, we honor it next after we drink the water. Then we name whatever fish we have, and then everyone takes a small bit before we eat the rest of the food. The next element is the game meat like deer, elk, and moose. That's how we honor the food we eat, especially the fish, because it is the next element after the water. The chinook salmon is more*

---

[8]Pat West and Brunilda Vargus, *A Subsistence-Culture Model for High Toxic Fish Consumption by Low Income Afro-Americans from the Detroit River* 16 (forthcoming 2002) (listing fisher's income as $5,000 - $9,999).

[9]Winona LaDuke, *All Our Relations: Native Struggles for Land and Life* 115 (1999).

favored because it is the strongest fish and the most tasty. Chinook Salmon is the fish we try to bring to the long house.[10]

As Hawaii's Thousand Friends relates:

> *Hawaiians, the indigenous people of these islands, rely on healthy aquatic ecosystems for their life-style. The depletion and contamination of these ecosystems has drastically impacted their health, food sources, economic well-being and ability to follow cultural, traditional and religious practices.*[11]

And, as Art Ivanoff, from the Alaska Native village of Unalakleet explains, their understandings of these practices and of the very meaning of the term "subsistence" are often quite different than the understanding of the dominant society:

> *We have a different definition [of subsistence]. Western society tends to look at it as something that's derogatory, before the poverty level. That's not how we define our lifestyle. It's something rich. It's spiritual. It's economic. It's social. It's getting together with your friends and your relatives going out there harvesting, and sharing with elders, sharing with widows, and that's a pride we get.*[12]

The harms occasioned by the degradation of aquatic habitats and the depletion of fisheries, moreover, are not only visited on the present generation. Part of the affront to the culture and social fabric of some communities and tribes for whom fish and fishing are vital comes from the diminished opportunities for inter-generational transfer of knowledge especially ecological knowledge about places and natural systems and for other aspects of inter-generational socialization. The acts of inter-generational transfer of customs and traditions surrounding catching, preparing, and consuming fish are themselves important to the maintenance of social and cultural health.[13] As an African-American fisher on the Detroit River explains:

---

[10]Dan Landeen and Allen Pinkham, *Salmon and His People: Fish and Fishing in Nez Perce Culture* 55 (1999).

[11]Hawaii's Thousand Friends (Written Comments, March 11, 2002).

[12]Art Ivanoff, Alaska Native Village of Unalakleet, *Comments to the National Environmental Justice Advisory Council* Vol. III-17 (Annual meeting transcript December 4, 2001); accord, Mary Kancewick & Eric Smith, *Subsistence in Alaska: Towards a Native Priority*, 59 UMKC Law Review 645, 650 (1991) ("Alaska Natives speak of subsistence not in terms of minimalism, but in terms of wealth; not in terms of something to be risen above, but in terms of something to aspire to and hold onto: 'Subsistence living, a marginal way of life to most, has no such connotation to the Native people of southeast Alaska. The relationship between the Native population and the resources of the land and the sea is so close that an entire culture is reflected.'"(quoting testimony of Nelson Frank, Tlingit, Sitka)).

[13]See, e.g., Pat West and Brunilda Vargus, *A Subsistence-Culture Model for High Toxic Fish Consumption by Low Income Afro-Americans from the Detroit River* 9-10, 18-21 (forthcoming 2002)

My stepdad taught me how to fish. He is from a little town in Mississippi. Most people around here who fish were from the South and our parents were from the South and they were used to fishing and then they taught their kids. When I was little we used to eat fish a lot but that was when the water was clean. . . . I do eat the fish that I catch.[14]

The Columbia River Inter-Tribal Fish Commission, for example, describes the extensive tribal ecological knowledge that was "transmitted to succeeding generations as part of their inheritance," and notes that "[p]lants, animals, and especially places were . . . repositories for historical, social, and spiritual lessons."[15] The concept of "risk" then, should include "cultural risk:"

> *Cultural risk [includes] ecological impacts that reduce or impair the inter-generational transfer of ecological knowledge used for implementing traditional holistic environmental management practices.*[16]

Indeed, for many members of communities of color, low-income communities, tribes, or other indigenous peoples, there are no real alternatives to depending on fish, aquatic plants, and wildlife. In some cases, for example, it is utterly impractical to suggest that people "switch" to "substitute sources of protein" when the fish on which they rely to put food on the table have become contaminated. Such suggestions are often unrealistic, given the many obstacles to the imagined alternatives: there may be no uncontaminated bays, lakes, or rivers for miles around; even if another fishing spot can be found just a little farther away, it may be difficult or impossible to reach without a car or other transportation   and it may cost too much for the gas or the bus or train ticket to get there; or another fishing spot may traditionally be someone else's fishing spot, such that it wouldn't be appropriate simply to go there; and there may be no adequate substitutes from other food sources at the grocery store   not being able to eat fish may mean having to look to foods that are poorer quality from a nutritional and health perspective. As Mark Davis, Coalition to Restore Coastal Louisiana, Baton Rouge, explains:

> *The advisories that are issued are just not relevant to the people here . . . it's as if no one believes that there really are subsistence fishers. Suddenly it is my responsibility as a risk-bearer to figure out what the advisories mean, what my level of risk is . . . as if there*

(discussing importance of inter-generational socialization for African-American community members in Detroit, many of whom brought practices surrounding fish and fishing with them as they and their families moved from the rural south to the industrial north).

[14]Id. at 20.

[15]Columbia River Inter-Tribal Fish Commission, *Cultural Context* available at http://www.critfic.org/text/TRP cul.htm.

[16]Columbia River Inter-Tribal Fish Commission, *Comments to EPA Administrator Carol Browner on the Draft Revisions to the Methodology for Deriving Ambient Water Quality Criteria for the Protection of Human Health* 10 (January 14, 1999).

*were a choice. People here walk or bike to a drainage ditch, to a bayou, to the
Mississippi River   how can these people be expected to go fish somewhere else?*[17]

An African-American fisher on the Detroit River explains:

*I think that mostly black people fish on the river (due to lack of money); if they have the
money they can go anywhere and fish   wherever they want. A lot of us don't have the
boats or the cars to get to the good fish. We settle for the fish here but it's all good. I still
get the fish. Some people fish because they have to fish. Fish is good food and it is cheap
but river fish is the cheapest and I don't blame people for eating it.*[18]

According to Angela Wilson, Founder, Environmental Justice Action Group, Portland, Oregon:

*It is unrealistic to think that the community members who fish in the Columbia Slough can
simply "eat peanuts and tofu," as the agencies suggest.*[19]

Hawaii's Thousand Friends explains:

*Fish, raw and cooked, is a staple of the Native Hawaiian diet. In an attempt to reduce the
alarmingly high percentage of Native Hawaiians with high blood pressure, diabetes, heart
disease and obesity, some physicians advocate returning to a historical Hawaiian diet, of
which eating fish is a major component. The EPA recommendation of only 12 ounces of
fish in one week is incompatible with most Native Hawaiian diets and with all those who
follow the physician-recommended diet.*[20]

Yin Ling Leung, Executive Director of Asians and Pacific Islanders for Reproductive Health,
California, summarizes:

*To our communities, being able to fish means being able to either put food on the table, or
basically eat a much less nutritious meal. I think that's a non-choice.*[21]

---

[17]Telephone Interview with Mark Davis, Coalition to Restore Coastal Louisiana (August 22,
2001).

[18]Pat West and Brunilda Vargus, *A Subsistence-Culture Model for High Toxic Fish Consumption
by Low Income Afro-Americans from the Detroit River* 16 (forthcoming 2002).

[19]Angela Wilson, Environmental Justice Action Group, Presentation at Public Interest
Environmental Law Conference, University of Oregon (March, 2001).

[20]Hawaii's Thousand Friends (Written Comments, March 11, 2002).

[21]Audrey Chiang, Asian Pacific Environmental Network, *A Seafood Consumption Survey of the
Laotian Community in West Contra Costa County, California* 1 (1998).

In some cases, too, not fishing and not eating fish are unimaginable for cultural, traditional, or religious reasons. For the fishing peoples of the Pacific Northwest, for example, fish and fishing are necessary for survival as a people — to fish is to *be* Nez Perce.[22] Fish and fishing are vital as a matter of cultural flourishing and self-determination. The importance of fish, especially salmon, to these peoples is reflected in language, in treaties, in past and present tribal fisheries management and environmental restoration efforts, and in the ongoing political and legal struggles for the survival of the salmon and the way of life that is bound up with the salmon. Don Samson, Umatilla, Executive Director, Columbia River Inter-Tribal Fish Commission, explains:

> *The reason I've been fishing is more for my own subsistence, to bring fish home. But maybe more importantly now these days is to maintain the tradition of fishing — of going up to the mountains where my father, my elders fished before me. So it's something that we've got to carry on — that's really why I fish. We've got to pass it on to our children. We have to have that for them in order to be Indians — in order to survive and carry on the things that were placed here for us, and carry on what our elders tell us and teach us.*[23]

Billy Frank, Jr., Nisqually, Chairman, Northwest Indian Fisheries Commission, explains:

> *Fishing defines the tribes as a people. It was the one thing above all else that the tribes wished to retain during treaty negotiations with the federal government 150 years ago. Nothing was more vital to the tribal way of life then, and nothing is more important now. . . .The tribes have fought too hard for too long to let the salmon and their treaty rights to harvest salmon go extinct. This summer and fall you will see tribal fishermen doing what they have always done — fish.*[24]

Of course, for many communities of color, low-income communities, tribes, and other indigenous peoples, the nutritional, economic, and traditional or cultural aspects of fishing, preparing and eating fish are interrelated. Members of these groups thus in many cases depend on fish for a combination of the above reasons. For example, a recent survey of first- and second-generation Asian and Pacific Islanders in King County, Washington — including members of

---

[22]See, e.g., Dan Landeen and Allen Pinkham, *Salmon and His People: Fish and Fishing in Nez Perce Culture* 156 (1999) (quoting Del White, Nez Perce: "People need to understand that the salmon is part of who the Nez Perce people are. It is just like a hand is a part of your body. The salmon have always been part of our religion. You can't separate the two.").

[23]Videotape: *My Strength is From the Fish* (Columbia River Inter-Tribal Fish Commission, 1994).

[24]Billy Frank, Jr., *A Statement from Billy Frank, Jr.* available at www.nwifc.wa.gov/esa/start.htm.

Cambodian, Chinese, Filipino, Hmong, Japanese, Korean, Laotian, Mien, Samoan, and Vietnamese ethnic groups   observes:

> *[Asian and Pacific Islanders] consider seafood collection and consumption as healthy activities that reflect a homelike lifestyle and may fish for economic necessity.*[25]

Similarly, in Green Bay, Wisconsin:

> *Eating fish forms a regular part of the diet and culture for the Asians (Hmong and Laotians) living in the Green Bay area.*[26]

And, in the Greenpoint/Williamsburg ("G/W") community in the Borough of Brooklyn in New York City:

> *In G/W, some anglers consume as many as two meals per day of fish caught in the East River, which forms the western boundary of G/W. Approximately 38 percent of the G/W population lives below the poverty line, suggesting that many of the anglers fishing in this community may be urban subsistence anglers who rely on fish caught in the East River as a free source of nutrition. In addition, fishing is a way of life rooted in the cultural heritage for many of the black and Hispanic anglers observed fishing on the piers in G/W, many of whom come from Carribean fishing cultures.*[27]

Finally, the health of humans and the health of aquatic ecosystems are intimately related, such that compromised aquatic ecosystems are of concern in and of themselves, with the contamination of fish, aquatic plants, and wildlife but some of the devastating effects. Water of sufficient quality and quantity is vital to sustain all life. To allow waters to be degraded and depleted is to undermine health, traditions, cultures, and economies. To allow waters to be degraded and depleted is to neglect obligations, including the obligation to sustain tribal homelands as contemplated by federal Indian treaties and other laws. As Frank Tenorio, Governor, San Felipe Pueblo, explained:

> *There has been a lot said about the sacredness of our land which is our body; and the values of our culture which is our soul; but water is the blood of our tribes; and if its life-*

---

[25]Ruth Sechena, et al., *Asian and Pacific Islander Seafood Consumption Study* (1999).

[26]Dyan M. Steenport, et al., *Fish Consumption Habits and Advisory Awareness Among Fox River Anglers*, Wisconsin Medical Journal (November 2000) available at www.wismed.org/wmj/nov2000/fish.html.

[27]Industrial Economics, Inc., *Community-Specific Cumulative Exposure Assessment for Greenpoint/Williamsburg New York* 3-1 (1999).

giving flow is stopped, or it is polluted, all else will die and the many thousands of years of our communal existence will come to an end.[28]

Consider in this vein, too, Langston Hughes's famous poem, "The Negro Speaks of Rivers:"

> *I've known rivers ancient as the*
> > *world and older than the flow of*
> > *blood in human veins.*
> *My soul has grown deep like the rivers.*
> *I bathed in the Euphrates when*
> > *dawns were young,*
> *I built my hut near the Congo and*
> > *it lulled me to sleep,*
> *I looked upon the Nile and raised*
> > *the pyramids above it,*
> *I heard the singing of the Mississippi*
> > *when Abe Lincoln went down to*
> > *New Orleans,*
> *And I've seen its muddy bosom turn*
> > *all golden in the sunset,*
> *I've known rivers;*
> *Ancient, dusky rivers;*
> *My soul has grown deep like*
> > *the rivers.*[29]

2. Contamination of Aquatic Ecosystems and the Fish, Plants, Wildlife, and People They Support

The rivers, streams, bayous, bays, lakes, wetlands, and estuaries that support the fish, aquatic plants, and wildlife on which communities and tribes depend have been allowed to become contaminated and depleted. The waters to which communities and tribes look to meet their nutritional, economic, traditional, cultural, religious and other needs also have become vectors of toxins. Contamination now renders communities' and tribes' everyday practices   their ways of living   a source of exposure to a host of substances toxic to humans and other living things. Depletion, too, threatens communities' and tribes' subsistence, traditional, cultural, and religious practices.

---

[28]Elizabeth Cheechio and Bonnie G. Colby, *Indian Water Rights: Negotiating the Future* 1 (June 1993) (quoting Frank Tenorio, Governor, San Felipe Pueblo, *Indian Water Policy in a Changing Environment* 2 (1982)).

[29]Langston Hughes, *My Soul Has Grown Deep: Classics of Early African American Literature*, "The Negro Speaks of Rivers" (John Edgar Wideman ed.).

Yet toxic chemicals and other contaminants have been and continue to be permitted to be emitted, discharged, dumped, or leaked into the air, water, soils, and sediments that together make up home to all life. Once in the environment, these contaminants behave in various ways: some move   traveling over distances or cycling between air and water; some linger   persisting for months or years; some biodegrade   becoming more or less toxic chemical successors; some bioaccumulate in the tissues of aquatic organisms, fish and wildlife   existing in increasing quantities higher up the "food chain." Eventually, humans that consume and use fish, aquatic plants, and wildlife may be exposed to the toxins concentrated in their tissues.

Toxic chemicals and other contaminants also contribute to the depletion of aquatic resources. These other threats (e.g., from logging, mining, grazing, and agricultural operations; from hydropower; from development) compromise water quality and quantity, destroy habitat for fish, aquatic plants and wildlife, and otherwise contribute to the depletion of the resources on which communities and tribes depend.

As a result, aquatic ecosystems are damaged from the Penobscot River to the San Francisco Bay, from Bayou d'Inde to the Great Lakes, from the Columbia Slough to the St. James River. These aquatic ecosystems are contaminated when mercury is emitted to the air from coal-fired power plants and other sources of fossil fuel combustion or from medical waste incinerators   this mercury is then deposited to surface waters and to soils. They are contaminated when PCBs are allowed to remain in sediments without being cleaned up   these PCBs persist for long periods of time and are released to waters, air and soils. They are contaminated when dioxins are discharged to the water from the industrial production of chlorinated organic chemicals   these dioxins are often contained for long periods in sediments and may, in turn, be resuspended to surface waters. These and multiple other sources and contaminants have wreaked incalculable harms to aquatic ecosystems and the fish, aquatic plants and wildlife they support.

James Ransom, Director, Haudenosuanee Environmental Task Force, recounts the destruction of the portion of the St. Lawrence River that is Akwesasne, home to the St. Regis Mohawk:

> *Akwesasne or St. Regis is like most Native communities. We were a fishing, farming, hunting, trapping, and gathering community. These lifestyles helped to support an earth-based value system. . . . We were sustainable societies. Everything we needed was provided by the natural world. We followed the natural laws. It required that we only take from the natural world what we need and that we use all that we take. . . This all changed for the Mohawks of Akwesasne in the 1950s. . . .In 1958, the St. Lawrence-FDR Power Project was constructed on the St. Lawrence River just upriver from Akwesasne. Low-cost hydroelectric power allowed two new industries to open, Reynolds Metal company, an aluminum smelter, and General Motors Powertrain, an automobile parts manufacturer. It allowed a third industry, ALCOA, an aluminum smelter, to expand operations.*
>
> *By the early 1960s, cattle within the territories of the Mohawks began feeling the effects of flouride poisoning from the aluminum smelters. By 1981, PCB contamination of the*

General Motors site came to light. In 1983, it became a federal superfund site. By 1987, PCB problems at ALCOA and Reynolds became known as well. By 1989, a six-mile stretch of the Grasse River and a two-mile stretch of the St. Lawrence River became a federal superfund site because of PCB contamination. . . .

In 1986, a 67-inch length, 200 pound lake sturgeon was caught by Mohawk fishermen in the St. Lawrence river. Parts of it were sent for PCB analysis. The results were alarming as 3.41 parts per million (ppm) of PCBs were found in the meat, 7.95 ppm in the eggs, and 10.20 ppm in the liver. The New York State PCB fish standard for human consumption is 2.0 ppm. . . .

Contamination of the St. Lawrence River resulted in a destruction of a subsistence lifestyle for the Mohawk people. It destroyed hunting, fishing, farming, trapping, and gathering activities. . . .[30]

At a meeting of Alaskan Natives from the northwest arctic region, Herman Toolie, Savoonga, expresses his concerns and the concerns of others in his village:

They have those   what do you call it?   PCBs? A lot of those were in the village. They found gallons in the village around Northeast Cape. There were transformers that were leaking. We don't know if they took them out of the ground or not. I guess they took them out. There used to be a lot of fish right there. We had our camp there not more than a mile away from the site. There used to be lots of fish there but no more. There is a whole bunch of concerns that these elders have. I wish I had a tape recorder and could tape them.[31]

In introducing its tribally-conducted fish consumption study, the Suquamish Tribe recounts the importance of fish and shellfish, even in the face of the degraded water quality and habitat of the Puget Sound:

The Suquamish culture finds its fullest expression in the acknowledged relationship of the people with the land, air, water and all forms of life found within the natural system. River systems, lakes and numerous small creeks historically supported abundant coho, chinook, sockeye and chum runs, with other salmonids and marine fish available as well. The same forests which sustained life in the riparian zones also harbored deer, bear, and other wildlife. Vast expanses of intertidal habitat supported shellfish. By virtue of the Treaty of Point Elliott, Suquamish rights to fish and interests in their habitat were recognized to include the marine waters of Puget Sound from the northern tip of Vashon

---

[30]James Ransom, Director, Haudenosuanee Environmental Task Force, *Proceedings of the American Fisheries Society: Forum on Contaminants in Fish* 25 (1999).

[31]Alaska Traditional Knowledge and Native Foods Database, *Native Concerns* available at www.nativeknowledge.org/db/concerns.asp.

Island to the Fraser River in Canada, including Haro and Rosario Straits and streams draining into the western side of central Puget Sound.

Increased levels of development as well as pollutants from residential, industrial, and commercial uses have resulted in degraded habitats and harvesting restrictions. There were eleven Superfund sites within the immediate area of the Port Madison Indian Reservation at the time the fish consumption survey was conducted.

Despite degraded water quality and habitat, tribal members continue to rely on fish and shellfish as a significant part of their diet. All species of seafood are an integral component of the cultural fabric that weaves the people, the water, and the land together in an interdependent linkage which has been experienced and passed on for countless generations.[32]

And in recounting the harms of intense industrialization along the lower Mississippi River and in St. James Parish, Louisiana, the United Church of Christ Commission for Racial Justice reports:

Also presented as a negative economic impact of polluting industries by local residents was the significant loss of wildlife and vegetation, which contribute to the subsistence living of many St. James Parish residents. Fruiting trees such as pecan, fig, peach, and others have died off. Fish, crayfish and oyster beds have been poisoned. And wildlife important for subsistence hunting, such as rabbit and deer, have disappeared. Not only have important food sources disappeared, but the ability of residents to gather and sell these for cash has also gone. With the decline in the prosperity of local residents, many local businesses have also left the area. A number of residents complained that they must now commute great distances simply to buy groceries and other necessities.[33]

3. Different Exposure Circumstances and Contexts Characterize Communities of Color, Low-Income Communities, Tribes, and Other Indigenous Peoples

Consumption and use of contaminated fish, aquatic plants, and wildlife is the primary route by which humans are exposed to many toxic contaminants. For example, consumption of contaminated fish is considered to be the single greatest route of exposure to PCBs and a major route of exposure to mercury. Consumption of contaminated fish is similarly a significant route of exposure to chlordane, dioxins, DDT, toxaphene, and a litany of over 40 other contaminants. Indeed, any contaminant that *persists* in aquatic environments and *bioaccumulates* in the fish and wildlife that are supported by aquatic environments may find its way to humans when they

---

[32]The Suquamish Tribe, *Fish Consumption Survey of the Suquamish Indian Tribe of the Port Madison Indian Reservation, Puget Sound Region* 4 (2000).

[33]Charles Lee, ed., United Church of Christ Commission for Racial Justice, *From Plantations to Plants: Report of the Emergency National Commission on Environmental and Economic Justice in St. James Parish, Louisiana* (1998).

consume or use these fish and wildlife. EPA has recognized that fish and wildlife consumption, in particular, is the chief route by which all humans are exposed to many of these "persistent and bioaccumulative toxins" or PBTs.

Consumption and use of contaminated fish, aquatic plants, and wildlife is an especially pressing concern for many communities of color, low-income communities, tribes, and other indigenous peoples, whose members may (1) consume fish, aquatic plants, and wildlife in greater quantities than does the general population; (2) consume and use different fish, aquatic plants, and wildlife than does the general population; (3) employ different practices in consuming and using fish, aquatic plants, and wildlife than does the general population; (4) consume and use fish, aquatic plants, and wildlife in cultural, traditional, religious, historical, economic, and legal contexts that differ from those of the general population.

When health and environmental agencies respond to the human health impacts from contaminated aquatic environments, they typically frame the issue as one of harm to individuals' physical health: the contaminants are carcinogens, or reproductive toxins, or endocrine disrupters, or have multiple human health "endpoints." Health and environmental agencies then manage these "health risks" by employing one or both of two general strategies: *risk avoidance* (whereby risk-bearers are encouraged or required to change the practices that expose them to environmental contamination, e.g. through fish consumption advisories, directed to those people who eat fish) or *risk reduction* (whereby risk-producers are required to cleanup, reduce, or prevent environmental contamination, e.g., through water quality standards, applied to industrial sources that discharge contaminants into surrounding waters). In both cases, agencies' decisions for the most part reflect the exposure circumstances and the cultural, traditional, religious, historical, economic, and legal contexts that describe members of the general population the "average American" or "the typical U.S. consumer." Importantly, these decisions often do not reflect the exposure circumstances or the traditional, religious, historical, economic, and legal contexts that describe members of communities of color, low-income communities, tribes, or other indigenous peoples.

To illustrate briefly a few of these considerations:

The EPA until quite recently based its environmental decisions on the assumption that humans eat just 6.5 grams of fish per day *roughly one 8-ounce fish meal per month*. Yet there is abundant evidence that people of color, low-income individuals, tribal members, and other indigenous people eat far greater quantities of fish. For example, a recent study by the Columbia River Inter-Tribal Fish Commission of members of four Columbia River tribes registered a mean fish consumption rate of 58.7 grams/day and a maximum fish consumption rate of 972.0 grams/day well over one hundred times the EPA value.[34] A recent study of ten Asian and Pacific Islander

---

[34]Columbia River Inter-Tribal Fish Commission, Technical Report 94-3, A Fish Consumption Survey of the Umatilla, Nez Perce, Yakama, and Warm Springs Tribes of the Columbia River Basin (1994); Columbia River Inter-Tribal Fish Commission, Comments to Administrator Browner on the Draft Revisions to the Methodology for Deriving Ambient water Quality Criteria for the Protection of Human Health 8 (1999).

groups in King County, Washington showed a mean fish consumption rate of 117.2 grams/day and a maximum values of 733.46 grams/day.[35]   Similarly, studies of anglers in both Alabama and Michigan registered markedly higher fish consumption rates for low-income African-Americans in Alabama, low-income African-Americans ate a mean of 63 grams/day;[36] in Michigan, low-income African-Americans (together with other "minority fishers and off-reservation Native Americans") consumed a mean of 43.1 grams/day;[37] a recent study of members of the Suquamish Tribe registered a mean fish consumption rate of 213.9 grams/day and a maximum fish consumption rate of 1,453.6 grams/day.[38] Although methodological differences in the various studies mean that these numbers cannot provide a precise basis for comparison, they nonetheless afford a sense of the large differences in the quantities of fish consumed by different groups. EPA has just revised its standard assumptions and now uses default values of 17.5 grams/day for the general population and 142.4 grams/day for subsistence populations. While these revised numbers are a marked improvement, they are still a source of concern for those groups whose members consume at the highest levels. The result is that when the fish are contaminated, those consuming at higher rates will be exposed to greater quantities of the contaminants that are present in the fish tissue.

EPA also typically makes assumptions about the species and parts consumed and about the methods of preparation that reflect that practices of the general population but often do not depict fully or accurately the practices of communities of color, low-income communities, tribes, or other indigenous peoples. For example, according to a recent survey of first- and second-generation Asian and Pacific Islanders in King County, Washington   including members of Cambodian, Chinese, Filipino, Hmong, Japanese, Korean, Laotian, Mien, Samoan, and Vietnamese ethnic groups:

> *[Asian and Pacific Islanders] consume a wide variety of seafood species, the most frequently consumed being shellfish. These seafood, depending on their feeding and habitat characteristics, and the tissue parts consumed pose varying chemical contaminant risks to APIs. For example, certain fat soluble chemicals, e.g., PCBs, are concentrated in the fat layer between the meat and the skin, potentially exposing such consumers to higher contaminant levels than those who simply eat the fillet. Eating the fillet with skin is clearly a common practice in the API community. . . . Overall, skin was consumed with the fillet 55% of the time. . . .*

---

[35]Ruth Sechena, et al., *Asian and Pacific Islander Seafood Consumption Study* (1999) [See Table 1 in Chapter One].

[36]Alabama Department of Environmental Management (1993) [See Table 1 in Chapter One].

[37]Patrick West, et al. (1995) [See Table 1 in Chapter One].

[38]Suquamish Indian Tribe (2000) [See Table 1 in Chapter One].

API community members appear to eat shellfish parts that are thought to contain higher concentrations of chemical contamination, e.g., clam stomachs or the hepatopancreas of crabs. Bivalve shellfish were consumed whole by 24% (geoduck) to 89% (mussels) of respondents depending on the species. The "butter" as well as the meat of crabs were consumed 43% of the time . . . .Finally, cooking water, both for finfish and shellfish are commonly used in cooking or directly consumed.[39]

According to a study of the Greenpoint/Williamsburg ("G/W") community in the Borough of Brooklyn in New York City:

[Hispanics and Caribbean Americans] consume considerable quantities of fresh shellfish, including parts of the fish not typically consumed (e.g., the highly contaminated hepatopancreas of blue crabs).[40]

According to Hawaii's Thousand Friends:

Hawaii's diverse ethnic population led to a mixing of traditions and foods, including many fish dishes. Japanese sashimi and Hawaiian poke, both raw fish dishes, are mainstays at most parties and traditional gatherings.[41]

According to an account of subsistence fishing on the Upper Kobuk River in Alaska:

Each summer, families from Shungnak and Kobuk move to camps to harvest salmon, whitefish, and sheefish. . . . upper Kobuk residents preferred to camp in the sheefish spawning areas because sheefish caught there had eggs, a local delicacy. . . .Although sheefish are caught throughout the summer, local residents prefer to catch them late in the season because the sheefish are fat, the eggs are ripe, and the fish can be left to age and freeze, a storage method preferable to drying.

Aged, frozen sheefish, an upper Kobuk delicacy, were eaten later in winter without further processing or preparation. By spring, these fish were known as ui.laaq (thawed, aged sheefish) a meal savored by upper Kobuk residents.

---

[39]Ruth Sechena, et al., *Asian and Pacific Islander Seafood Consumption Study* (1999)

[40]Industrial Economics, Inc., *Community-Specific Cumulative Exposure Assessment for Greenpoint/Williamsburg New York* 2-21 (1999).

[41]Hawaii's Thousand Friends (Written Comments, March 11, 2002).

Fresh sheefish were baked, boiled, or fried. The large intestines, full of fat, were boiled. Fish oil (qaluum uqsruq) was separated from the boiled water with a large spoon and served with cooked sheefish.[42]

Ron Oatman, Nez Perce, recalls:

We used to collect the eggs from the suckers and Mom would fry them up with the rest of the fish. We always thought this quite good.[43]

Again, the result in many cases is that when the fish are contaminated, those consuming in accordance with different practices will be exposed to greater quantities of the contaminants.

Moreover, the approach employed by EPA and other environmental agencies proceeds as if humans were exposed to one contaminant at a time. However, members of communities of color, low-income communities, tribes, and other indigenous peoples are often exposed to multiple contaminants (and by multiple routes) at the same time; this is so to a greater extent than for the general population. For example, according to Barbara Harper, Fourteen Confederated Tribes and Bands of the Yakama Nation, and Stuart Harris, Confederated Tribes of the Umatilla Indian Reservation:

[I]t is the norm, at least in the Columbia River system, for over 100 contaminants to be identified in fish tissues.[44]

Environmental agencies also proceed as if all humans similarly enjoyed relative health and access to basic health care and nutrition. However, members of communities of color, low-income communities, and tribes often have relatively poorer background health and lesser access to health care and nutrition than is enjoyed by the general population. Other "co-risk" factors, too, affect how humans respond when they are exposed to environmental contaminants and often these co-risk factors are different for members of affected communities and tribes.

Health and environmental agencies generally assume that all humans are similarly able to turn to substitutes when fish, aquatic plants, and wildlife have become contaminated. While this substitution may pose few difficulties for members of the general population, it may be impractical or impossible for economic, cultural, religious and/or other reasons for some members of communities of color, low-income communities and tribes. For example, for some tribal peoples,

------

[42]Susan Georgette and Hannah Loon, *Subsistence and Sport Fishing of Sheefish on the Upper Kobuk River, Alaska* (1990) available at www.nativeknowledge.org/db/files/tp175.htm.

[43]Dan Landeen and Allen Pinkham, *Salmon and His People: Fish and Fishing in Nez Perce Culture* 95 (1999).

[44]Barbara Harper and Stuart Harris, *Proceedings of the American Fisheries Society: Contaminants in Fish,* "Tribal Technical Issues in Risk Reduction Through Fish Advisories" 19 (1999).

as Barbara Harper, Fourteen Confederated Tribes of the Yakama Nation, and Stuart Harris, Confederated Tribes of the Umatilla Indian Reservation, explain:

> [T]here are likely to be no acceptable 'tradeoffs.' Tribal peoples may not have an option of avoiding fish consumption for cultural or religious reasons as well as economic reasons. . . . The cultural use of fish is not a 'perceived benefit of fish consumption.' It is a baseline situation that is not an option or a choice, but an absolute requirement.[45]

These considerations and others place in question the appropriate role of fish consumption advisories in protecting those who would consume fish, aquatic plants, and wildlife from the serious harms of exposure   harms including the risk of cancer, neurological damage, endocrine disruption, and a host of other ills. To the extent that fish consumption advisories form an appropriate part of agencies' response to contaminated aquatic environments, however, there is reason to be concerned that health and environmental agencies generally employ the language and methods of communication that are likely to reach and be understood by the members of the general population, but often fail to reach and cannot be understood by members of affected communities. This is particularly likely when agencies distribute advisories in English to those who have limited English proficiency, or when agencies post advisories on the Internet but those affected cannot afford and do not otherwise have access to a computer. There has been recent progress here, however, as EPA and other agencies in some cases have translated their advisories into the language(s) of those affected and have sought to learn which methods of communication would be most likely to reach communities likely to be among the most exposed.

4. Environmental Agencies Have Made Considerable Progress; However, Many Aspirations and Obligations Remain Unfulfilled

EPA and other agencies have made considerable progress toward addressing degraded and depleted aquatic ecosystems, and, more recently, toward attending to the needs and rights of communities of color, low-income communities, tribes, and other indigenous peoples. Aquatic ecosystems are significantly less contaminated than they were three decades ago, when the Clean Water Act was passed. According to EPA estimates, whereas in 1972 only 36% of the rivers, lakes, and estuaries within the United States were clean enough to support "fishable-swimable" uses, today roughly 60% of lakes, rivers, and estuaries are clean enough to support these uses.[46] EPA and other agencies have also made progress in attending to the different circumstances of exposure that often describe members of communities of color, low-income communities, tribes, and other indigenous peoples; in evidencing awareness of their different languages, traditions, and cultures; and in addressing their claims to participation and consultation when EPA and other agencies make decisions affecting their lives and resources.

---

[45]Id. at 21 (1999).

[46]Zygmunt J.B, Plater, et al., *Environmental Law and Policy: Nature, Law, and Society* 503 (2d ed. 1998).

Yet, by EPA's own account, there is much yet to be done. EPA's Strategic Plan issued in September 2000 (2000 EPA Strategic Plan) acknowledges that much more work is needed to protect effectively American's rivers, lakes, wetlands, aquifers, and coastal and ocean waters so that they will sustain fish, plants, and wildlife as well as recreational, subsistence, and economic activities.[47] There EPA notes that "[a]s of 1998, about 40 percent of the assessed waters in the United States were degraded to the point that they did not support their designated use."[48] Additionally, more than 50% of the Nation's wetlands--some 100 million acres--have been lost since European settlement.[49] And, "polluted water and degraded aquatic ecosystems threaten the viability of all living things and vigor of the nation's economy."[50] In 2000, the number of fish consumption advisories rose by 187, representing a 7% increase over 1999, and the number of acres of lakes under advisories increased from 20.4% in 1999 to 23% in 2000, a total of 63,288 lakes.[51] All of the Great Lakes and their connecting waters and 71% of coastal waterways were under advisory in 2000.[52]

Thus, EPA has yet to fulfill the aspirations set for it in the Clean Water Act and elsewhere. The CWA, for example, aspires "to restore and maintain the chemical, physical, and biological integrity of our Nation's waters;" it aspires to do this by, among other things, eliminating the discharge of pollution into navigable waters "by 1985."

EPA also has yet to uphold fully its obligations to communities of color, low-income communities, tribes, and other indigenous peoples under various treaties, the federal trust responsibility, Title VI of the Civil Rights Act of 1964, and Executive Order 12898.

B. WHAT ARE THE POLICY IMPLICATIONS OF THE ABOVE?

Together, the chapters of this Report respond to the policy charge to NEJAC:

How should EPA improve the quality, quantity, and integrity of our Nation's aquatic ecosystems in order to protect the health and safety of people consuming or using fish, aquatic plants, and wildlife?

---

[47]U.S. Environmental Protection Agency, Office of the Chief Financial Officer, *Strategic Plan* 19 (No. 190-R-00-002) (September 2000) available at www.epa.gov/ocfopage/plan/2000strategicplan.pdf.

[48] Id. Note that this figure does not include unassessed waters – some of which may not meet these standards.

[49] Id.

[50] Id.

[51]*U.S. Environmental Protection Agency Fact Sheet Update: National Listing of Fish and Wildlife Advisories* 1 (EPA-823-F-01-010) (April 2001).

[52]Id.

Chapter One focuses on the tools that environmental agencies use to define, evaluate and respond to the adverse health impacts from contaminated aquatic environments. It discuses the research methods agencies use to obtain information about the lives, practices, and circumstances of affected communities and tribes, as well as the risk assessment approaches agencies use to evaluate these impacts.

The next two chapters examine agencies' responses   the "risk management" approaches that they employ to address the health impacts of contaminated aquatic environments. Chapter Two discusses agencies' risk reduction strategies, whereby risk-producers are required to cleanup, reduce, or prevent environmental contamination. This chapter examines the legal authorities that might be invoked more effectively to sustain healthy aquatic ecosystems and to protect the health and safety of people consuming or using fish, aquatic plants, and wildlife.

Chapter Three then discusses agencies' risk avoidance strategies, whereby risk-bearers are asked to change their lives and practices in order to avoid exposure to harmful contaminants. This chapter focuses on fish consumption advisories and asks what role they should play in efforts more effectively to protect the health and safety of people consuming or using fish, aquatic plants, and wildlife. In so doing, it considers how agencies can identify, acknowledge and meet the real needs of those who are affected among communities of color, low-income communities, tribes, and other indigenous peoples. This chapter discusses means by which agencies can ensure community participation and tribal consultation. It also discusses ways agencies can work to make communities whole once the fish, aquatic plants, and wildlife on which they depend have already become contaminated. This chapter, in particular, responds to questions posed to the NEJAC by the EPA Office of Water in October, 2001, requesting advice on improving its risk communication efforts and on updating its *Guidance for Assessing Chemical Contaminant Data for Use in Fish Advisories, Volume IV: Risk Communication.*[53] Various aspects of these questions are also addressed throughout the Report.

Chapter Four examines issues unique to American Indian tribes, Alaskan Native villages, and their members. Although tribes and their members share many of the concerns discussed in the first three chapters, their unique political and legal status warrants separate treatment.

---

[53]Memorandum from James Hanlon, Acting Deputy Assistant Administrator, Office of Water, to Barry Hill, Director, Office of Environmental Justice (October 4, 2001).

CHAPTER I: RESEARCH METHODS AND RISK ASSESSMENT APPROACHES

How should EPA improve its research methods and risk assessment approaches to address degradation of aquatic ecosystems and adverse impacts to human health from consuming or using contaminated fish, aquatic plants, and wildlife for subsistence, cultural, traditional, and religious activities and purposes?

When health and environmental agencies respond to the harms from contaminated aquatic environments, they typically frame the issue as one of "human health risks" specifically, harm to individuals' physical health: the contaminants are carcinogens, or reproductive toxins, or endocrine disrupters, or have multiple human health "endpoints."

Health and environmental agencies then manage these "health risks" by employing one or both of two general strategies: *risk avoidance* (whereby risk-bearers are encouraged or required to change the practices that expose them to environmental contamination, e.g. through fish consumption advisories, directed to those people who eat fish) or *risk reduction* (whereby risk-producers are required to cleanup, reduce, or prevent environmental contamination, e.g., through water quality standards, applied to industrial sources that discharge contaminants into surrounding waters).[54] Risk reduction strategies will be the focus of discussion in Chapter 2; risk avoidance strategies will be the focus of discussion in Chapter 3.

For both strategies, agencies need to get a sense of the practices that expose humans to environmental contaminants (e.g., how much fish do they eat? what kinds of fish? how is it prepared?) and the underlying health and other circumstances of those exposed (e.g., are they young or old? do they have other preexisting health conditions? do they have access to adequate health care?). In gathering this information and, more generally, in fashioning their responses to contamination, agencies' efforts have until quite recently reflected the lives, practices, and circumstances of the "average American" or "the typical U.S. consumer."[55] Importantly, they often have not reflected the lives and circumstances of communities of color, low-income communities, tribes, and other indigenous peoples. That is, agencies' efforts overall have tended to reflect the cultural, traditional, religious, historical, economic, and legal contexts that describe members of the general population. Specifically, agencies' efforts have assumed (1) the exposure circumstances of members of the general population; and (2) the susceptibilities and co-risk factors of members of the general population.

---

[54]Catherine A. O'Neill, *Risk Avoidance and Environmental Justice* (forthcoming).

[55]See, e.g., U.S. Environmental Protection Agency, *Note to Correspondents: EPA Issues 1996 Fish Advisory Data* (1997) ("The typical U.S. consumer eating fish in moderation from a variety of sources and eating a variety of species is not believed to be at increased risk . . .").

This Chapter will focus on the tools environmental agencies use to define, evaluate and respond to the adverse health impacts from contaminated aquatic environments: the *research methods* agencies use to obtain information about the lives, practices, and circumstances of affected communities and tribes, and the *risk assessment approaches* agencies employ to evaluate and address these health impacts. Along the way, it will highlight issues that bear as well on agencies' approaches to *risk management* and *risk communication*, although these questions will be taken up at greater length later in the Report.

Part A of the chapter discusses briefly the prior question: what is meant by "adverse impacts to human health?" The next four parts examine exposure. Part B looks at fish consumption rates and how these differ as between the general population and higher-consuming "subpopulations" such as communities of color, low-income communities, tribes, and other indigenous peoples. Part C examines standard assumptions about the fish, plant and wildlife species people consume and use; the parts of these species they use; and the preparation methods they employ. It considers the differences in these practices among various affected groups and how this affects estimates of exposure. Part D raises the point that communities of color, low-income communities, tribes, and other indigenous peoples consume and use fish, plants and wildlife in different cultural, traditional, religious, historical, economic, and legal contexts than the "average American." Part E takes up the issues of aggregate or multiple exposures and cumulative risks. Part F turns from exposure to issues of susceptibility and co-risk factors. Part G explores suppression effects and their implications. Part H addresses research methods relevant to risk assessment, management, and communication involving contaminated fish and aquatic environments. Finally, Part I considers refinements and alternatives to risk-based approaches.

A. DEFINING ADVERSE IMPACTS TO HUMAN HEALTH

How can EPA in its various functions ensure that cultural, traditional, religious practices are being considered in defining and evaluating health risks with respect to all people, including minority and low-income communities, and tribes?

When health and environmental agencies evaluate and respond to the human health risks from contaminated aquatic environments, they typically invoke a particular conception of "human health."[56] This conception tends to be that of the dominant society, for whom "human health" is taken in the narrow, individual and physiological sense of the term. So defined, agencies look to toxicological and epidemiological data that connect environmental contaminants such as mercury or PCBs to human health "endpoints" such as neurological damage or cancer. Agencies cite determinations (by legislatures, courts, or their own or other agencies) as to "acceptable" increases in the risk of occurrence of such "endpoints," and from there work backward to decide how much mercury to permit to be emitted into the air or what quantity of PCBs to allow to remain in

---

[56]Agencies also sometimes (although less often) respond to "ecological risks;" these are typically considered separately from human health risks, and do not include attention to social, cultural, or other related harms.

contaminated sediments after cleanup. These decisions then get incorporated into standards or permits or cleanup requirements.

This definition of the adverse impacts, however, may not reflect the perspectives of those affected. For some of those affected, the harms from contamination are not only physical, but psychological, social, and cultural. For some of those affected, the affront is not only to an individual but to a group the threat is not only to the physical survival of a person, but to the cultural flourishing of a people. Stuart Harris, Confederated Tribes of the Umatilla Indian Reservation, and Barbara Harper, International Institute for Indigenous Resource Management, explain:

> *For example, Native American communities are inseparable from their lands and resources, so evaluation of their risks from contamination must integrate human physiological and mental health, ecological health, socio-economic health, and cultural and spiritual health within a single framework. This does not mean simply adding a quality of life component and calling it cultural risk, or using an exposure scenario that reflects additional routes of exposures. Rather, it means beginning the assessment by understanding the entire eco-cultural system (people and biota interlocked in a co-adapted system of behaviors and ecologies that is sustainable over time but which is now severely strained even without the addition of contamination). . . .*
>
> *The individual and collective well-being of tribal members is often derived from membership in a healthy community that has access to ancestral lands and traditional resources and from having the ability to satisfy personal responsibility to participate in traditional community activities and to help maintain the spiritual quality of our resources.[57]*

Environmental justice means noticing and acknowledging not only the harms that are perceived by the dominant society, but also the harms that are felt by communities of color, low-income communities, tribes, and other indigenous peoples. Often, these harms will have quite different dimensions than those felt by the dominant society and reflected in agencies' definition and evaluation of the problem. EPA and other agencies need to reexamine methods and models employed in evaluating adverse health impacts from environmental contamination.[58]

----

[57]Stuart G. Harris and Barbara L. Harper, *Using Eco-Cultural Dependency Webs in Risk Assessment and Characterization of Risks to Tribal Health and Cultures*, 2 Environmental Science & Pollut. Res. 91, 91-92 (Special Issue, 2000).

[58]Elizabeth D. Nobmann, *Nutritional Benefits of Native Foods*, available at www.nativeknowledge.org/db/files/aboutnt2.htm (describing Alaskan Native's understanding of "nutrition" in the broadest sense and recounting a call for "models that addressed social, emotional, spiritual and cultural issues as well as physical health" by attendees of the Alaska-Russia Native People's Health and Social Issues Conference in 1992).

B. EXPOSURE: FISH CONSUMPTION RATES

Several factors determine (1) whether and how an individual comes in contact with environmental contaminants and (2) to what extent that individual suffers adverse health effects as a result of this contact. The first set of factors describes one's circumstances of *exposure*. The second set of factors describes one's *susceptibilities and co-risk factors*. Although more information needs to be gathered about the differences among various "subpopulations" with respect to both exposure and susceptibilities, existing data show important differences between the general population and communities of color, low-income communities, tribes, and other indigenous peoples. Questions of exposure will be addressed in Parts B, C, D and E, below; questions of susceptibility will be addressed in Part F.

Humans are exposed to environmental contaminants through a variety of routes: they inhale toxic air contaminants; they drink contaminated groundwater; they absorb pesticides through our skin; they eat fish that swim in and bioaccumulate toxins from contaminated surface water and sediments. As noted above, fish consumption is the primary route of exposure for many toxic contaminants, including those that are now present in and permitted to be released to aquatic environments. All else being equal, the higher the level of fish one consumes, the greater one's exposure to any contaminants in the environment that the fish uptake, and the greater one's risk of adverse health effects.

EPA and other agencies use exposure data to set environmental standards for aquatic environments that support fish and other species consumed by humans: they set water quality standards to determine how much contamination will be permitted to be released now and in the future; they set cleanup standards to determine to what level surface waters and sediments must be cleaned up once they are already contaminated. They also use exposure data to estimate risk in order to determine whether to issue fish consumption advisories. When EPA and other agencies use risk assessment to set environmental standards, they start from a level of risk that has been deemed "acceptable" or a threshold level of exposure that is believed not to result in adverse health effects. They then consider the toxicity of the contaminant in question (e.g., dioxin) and the various elements of humans' exposure to that contaminant (e.g., how much fish do people consume? for how many years do people live and consume fish at these rates? to what extent does the contaminant in question bioaccumulate in the fish tissue consumed?). Working from these inputs, agencies determine how much of the contaminant to allow to be discharged to or to remain in aquatic environments. Note that when agencies set standards in this way, they typically rely on values for each of the inputs that reflect the characteristics and practices of the general population. These values often do not reflect the characteristics and practices of affected communities and tribes, which often lead to greater exposures for these groups. This is problematic in that the resulting standards will not protect these more highly-exposed groups.

1. Evidence of Different Consumption Practices

While there is considerable evidence that different groups have different fish consumption practices, these differences have until recently been demonstrated chiefly by "anecdote" rather than by empirical study. Even today, there are many more instances in which practices that include high rates of fish consumption and/or consumption from seriously contaminated waters are evidenced by local knowledge, direct observation, or "anecdote" rather than by formal study. Thus, for example, as Yalonda Sindé, Executive Director of the Community Coalition for Environmental Justice, Seattle, reports:

> *We know there are people out there fishing on the Duwamish. People in the neighborhood see them out there.*[59]

The Duwamish waterway is highly contaminated and under advisory for a host of industrial chemicals; signs are posted warning against eating all bottom fish, all shellfish, and seaweed. Similarly, as Bowden Quinn of the Grand Cal Task Force reports:

> *Although we don't have any hard data, there is anecdotal evidence of people subsistence fishing on the Calumet River. People do fish and they likely eat the fish they catch . . . despite a "Class 5" restriction on the River, which means "Do Not Eat the Fish."*[60]

The Calumet Region is home to steel manufacturing facilities, petroleum refineries, chemical manufacturing facilities and a host of other heavy industries, and has been described as "one of the nation's most polluted areas."[61] And, Ora Rawls, Executive Director, Mississippi Rural Development Council, reports:

> *Fish consumption (volume) has been underestimated. As I shared with a DEQ (EPA) official, many individuals (African American) eat fish two to three times a week in rural areas, as often as five times a week. Where I lived on the Coast (Gulport/Biloxi), four to five times a week. This volume is from personal fishing (streams, lakes, ponds), not from retail sales data that is used to capture consumption patterns.*[62]

---

[59]Personal Interview with Yalonda Sindé, Executive Director, Community Coalition for Environmental Justice, Seattle, Washington (October 16, 2001).

[60]Telephone Interview with Bowden Quinn, Executive Director, Grand Cal Task Force (October 10, 2001); accord, Telephone Interview with Alex DaSilva, Remedial Action Coordinator, Indiana Department of Environmental Management (October 10, 2001).

[61]Bill Eyring, Center for Neighborhood Technology, *The Neighborhood Works,* "Industry's Polluted Legacy: The Calumet Region" 10 (October/November 1993).

[62]National Risk Communication Conference, Proceedings Document II-17-19 (2001).

Anecdotal evidence similarly describes people fishing on and consuming fish from Lake Erie and the Cuyahoga River in Cleveland;[63] from the Mississippi River in East St. Louis;[64] from the Columbia Slough in Portland, Oregon;[65] and from the Mississippi River between New Orleans and Baton Rouge.[66]

There are, however, several formal fish consumption studies that demonstrate that members of various communities of color, low-income communities, tribes, and other indigenous peoples consume far greater quantities of fish than do members of the general population. Further, these studies show that there are differences as well *among* these various communities, groups, or peoples. They also support the observation that the intersection of poverty and identity or group membership may be an important factor in accounting for differences in fish consumption practices. Table 1 presents a sampling of the fish consumption rates gathered by recent studies, selected to illustrate these characteristics of the data in the context of various subpopulations (e.g., Native American, Alaskan Native, Asian/Pacific Islander, African-American, southern, and urban subpopulations). Note that the values presented here are not directly comparable because of design and other differences among the studies. (For example, some studies include shellfish whereas others include only finfish; some studies provide *per capita* values which include those who do not eat fish along with those who do whereas other studies provide values for fish-consumers only.) These values are provided only to give some sense of the relatively higher consumption rates of communities of color, low-income communities, tribes, and other indigenous peoples compared to the general population (as well as some sense of the differences among and within these groups).[67]

---

[63]Telephone Interview with Patrick C. West, Professor Emeritus of Natural Resources/Environmental Sociology, University of Michigan School of Natural Resources (October 23, 2001).

[64]Id.

[65]Videotape: The Water in Our Backyard (City of Portland, Bureau of Environmental Services).

[66]Telephone Interview with Mary Lee Orr, Louisiana Environmental Action Network (October 17, 2001).

[67]Some of these values, moreover, were generated for this purpose only and should *not* be cited or used without consulting the studies and their authors. In some cases, these numbers were generated in reliance on assumptions that may or may not be shared by the study authors (e.g., conversion methods for values originally given in g fish/kg bodyweight/day).

Table 1: Quantified Evidence of Fish Consumption

Study Authors (Date)	Sample Population	50th Percentile (g/day)	Mean (g/day)	90th Percentile (g/day)	95th Percentile (g/day)	Max. Value (g/day)*
Duncan (2000)	Suquamish Indian tribe	132.1	213.9	489.0	796.9	1453.6
Sechena (1999)	Ten Asian & Pacific Is ander groups, King Co., WA	89	117.2	242	---	733.46
Chiang (1998)	Laotian Groups (Mien, Lao, Khmu, Thadum), West Contra Costa Co., CA	9.1	18.3	42.5	85.1	182.3
Toy, et a . (1995)	Squaxin Is and and Tu a ip tribes	35.6 - 48.7	60.6 - 82.9	159.7 - 221.7	205.1 - 280.5	391.4
West, et a . (1995)	Michigan fishers	---	14.7	---	---	---
	Low-income African Americans and off-reservation Native Americans	---	43.1	---	---	---
CRITFC (1994)	Nez Perce, Umati a, Y akama, and Warm Springs tribes	29.0 - 32.0	58.7	97.2 - 130.0	170.0	972.0
A abama DEM (1993)	A abama Fishers	---	44.8	---	50.7	---
	B ack ang ers with income < $15,000	---	63	---	---	---
De enbarger, et a . (1993)	Houma, LA consumers	65	---	---	---	---
Nobmann, et a . (1992)	A askan Natives from 11 communities	---	109	---	---	---
Puffer, et a . (1982)	Los Ange es Harbor fishers	37	---	225	338.8	---

* Note: In some studies, these maximum va ues were treated as out iers and adjusted downward.

In addition to the studies presented here, several other studies provide further formal, quantified evidence of differences in fish consumption practices among communities of color, low-income communities, tribes, other indigenous peoples, and the general population.[68]

Significantly, the fish consumption rates presented in Table 1 are markedly higher, at virtually every point of comparison, than those relied upon by agencies to set water quality standards, to set cleanup standards for surface water and sediments, and to gauge baseline consumption to estimate health risks and the need for fish consumption advisories. As elaborated below, EPA until quite recently employed a fish consumption rate of 6.5 grams/day for all populations. EPA now employs a fish consumption rate of 17.5 grams/day for the general population and recreational fishers, and 142.4 grams/day for subsistence fishers.[69] These are 90th and 99th percentile values, respectively, from a study of the general population (fish consumers and non-consumers alike). That is to say, EPA targets protection at the 90th percentile of the general population (a point discussed further below). Compare these values with the 90th percentile of Asian and Pacific Islanders in King County, at 242 g/day or the 90th percentile of the Suquamish Indian tribe, at 489 g/day, or the 90th percentile of fishers in the Los Angeles Harbor, at 225 g/day. Consider, too, that whereas those Asian and Pacific Islanders in King County consuming at the average (mean) rate may be adequately protected were the relevant environmental standards to reflect EPA's default for subsistence fishers (142.4 g/day), those consuming at the maximum rate   733.46 g/day would be grossly underprotected. They would fare even worse were the relevant environmental standards to reflect EPA's default for the general population (17.5 g/day). Those consuming at the maximum rate for the Suquamish Tribe (1453.6 g/day), the Laotian communities in West Contra Costa County (182.3 g/day), the Squaxin Island and Tulalip tribes (391.4 g/day), and the four Columbia River tribes (972 g/day) would be similarly underprotected   and, as discussed below, consumption at these rates may reflect the very practices that these affected groups would want to see perpetuated and protected for cultural, traditional, religious, economic, and other reasons.

However, as this survey of the available data reveals, there are many communities, groups, or peoples for which empirical studies have not yet been conducted. In addition, there is still relatively little data about the intersection of factors such as ethnicity or group membership and income. And, for some groups, there is the matter of acute or peak consumption rates   very high rates of consumption for shorter periods, such as during ceremonies, religious and other holidays (e.g., Lent, during which Roman Catholics may consume 2 or more fish meals per week), or

---

[68] Among these are studies of fish consumption in Santa Monica (CA); in the state of New York; on the Hudson River (NY); in Detroit (MI); in Lake Coeur d'Alene (ID); on Commencement Bay (WA); on the Savannah River (GA); in the state of Florida; on Lake Ontario; in American Samoa; on the Fox River (WI); among Wisconsin Chippewa Indians; among the Miccousukee Indian Tribes of South Florida; and among Native Americans living near Clear Lake, California. EPA canvassed these and other studies in preparing its AWQC Methodology. See, U.S. Environmental Protection Agency, Ambient Water Quality Criteria Derivation Methodology Human Health, Technical Support Document 89-103 (July 1998).

[69] It is not clear precisely which groups EPA means to include when it refers to "subsistence fishers."

harvest seasons (e.g. salmon runs, during which some Alaskan Natives consume 80-100 pounds of fish per month) — about which less may be known and for which, in any event, current risk assessment methods may fail to account. As Delores Garza, Alaska Native Science Commission, explains:

> [W]e eat much more [fish, wildlife, and plants] than is listed [by EPA and other agencies], but we also eat it in a very short time period. That's when strawberries are fresh, when corn is fresh, when salmon run — you eat nothing but salmon. So you don't eat one steak per month or one filet per month. You eat salmon for breakfast, for lunch, and for dinner for a month, and then you go to your next resources and you eat that same amount of that resource.[70]

Similarly, the Swinomish Indian Tribal Community, comments:

> Not only should the EPA add multiple exposures and cumulative risks to health risk calculations done, but they should also publish and distribute methodology to Tribes who employ their own fish consumption rates, based on local data. Moreover, calculations and procedures to determine acute and chronic events ought to be explicitly described so that health risks can be determined from one high consumption event, for instance during a traditional ceremony, as well as over the long term.[71]

In many cases, communities, groups, or tribes would be interested in conducting such studies, but lack the financial and/or technical resources to do so. Although anecdotal data may be plentiful, non-quantified data are difficult to incorporate into risk assessment as currently practiced; moreover, environmental agencies are unlikely to accept data that have not been quantified according to accepted norms (e.g., for statistical analysis, peer review, etc.). These are research needs that should be addressed. This point is discussed further in Part H, below.

2. EPA's Revised Fish Consumption Rates

Until recently, EPA used a standard or "default" assumption for the fish consumption rate (FCR) that would be factored into estimates of health risk: 6.5 grams/day.[72] This is about one 8-ounce fish serving *per month* — an amount that is outdated and inaccurate even for the general population. And, this amount grossly underestimates the consumption rates for many communities of color, low-income communities, tribes, and other indigenous peoples.

---

[70]Delores Garza, Alaska Native Science Commission, *Testimony to National Environmental Justice Advisory Council* Vol III-89-90 (Annual Meeting Transcript) (Dec. 4, 2001).

[71]Swinomish Indian Tribal Community, *Comments on the National Environmental Justice Advisory Council's Draft Fish Consumption Report* (Feb. 5, 2002).

[72]Consent Decree Water Criteria, "Guidelines and Methodology Used in the Preparation of Health Effect Assessment" 45 Fed. Reg. 79,347, App. C (1980).

Recognizing this, EPA revised its default assumption in the fall of 2000, as part of an updated Methodology for Deriving Ambient Water Quality Criteria for the Protection of Human Health ("AWQC Methodology").[73] Although in many cases federal and state water quality criteria currently in effect reflect the old 6.5 grams/day default, EPA now recommends the following default FCRs:

General population	17.5 grams/day
Recreational fishers	17.5 grams/day
Subsistence fishers	142.4 grams/day

EPA will use the 17.5 grams/day value when it derives or revises national criteria pursuant to CWA 304(a).[74] EPA will also consider these values when it reviews water quality standards set by states and authorized tribes,[75] as part of a four-part preference hierarchy:

(1) Use local data;
(2) Use data reflecting similar geography/population groups;
(3) Use data from national surveys; and
(4) Use EPA's default intake rates.

EPA "strongly emphasizes that States and authorized Tribes should consider developing criteria to protect highly exposed population groups and use local or regional data over the default values as more representative of their target population group(s)."[76]

EPA's default value of 17.5 grams/day for the general population and for recreational fishers reflects the 90th percentile value of 17.53 grams/day for freshwater and estuarine ingestion by adults, taken from the USDA's CSFII Survey for the years 1994 to 1996. EPA's default value of 142.4 grams/day for subsistence fishers reflects the 99th percentile value of 142.41 grams/day for freshwater and estuarine ingestion by adults, taken from the USDA's CSFII Survey for the years 1994 to 1996. EPA states that it "believes that the assumption of 142.4 grams/day is within

---

[73]U.S. Environmental Protection Agency, *Methodology for Deriving Ambient Water Quality Criteria for the Protection of Human Health* (October 2000) ["AWQC Methodology"].

[74]Under CWA 304(a), the EPA is to develop "criteria" – scientific information and guidance for use by the states and authorized tribes and the EPA itself in establishing water quality standards pursuant to CWA 303(c). Under CWA 303(c), states and authorized tribes have primary responsibility for establishing water quality standards. EPA is charged with reviewing these standards. EPA may promulgate superceding federal standards if a state's or tribe's standards are not consistent with the CWA and its implementing regulations, or if the EPA determines that national standards are necessary. In either event, EPA relies on the criteria it developed under CWA 304(a) as it undertakes review or promulgates standards itself.

[75]See id.

[76]AWQC Methodology at 4-25.

the range of *average* consumption estimates by subsistence fishers based on the studies reviewed."[77]

For states or tribes exercising any of the first three preferences, EPA remarks: "States and authorized Tribes may use either high-end values (such as the 90th or 95th percentile values) or average values for an identified population they plan to protect (e.g., subsistence fishers, sport fishers of the general population). EPA generally recommends that arithmetic mean values should be the lowest value considered by States or Tribes when choosing intake rates for use in criteria derivation. When considering geometric mean (median) values from fish consumption studies, States and authorized Tribes need to ensure that the distribution is based on survey respondents who reported consuming fish because surveys based on both consumers and nonconsumers can often result in median values of zero. If a State or Tribe chooses values (whether central tendency or high-end values) from studies that particularly target high-end consumers, these values should be compared to high-end fish intake rates for the general population to make sure that the high-end consumers within the general population would be protected by the chosen intake rates."[78]

Several aspects of the CSFII data and EPA's AWQC Methodology are worth discussing. First, while EPA's new default values represent a vast improvement over the old 6.5 g/day default, the new default values are problematic in that they aim to protect the general population at the 90th percentile, but to protect subsistence fishers only at a level somewhere "in the range of *average* estimates." This choice provides disparate levels of protection to the general population, on the one hand, and subsistence subpopulations, on the other. Taking this view, it is unclear why EPA's default values do not set protection for subsistence subpopulations at the 90th percentile as they do for the general population   rather than at the average. Moreover, from the perspective of some groups or tribes, it is the very highest consumers that warrant particular attention and protection, because it is these individuals who are consuming at levels and in accordance with practices that are most consonant with the group's or tribe's traditional, cultural, religious or spiritual beliefs. Taking this view, it may be appropriate in some cases for states, tribes, and the EPA to use values that target protection at the 95th or 99th percentile, or even at the maximum value, for particular subsistence subpopulations.

Second, to EPA's credit, the AWQC Methodology's four-part hierarchy recommends using local data as a first choice, data reflecting similar geography/population groups as a second choice, and relying on EPA's default values only as a fourth and last choice. That having been said, the reality is that many states still rely on EPA's default values because they (and the affected communities and tribes within their borders) simply don't have any local data on which to

---

[77]AWQC Methodology at 4-27; but compare Catherine A. O'Neill, *Variable Justice: Environmental Standards, Contaminated Fish, and "Acceptable" Risk to Native Peoples*, 19 Stanford Environmental Law Journal 3, 59 (2000) (noting that EPA appears to offer conflicting accounts of what it means to be a "subsistence" fisher and that "EPA nowhere makes clear precisely who it views to be included in this grouping or to which studies it refers for the 'range of averages.'")

[78]AWQC Methodology at 4-26.

rely often due to a lack of resources.[79] If using local data is to be a meaningful first choice, more resources need to be devoted to gathering this data, a point taken up at greater length below.

Third, EPA notes that the default values and the four-part preference hierarchy assume data reflecting consumption of freshwater and estuarine species only. For states or tribes exercising any of the first three preferences, EPA recommends that consumption of marine species be treated as an "other source of exposure." The effect of choosing to exclude marine species is to decrease the resulting default fish consumption rates (and, ultimately, to render any standard based on these defaults or recommendations less protective). Of note, too, EPA deemed salmon to be marine, although they are anadromous, spending a portion of their lifecycles in freshwater and/or estuarine environments. EPA estimates that the effect of this exclusion is to decrease the resulting default FCRs by approximately 13%.[80]

Fourth, the EPA's default values are based on *per capita* consumption rates from the general population — that is, "fish consumption" rates that include fish consumers and fish nonconsumers alike. The CSFII study on which the EPA's defaults are based for its Draft AWQC Methodology surveyed 11,912 individuals annually for 3-day periods.[81] Of the 11,912 participants, only 3,972 actually ate fish during the three days surveyed.[82] These were the fish consumers; their fish consumption rates were recorded. The 7,940 participants who didn't eat fish during the three-day period were the fish nonconsumers; their fish consumption rates were entered as "0." The CSFII study then generated two sets of figures: a set considering only the fish consumers and a set considering both the fish consumers and the fish nonconsumers. EPA chose to base its default values on the latter, *per capita* figures. Importantly, the effect of this choice is again to decrease the resulting default FCRs — with so many "zero" values factored in, the point estimates are decreased at every point of comparison. So, for example, whereas the mean value for fish consumers is 106.39 g/day, the mean value once fish nonconsumers are also included sinks to 18.01 g/day; similarly, whereas the 99th percentile value for fish consumers is

---

[79]Telephone Interviews with Denis Borum, Environmental Scientist, Office of Science and Technology, Office of Water, U.S. Environmental Protection Agency (Nov. 23, 1999 and March 15, 2002).

[80]Draft AWQC Methodology at 43,804.

[81]1 & 2 U.S. Department of Agriculture, Continuing Survey of Food Intake by Individuals (1998) [hereinafter 1 CSFII Study and 2 CSFII Study]. Note the caveat that the Draft AWQC Methodology references the CSFII study data for 3-day periods for the years 1989, 1990, and 1991, whereas the Final AWQC Methodology references the CSFII data for the years 1994, 1995, and 1996. The numbers in the paragraph are taken from the *Draft* AWQC Methodology, and the 1989-1991 data, which were available to the Fish Consumption Workgroup. While the numbers may be slightly different for the 1994-1996 data (on which EPA based its final AWQC Methodology, the phenomenon described here applies generally to the choice between *per capita* rates versus rates that include fish consumers only and is likely borne out by the 1994-1996 data as well.

[82]1 CSFII Study at IV-8 and IV-16. See caveat, id.

399.26 g/day, the 99th percentile value drops to 142.96 g/day.[83] It is unclear why EPA, in setting out to fashion water quality criteria that are protective of the health of humans who are exposed to contaminants through the fish ingestion route, chooses to consider the fish consumption practices of those who do not eat fish at all. People who don't eat fish aren't in any danger of being exposed via this route. And people who do eat a lot of fish will be underprotected by diluted FCRs influenced by so many "zero" values. This choice is akin to including non-smokers in a study of the direct (not indirect) exposure to nicotine, or setting occupational safety standards to protect non-workers from on-the-job hazards.

Finally, the CSFII participants were selected from the forty-eight contiguous states only. The authors of the CSFII study note that the exclusion of Alaska and Hawai'i may result in depressed fish consumption values given that Alaska and Hawai'i "could potentially contain" a larger percentage of subsistence and other higher-consuming groups than the forty-eight contiguous states. Given the available data regarding fish consumption practices in Alaska and Hawai'i, this is almost certainly the case. Moreover, as affected groups in Alaska and Hawai'i have emphasized, this exclusion is inappropriate not only as a matter of science, but also as a matter of justice.[84]

Taken together, these choices mean that EPA's default values are less protective of higher-consuming and subsistence subpopulations. Given that these subpopulations are in the main comprised of particular communities of color, low-income communities, tribes, or other indigenous peoples, these choices are deeply troubling. Even in those cases where a state or a tribe undertakes any of the first three options in the four-part hierarchy, they must demonstrate "consistency with the principles" of the guidance provided by EPA in order to satisfy EPA review under CWA 303(c). Thus, all of the choices EPA has made in setting its own default values in effect become recommendations for the states or tribes to do the same (or face having to justify departures).

3. Fish Consumption Rates Reflected in Current Water Quality Criteria and Standards[85]

As noted above, EPA has recently revised its default assumption for the fish consumption rate to capture more accurately current national consumption patterns. States and authorized tribes, moreover, have always been free, subject to EPA approval, to depart upward from EPA's

---

[83]2 CSFII Study at IV- 9 (table A-4) and IV-17 (table B-4). Note that these values are for "all fish;" recall that EPA's default values are based not on all fish, but only on freshwater and estuarine fish. See caveat, id.

[84]See, e.g., Hawaii's Thousand Friends (Written Comments, March 11, 2002).

[85]See discussion of water quality criteria under CWA 304(a) and 303(c), at note 74. Note that the term "water quality criteria," as used in CWA 303(c), is part of the definition of a "water quality standard," which is comprised of (1) designated uses of a water quality segment, together with (2) water quality criteria necessary to support those uses. The term "water quality criteria" or "criteria" is also used to refer to the scientific information and guidance to states and tribes provided by the EPA pursuant to CWA 304(a). It is to the former usage that this section of this Report refers.

default numbers to reflect their higher-consuming populations. And under EPA's revised AWQC Methodology, states and tribes are now expressly encouraged to do so. Nonetheless, the question remains to what extent do the water quality standards *currently in effect* (whether developed by EPA, various states or tribes) reflect fish consumption rates higher than the old 6.5 grams/day default?

Although a handful of states have developed their own default fish consumption rates for use in developing water quality criteria and standards (e.g., WA, NY, MN, others), by and large, states have relied on EPA's default of 6.5 grams/day. Note that EPA, for its part, has never disapproved state water quality criteria or standards developed using the 6.5 grams/day value on the basis that this FCR did not adequately reflect higher-consuming or subsistence fishers affected by that state's standards.[86] As a result, a significant number of the state-issued water quality criteria and standards currently in effect rely on the 6.5 grams/day value.[87]

When EPA develops national water quality criteria or when it steps in to develop water quality criteria for states or tribes,[88] it looks to its own default values. Because EPA's revisions have only been in place since fall of 2000, it is perhaps not surprising that many of the criteria currently in effect still reflect EPA's old default value of 6.5 grams/day.[89]

Taken together, a significant portion of water quality criteria and standards currently in effect still rely on the 6.5 grams/day value. As has been noted, this value grossly underestimates consumption by many communities of color, low-income communities, tribes, and other indigenous peoples, and is thus no longer scientifically defensible.

C. EXPOSURE: ASSUMPTIONS ABOUT SPECIES, PARTS, PREPARATION

As noted above, the fish, aquatic plant, and wildlife consumption and use practices of communities of color, low-income communities, tribes, and other indigenous peoples differ from those of the general population. These differences in practices refer not only to the quantities of fish, plants and wildlife consumed, but also to the species consumed; the fish, animal or plant parts used; and the preparation methods employed. The studies upon which EPA and other agencies base their risk assessment and risk management decisions, however, typically make assumptions about species consumed, parts used, and preparation methods employed that reflect the practices of the general population but do not depict fully or accurately the practices of affected communities and tribes. For example, agencies typically assume that people eat or prefer certain

---

[86]Rich Healy, U.S. Environmental Protection Agency, Office of Water (Fish Consumption Workgroup Conference Call, June 26, 2001).

[87]Telephone Interview, Dennis Borum, Environmental Scientist, Office of Science and Technology, Office of Water, U.S. Environmental Protection Agency (March 15, 2002).

[88]The only example here is the case of the Confederated Tries of the Colville Reservation.

[89]Telephone Interview, Dennis Borum, Environmental Scientist, Office of Science and Technology, Office of Water, U.S. Environmental Protection Agency (March 15, 2002).

species, and that they refrain from eating a host of others, including "unusual" species such as sea urchin, sea cucumbers or bottom-feeding fish. Agencies typically assume that people eat only the fillet of finfish, and that they do not eat the fat, head, skin, bones, eggs, or internal organs. Agencies typically assume that people dispose of the drippings or cooking fluid. One result is that agencies set water quality standards and issue consumption advisories that are founded on an inaccurate picture of affected communities' and tribes' exposure. In most cases, the resulting standards will therefore not be sufficiently protective of members of these groups, whose different practices often expose them to additional sources of contaminants beyond those considered by the agencies. For example, lead accumulates in the bones, and most PCBs and most other persistent and bioaccumulative toxins accumulate in tissue with high lipid content, such as fat or eggs. Also, consumption advisories may include irrelevant or inappropriate information or recommendations, a point taken up in Chapter Three.

There is considerable evidence that different groups have different practices with respect to species consumed, parts used, and preparation methods employed. Much of this evidence is contained in local knowledge, direct observation, or "anecdote," rather than in formal studies, although there is a growing body of empirical work that confirms what affected communities and tribes know to be the case. For example, an African-American fisher on the Detroit River explains:

> *I keep sheephead and carp [which are bottom-feeding fish] because I have a large family to feed.*[90]

According to a study by the Squamish Tribe:

> *Children still teethe on dried clams . . .*[91]

According to a study recounting subsistence consumption practices in the Chignik Lake area, Alaska:

> *In exchange for the "red" salmon, Chignik Lake [people] received shellfish such as chitons (bidarkies), sea urchins (uduks), and butter clams from Perryville and Ivanof Bay people, resources Chignik Lake people have to travel far to get.*[92]

---

[90]Patrick C. West and Brunilda Vargus, *A Subsistence-Culture Model for High Toxic Fish Consumption by Low Income Afro-Americans from the Detroit River* 5 (forthcoming).

[91]The Suquamish Tribe, *Fish Consumption Survey of the Suquamish Indian Tribe of the Port Madison Indian Reservation, Puget Sound* 9 (2001).

[92]Lisa Hitchinson-Scarbrough and James A. Fall, *An Overview of Subsistence Salmon and Other Subsistence Fisheries of the Chignik Management Area, Alaska Peninsula, Southwest Alaska* (1996) available at www.nativeknowledge.org/db/files/tp230.htm.

According to a study of fishers on the Lower Fox River in the Green Bay, Wisconsin area:

> *Of those who reported eating the fish, Caucasian anglers reported that they like to eat the walleye . . . Most Asian [Hmong and Laotian] anglers reported that they prefer to eat the White Bass. White Bass is on the list of "Do Not Eat" fish in the fish advisory.*[93]

According to a study of the subsistence hooligan fishery on the Chilkat and Chilkoot Rivers in Alaska:

> *Historically, hooligan oil was used primarily for eating with other foods, but also for preserving certain berries, roots, herbs, and salmon eggs. It was commonly mixed with fresh berries. It was also consumed at feasts.*
>
> *In 1990 and 1991, processors dipped crackers, raw vegetables, dry fish, or meat into the fresh oil while it was still cooking in the vats. Pieces of hooligan meat were scooped up and eaten from cooking vats. One processing group served fresh hooligan oil accompanied by an array of other wild or fresh foods including smoked seal, smoked salmon, and raw fruits and vegetables. Throughout the year, the oil generally was eaten as a condiment with foods. It was added to boiled fish and meat, and spread or dipped with a variety of foods. Herring eggs, other fish eggs, boiled fish, and black seaweed were often eaten with hooligan oil. It was used for frying red sea ribbons in early summer. Year-old oil was whipped and mixed with cranberries, or cranberries and coho or sockeye salmon eggs. The aged oil was preferred, as it tended to whip more easily than freshly rendered oil.*[94]

Velma Veloria, Washington State Representative, observes:

> *Culturally, in the Filipino community, we eat the fin that many cut off, along with the belly fat. We love the fat. We fry it up to make soup.*[95]

---

[93]Dyan M. Steenport, et al., *Fish Consumption Habits and Advisory Awareness Among Fox River Anglers*, Wisconsin Medical Journal (November 2000) available at www.wismed.org/wmj/nov2000/fish.html.

[94]Martha F. Betts, *The Subsistence Hooligan Fishery of the Chilkat and Chilkoot Rivers* (1994) available at www.nativeknowledge.org/db/files/tp213.htm.

[95]Velma Veloria, FCW Conference Call (Oct. 23, 2001).

According to a study of the Greenpoint/Williamsburg ("G/W") community in the Borough of Brooklyn in New York City:

> *[Hispanics and Caribbean Americans] consume considerable quantities of fresh shellfish, including parts of the fish not typically consumed (e.g., the highly contaminated hepatopancreas of blue crabs).*[96]

According to a study of lead contamination in the Spokane River from the Idaho state line to the Seven Mile Bridge:

> *Russians and other immigrants said they use the whole fish, including bones and internal organs, in fish stews. The lead concentrates in bone and brains, the fish study showed.*[97]

According to a study recounting consumption practices in Bristol Bay, Alaska:

> *A variety of parts of the salmon were used for human consumption by Naknek River residents during the study period. Some parts, such as fillets, are used from every fish. Other parts, such as milt, were used on an occasional basis. . . .*
>
> *[Fillets] were frozen, salted, canned, smoked, dried, or eaten fresh. Heads, particular for those kings or large sockeyes, were used by many households. Fish head chowder was the most common method of preparation. Among those persons who used fish heads, it was ranked a favorite part of the fish, particularly of the king salmon.*
>
> *Eggs were frequently used, either as bait or eaten. If eaten, eggs were boiled or prepared as caviar. Fried milt was also used as food. . . . Milt can be frozen, but most reported using it fresh. The backbone was used two ways, either when a whole fish was canned or as 'gumchuk.' Gumchuk is the local term for a backbone that is hung until the outside layer of meat is dry, while the inside portion remains moist. It is then stored in a freezer. The dried backbone piece is boiled for eating. The backbone itself is not eaten, but sucked to extract the marrow and juices. The second method of preserving the backbone was canning. This method of processing disintegrates the backbone which is then eaten along with the meat.*
>
> *Other salmon parts were used on a less frequent basis by local Naknek River residents. Some households fixed salmon tails. These were either dried or smoked, or more*

---

[96]Industrial Economics, Inc., *Community-Specific Cumulative Exposure Assessment for Greenpoint/Williamsburg New York* 2-21 (1999).

[97]Karen Dorn Steele, *Agencies Warn of Lead in River's Fish Advisory; Targets Fish Consumption of Contaminated Fish Caught in Stretch of Spokane River*, The Spokesman Review A1 (Jun. 21, 2000).

frequently, salted, soaked out, and boiled. Tips were mainly salted and then boiled. The stomachs were cleaned and boiled by a few households. Livers and hearts were fried.[98]

According to a study by the Suquamish Tribe:

> *Nectar resulting from shellfish preparation methods was commonly used. Sixty-four percent of respondents reported drinking the nectar and 24% reported using it in cooking, in contrast to 19% who reported that they "threw it out."*[99]

Finally, as noted above, according to a recent survey of first- and second-generation Asian and Pacific Islanders in King County, Washington including members of Cambodian, Chinese, Filipino, Hmong, Japanese, Korean, Laotian, Mien, Samoan, and Vietnamese ethnic groups:

> *[Asian and Pacific Islanders] consume a wide variety of seafod species, the most frequently consumed being shellfish. These seafood, depending on their feeding and habitat characteristics, and the tissue parts consumed pose varying chemical contaminant risks to APIs. For example, certain fat soluble chemicals, e.g., PCBs, are concentrated in the fat layer between the meat and the skin, potentially exposing such consumer to higher contaminant levels than whose who simply eat the fillet. Eating the fillet with skin is clearly a common practice in the API community. . . . Overall, skin was consumed with the fillet 55% of the time. . . .*
>
> *API community members appear to eat shellfish parts that are thought to contain higher concentrations of chemical contamination, e.g., clam stomachs or the hepatopancreas of crabs. Bivalve shellfish were consumed whole by 24% (geoduck) to 89% (mussels) of respondents depending on the species. The "butter" as well as the meat of crabs were consumed 43% of the time . . . .Finally, cooking water, both for finfish and shellfish are commonly use in cooking or directly consumed.*[100]

Yet, the studies upon which EPA and other agencies base their risk assessment and risk management decisions often make assumptions about species consumed, parts used, and preparation methods employed that do not reflect these practices. Consider the following description of a study of Los Angeles Harbor fishers by Puffer, et al.:

> From January to December of 1980, 1059 interviews with sportfishers were conducted in several fishing areas of the Los Angeles Harbor area. No fisher was sampled more than once. Data was collected on the following: amount of fish caught on the day of the interview, the primary use of the fish (whether it was eaten by the fisher's family, given

---

[98] Judith M. Morris, *The Use of Fish and Wildlife Resources by Residents of the Bristol Bay Borough, Alaska* (1985) available at www.nativeknowledge.org/db/files/tp123.htm.

[99] The Suquamish Tribe, *Fish Consumption Survey of the Suquamish Indian Tribe of the Port Madison Indian Reservation, Puget Sound* 51 (2001).

[100]Ruth Sechena, et al., *Asian and Pacific Islander Seafood Consumption Study* (1999)

away, thrown back, etc.), frequency of fishing, and other variables. Based on this data *and assuming that only an edible portion (1/4 to ½) of the caught fish would be eaten,* median and 90th percentile consumption rates of 37 grams per day and 225 grams per day were determined.[101]

If the fishers studied were members of a group that viewed the "edible portion" of the fish to include more parts or a greater portion of the fish than assumed by the study authors, this consumption would not have been registered and the resulting consumption rates would be lower than the actual consumption rates of those studied. Although there is no way to know for exactly how many of the fishers studied this would be the case; however, given that a significant number of the fishers studied were what the authors characterized as "Orientals/Samoans," it would at least be true for some. Importantly, as noted above, it is also often the case that the different parts consumed by communities of color, low-income communities, tribes, and other indigenous peoples are the very parts that accumulate the toxins. For both of these reasons, these groups' exposure is often underestimated by agencies relying on conventional studies and methods.[102]

Of note is that the CSFII study on which the EPA bases its default fish consumption rates similarly relies on a variety of assumptions that tend to reflect the consumption practices of the general population. The CSFII study asks participants to categorize and quantify their food intake according to a list of approximately 6,600 different food codes, of which 460 relate to fish and shellfish.[103] The participants' responses are then matched with standard recipes contained in the U.S. Department of Agriculture recipe file, in order to adjust the responses to reflect the quantity of fish contained in the particular dish, assuming standard quantities and preparation methods.

The differences noted here have implications for EPA's risk assessment and risk communication decisions. When agencies set water quality standards that are founded on an inaccurate picture of affected communities' and tribes' exposure, the standards will not be sufficiently protective of members of these groups. Although the examples above provide a sense of the growing body of evidence of differences in consumption practices as between the general population and communities of color, low-income communities, tribes, and other indigenous peoples, there is still a need for systematic study for many of these groups. Further, there is no place in EPA's current risk assessment methods to account for these different practices and the higher level of exposure they entail. The fact that often extraordinary levels of exposure e.g., exposure to the large amounts of contaminants accumulated in the hepatopancreas of crab are

---

[101]U.S. Environmental Protection Agency, Office of Water, *Ambient Water Quality Criteria Derivation Methodology Human Health: Technical Support Document* 96 (1998) (emphasis added).

[102]Note that the extent to which exposure is likely to be underestimated depends in part on whether bioconcentration or bioaccumulation factors are determine using whole fish or merely "edible portions" of fish.

[103]1 U.S. Department of Agriculture, *Continuing Survey of Food Intake by Individuals* II-1-4 (1998).

simply unaccounted for by EPA and other agencies when they set environmental standards is extremely troubling to affected communities whose health is thereby relatively underprotected.

Finally, when agencies issue consumption advisories founded on a misunderstanding of affected communities' baseline practices, they may include irrelevant or inappropriate information or recommendations. This issue will be discussed at greater length in Chapter Three.

D. EXPOSURE: CONSUMPTION PRACTICES IN CONTEXT

The contamination of fish, aquatic plants, and wildlife is especially troubling to many communities of color, low-income communities, tribes, and other indigenous peoples because these groups consume and use these resources in different cultural, traditional, religious, historical, economic, and legal contexts than the "average American." Thus, it is not only that there are differences in the quantities of fish consumed or in the species, parts, and preparation methods used, but also that there differences   sometimes profound differences   in the place that these practices occupy in the lives of these people and groups. This is abundantly demonstrated by both testimonial and social scientific evidence. These practices are, in an important sense, *indispensable* to many of these communities and tribes. These differences need to be understood (as best as is possible, given that there may be difficult issues of cross-cultural translation) and accommodated in risk assessment, risk management, and risk communication approaches.

In order to gain a full sense of the circumstances of exposure for many communities of color, low-income communities, tribes, and other indigenous peoples, it is necessary to understand the cultural context in which exposure occurs. A handful of recent community- or tribally-conducted studies have demonstrated the importance of context for understanding exposure. (The necessity of community and tribal involvement in these and other studies is taken up below, in Section H.) For example, the recent consumption study conducted by the Suquamish Tribe commences with an account of "Cultural Patterns and Practices Affecting Suquamish Seafood Consumption," and notes the importance of *"[t]he stories that are woven into the statistics presented in this report."*[104]

It is not only a matter of reconsidering approaches to research, but also a matter of reevaluating approaches to risk assessment and risk management. Tradeoffs or cost-benefit analyses that may be appropriate in other contexts may thus be inappropriate where those affected engage in fishing and fish consumption for the interrelated cultural, traditional, religious, historical, and economic reasons that characterize many affected groups' practices. Additionally, such tradeoffs may run afoul of legal obligations to particular groups, e.g., civil rights-based protections or trust- and treaty- based protections.

Importantly, this discussion has implications for agencies' choices among various risk management tools. In some cases, for some affected groups, it will simply not be appropriate to

---

[104] The Suquamish Tribe, *Fish Consumption Survey of the Suquamish Indian Tribe of the Port Madison Indian Reservation, Puget Sound Region* 5-9 (2000).

ask members to avoid risks by reducing their consumption, by switching to alternative species or fishing locations, by avoiding certain fish parts, or by adopting different preparation methods. Some or all of these practices may be prescribed for cultural, traditional, religious, historical, and/or economic reasons. This issue will be discussed again in Chapter Three, but it should be recognized that its implications are broader.

E. MULTIPLE EXPOSURES AND CUMULATIVE RISKS

Agencies currently employ risk assessment methods that evaluate the risks of environmental contamination as if humans were exposed to only a single contaminant at a time, by a single route of exposure. Humans, however, are often exposed to multiple contaminants at a time or in succession, and often via more than one route of exposure. These contaminants may have synergistic (or antagonistic) effects in combination, yet very little is known about these effects and agencies do not take them into account.

It is the case, moreover, that members of communities of color, low-income communities, tribes, and other indigenous peoples are more likely to be exposed to multiple contaminants via multiple routes and pathways than are members of the general population. As Stuart Harris, Confederated Tribes of the Umatilla Indian Reservation, and Barbara Harper, Fourteen Confederated Tribes and Bands of the Yakama Nation, observe:

> *The issue of multiple contaminants is significant, and it is the norm, at least in the Columbia River system, for over 100 contaminants to be identified in fish tissues. While only a few might be at concentrations that trigger an action in any given fish, the combined risk for one fish or for the many species which comprise the native diet can be quite high. If these chemicals are in the fish, they are also in the water and/or sediment, so other routes of exposure are important. The toxicity of a mixture of dozens of carcinogens plus dozens of noncarcinogens . . . needs to be examined.*[105]

Similarly, communities along the Mississippi River Corridor between New Orleans and Baton Rouge, whose members are largely African American and/or low-income, are exposed to an unconscionable level and mix of contaminants, via several routes and pathways.[106] These multiple affronts include exposure to a host of toxic air pollutants (emitted at levels *several times* the levels elsewhere in the United States);[107] to mercury and numerous other contaminants in the fish, oysters and crayfish that are often staple foods;[108] and to vinyl chloride and other contaminants in

---

[105]Barbara Harper and Stuart Harris, *Tribal Technical Issues in Risk Reduction Through Fish Advisories*, Proceedings of the American Fisheries Society, Forum on Contaminants in Fish 17,19 (1999).

[106]Charles Lee, ed., United Church of Christ Commission for Racial Justice, *From Plantations to Plants: Report of the Emergency National Commission on Environmental and Economic Justice in St. James Parish, Louisiana* (1998).

[107]Id.

[108]Telephone Interview, Barry Kohl, Department of Geology, Tulane University (Oct. 17, 2001); Louisiana Department of Environmental Quality and Louisiana Department of Health and Hospitals,

drinking water.[109] And northern Ojibwa tribes are exposed to mercury via multiple resource pathways, given its uptake by fish and its presence in and on wild rice.

EPA and other agencies have begun to look at how to address multiple exposures and cumulative risk. For example, and to its credit, EPA's Office of Policy has recently conducted a cumulative exposure project to begin to assess the total exposure of more than 100 contaminants across multiple pathways; one component of this project is a community-specific study in the Greenpoint/Williamsburg community in Brooklyn, NY, designed to assess exposures to a variety of contaminants via fish consumption, water ingestion, air inhalation, and lead exposure.[110] This urban community is one of the poorest in New York City; it is comprised of substantial African American, Hispanic (including Caribbean American), Polish, Italian, and Hasidic subpopulations.[111] It is well recognized, however, that many of the issues of multiple exposures and cumulative risks remain unaddressed for the bulk of risk assessments currently being conducted.

F. SUSCEPTIBILITY AND CO-RISK FACTORS

Even if it were the case that all individuals' exposure circumstances were the same that they came in contact with the same environmental contaminants, by the same routes, at the same frequency, for the same duration they might not suffer the same adverse health effects as a result of this contact due to differences in their susceptibilities and differences in the extent to which their life circumstances allowed them to be prepared for and recover from the insult of an environmental contaminant, i.e. in their "co-risk" factors.

One might be more or less susceptible to a given level or "dose" of an environmental contaminant depending on one's life stage (e.g., children or the elderly may be more susceptible); one's prior exposure to the same or other contaminants (e.g. those who have become sensitized through prior exposures and now have more severe responses); one's genetic makeup (e.g., genetic susceptibilities that occur in a small but significant percentage of the population); or one's existing conditions or diseases (e.g., asthmatics). Although very little is known about the coincidence of some of these factors genetics, for example and whether one is a person of

---

Human Health Protection Through Fish Consumption and Swimming Advisories in Louisiana available at www.deq.state.la.us/surveillance/mercury/fishadvi.htm (listing advisories statewide, many of wide apply to the waters of the Mississippi River Corridor).

[109]See, e.g., Chris Frink, *State Knew Well was Contaminated*, The Advocate Online available at www.theadvocate.com/news/story.asp?storyid=20619; Telephone Interview, Mary Lee Orr, Louisiana Environmental Action Network (October 17, 2001).

[110]Industrial Economics, Inc., *Community-Specific Cumulative Exposure Assessment for Greenpoint/Williamsburg New York* 1-1- 1-5 (1999).

[111]Id. at 1-2.

color, a low-income person, or a Native American, it is fair to say that there is a significant correlation for others   prior exposures, or access to adequate health care, for example.[112]

One may also be more or less able to prepare for and recover from exposure to given level or "dose" of an environmental contaminant depending on the various resources an individual, community, group, or tribe can call upon and depending on other aspects of one's life circumstances. Thus, one may be more or less able to withstand and recover from a toxic insult depending on one's income, the quality of one's baseline diet, whether one is employed, whether one has access to adequate health care, whether one has adequate insurance, and whether one's community or tribe can assist to provide coping systems.

Current risk assessment, risk management and risk communication methods do not account adequately for susceptibilities and co-risk factors that affect individuals' responses to the environmental contaminants with which they come in contact. This is especially troubling to the extent that current risk estimates are made assuming the life circumstances of the general population or the affluent and fail thereby to account for the particular susceptibilities and co-risk factors that tend to be clustered in or characterize various communities of color, low-income communities, tribes, and other indigenous peoples. To take but a single co-risk factor by way of example, consider that of the respondents surveyed in a recent study of Asian and Pacific Islander communities in King County, Washington, 90% of Samoans, 62% of Vietnamese, 60% of Mien, 50% of Cambodians and 45% of Laotians live under the federal poverty line.[113] Among American Indians and Alaskan Natives, one in three lives below the federal poverty line.[114] Here again, more data need to be gathered about the particular susceptibilities and co-risk factors relevant to communities of color, low-income communities, and tribes. And here, too, EPA's and other agencies' risk assessment, management and communication methods need to be able to incorporate and address differences in susceptibilities and co-risk factors.

G. SUPPRESSION EFFECTS AND THEIR IMPLICATIONS

A "suppression effect" occurs when a fish consumption rate (FCR) for a given population, group, or tribe reflects a current level of consumption that is artificially diminished from an appropriate baseline level of consumption for that population, group, or tribe. The more robust baseline level of consumption is suppressed, inasmuch as it does not get captured by the FCR.[115]

---

[112]See e.g., Robert R. Kuehn, *The Environmental Justice Implications of Quantitative Risk Assessment*, 1996 University of Illinois Law Review 103.

[113]Ruth Sechena, et al., *Asian and Pacific Islander Seafood Consumption Study* (1999).

[114]See Chapter 4 for a more complete discussion of the susceptibilities and co-risk factors of American Indians and Alaskan Natives.

[115]This effect was recognized and named in an early survey of Michigan sport anglers, and cited by the study's authors as a basis for adjusting the observed FCR upward. Patrick West, et al., *Michigan Sports Anglers Fish Consumption Survey: Supplement I, Non-Response Bias and Consumption Suppression Effect Adjustments* (School of Natural Resources, University of Michigan, Ann Arbor; Natural Resource Sociology Research Lab, Technical Report No. 2 (1989).

There are two circumstances in which suppression effects have implications for an environmental justice policy that seeks to sustain healthy aquatic ecosystems and to protect the health and safety of people consuming fish, shellfish, aquatic plants, and wildlife for subsistence, traditional, cultural, or religious purposes. In the first, a suppression effect may arise when an aquatic environment and the fish it supports have become contaminated to the point that humans refrain from consuming fish caught from particular waters. Were the fish not contaminated, these people would consume fish at more robust baseline levels. In the second, a suppression effect may arise when fish upon which humans rely are no longer available in historical quantities (and kinds), such that humans are unable to catch and consume as much fish as they had or would. Such depleted fisheries may result from a variety of affronts, including an aquatic environment that is contaminated, altered (due, among other things, to the presence of dams), overdrawn, and/or overfished. Were the fish not depleted, these people would consume fish at more robust baseline levels.

The implications for environmental justice policy will depend in part upon which of these two scenarios accounts for the suppression effect observed. They will also depend upon how the more robust "baseline" level is defined an exercise that itself raises important environmental justice issues. This question of an appropriate "baseline" will in turn be related to the particular group affected. In many cases, for example, a tribe will be able to cite a historical "point of reference" that would describe an appropriate baseline in terms of environmental quality, geographic delineation, and treaty rights.[116] In each case, there would be important questions of history, culture, and aspiration that would need to be considered in determining an appropriate baseline; that is to say, an appropriate baseline might mean examination into what people *had* consumed as well as aspiration for what people *would* consume were there "fair access for all to a full range of resources,"[117] or were the conditions fulfilled for full exercise of treaty- and trust-protected rights and purposes.

When environmental agencies employ a FCR that does not capture fully the consumption that is suppressed under either scenario in which suppression effects occur they set in motion a sort of downward spiral whereby the resulting environmental standards permit further and further contamination or depletion of the fish and so diminished health and safety of people consuming fish, shellfish, aquatic plants, and wildlife for subsistence, traditional, cultural, or religious purposes. These effects play out somewhat differently in each of the two scenarios, as elaborated below.

---

[116]Moses Squeochs, Director, Environmental Program, Fourteen Confederated Tribes and Bands of Yakama Nation (C3G Conference Call, August 3, 2001). For the Tribes and Bands of the Yakama Nation, for example, this point of reference would be 1855. Id.

[117]Principles of Environmental Justice, Proceedings of the First National People of Color Environmental Leadership Summit (1991).

1. Contamination

Health and environmental agencies have increasingly responded to contaminated aquatic environments by issuing fish consumption advisories warning humans to limit or stop their consumption of fish from polluted waters.[118] In many cases, individuals have responded to these advisories and/or to a greater general awareness of the dangers of consuming contaminated fish by eating less fish.[119] The extent to which individuals respond to fish consumption advisories by reducing their consumption varies.[120] In some cases, this is due to the fact that advisories are more effectively communicated to some affected populations than others. Among other things, advisories may not be communicated in culturally or language-appropriate ways. In other cases, this is due to the fact that, for cultural, traditional, spiritual, economic, and/or other reasons, the individuals to whom the advisories are addressed do not respond by reducing their consumption.

When environmental agencies set or approve water quality standards that are meant to be protective of human health, agencies look to gauge humans' exposure by how much fish they are consuming, i.e. their fish consumption rate. Agencies estimate or measure this FCR, and on this basis determine how much pollution can remain in or be discharged to the relevant waters and sediments and still result in what have been deemed "acceptable" levels of contamination and risk to human health. Notably, the FCRs on which agencies rely are meant to represent *current* rates of fish consumption, rates that may reflect a suppression effect as outline above.

When environmental agencies set or approve water quality standards that rely on a picture of exposure that takes people to be eating smaller quantities of fish, agencies will permit relatively greater quantities of pollutants to remain in or be discharged to the waters and sediments. That is to say, agencies will set less protective standards. The downward spiral thus begins, as these aquatic environments and the fish they support will be permitted to become increasingly contaminated, and some individuals in turn might be expected to respond by reducing their fish consumption even further. The downward spiral would continue, as agencies would then register this even lower rate of consumption, set new standards assuming that little or no human exposure to contaminants occurs via fish consumption, and permit even greater quantities of pollutants in aquatic ecosystems.

----

[118]U.S. Environmental Protection Agency, Office of Water, Update: National Listing of Fish and Wildlife Advisories 2 (April 2001), available at www.epa.gov/ost/fish.

[119] See, e.g., Telephone interview with Shawn Martin, Clean Water Manager, St. Regis Mohawk Tribe Environment Division (July 12, 2001).

[120]Studies suggest varying degrees of both (1) awareness of fish consumption advisories by members of the public and (2) "compliance" with fish consumption advisories through changed fish consumption practices even when members of the public are aware of fish consumption advisories. See e.g., John Tilden et. al, Health Advisories for Consumers of Great Lakes Sport-Fish: Is the Message Being Received?, 105 Environmental Health Perspective 1360 (Dec. 1997); Hugh F. MacDonald and Kevin J. Boyle, Effect of a Statewide Sport Fish Consumption Advisory on Open-Water Fishing in Maine, 17 Journal of Fisheries Management 687 (1997).

2. Depletion

Many species of fish upon which people have traditionally relied are no longer readily available, due to habitat degradation and diminishment, ecosystem alteration, overfishing, and other causes. In the Pacific Northwest, for example, compromised aquatic ecosystems mean that fish are no longer available for tribal members to take, as they are entitled to do in exercise of their treaty rights. These numerous affronts have resulted in 24 salmon and steelhead runs being listed as endangered or threatened under the Endangered Species Act, and other fisheries being depleted. With fewer fish available to be taken, many tribal members have been prevented from consuming fish at the level that they would have were they able to exercise their treaty rights to the fullest extent.[121]

Again, when environmental agencies set or approve water quality standards that rely on a picture of exposure that takes people to be eating smaller quantities of fish, agencies will permit relatively greater quantities of pollutants to remain in or be discharged to the waters and sediments. Thus, tribal members are not only left with fewer fish to take and consume, but those that remain will be permitted to become increasingly contaminated. If fish stocks continue to decline, a variation on the downward spiral described above can be expected, with lower FCRs resulting from the fact that there are simply fewer fish to be consumed. Again, agencies would then register this even lower rate of consumption, set new standards assuming that little or no human exposure to contaminants occurs via fish consumption, and permit even greater quantities of pollutants in aquatic ecosystems.

It should be noted, too, that contamination is related to depletion. To take but one example, among the contaminants that have contributed to the decline and listing of salmon populations in the Pacific Northwest are numerous pesticides. Recent studies have shown that pesticides disrupt the ability of salmon to develop properly and to home to their natal streams; these harmful effects are in addition to their toxic effects on humans and other animals that consume fish.[122]

3. Evidence of Suppression Effects

There is limited evidence regarding the existence and extent of suppression effects. This is likely due in part to the fact that this term for the phenomenon hasn't been widely used   indeed, although diminished fish consumption due to contamination and/or depletion has been observed in numerous contexts, it is believed that this Report is the first document to bring these observations together under a single umbrella term. Nonetheless, there is a growing body of evidence of suppression effects due to contamination and/or to depletion. Among other sources of data are recent studies conducted to evaluate the effectiveness of fish consumption advisories for

---

[121]   Telephone Interview with Kelly Toy, Shellfish Biologist, Tulalip Tribes (November 9, 1999).

[122]   See, e.g., Oregon Pesticide Action Network, *Diminishing Returns: Salmon Decline and Pesticides* (1999).

contaminated waters. To the extent that such studies find that people have "complied" with advisories by eliminating or lowering their consumption of fish, they provide evidence of a suppression effect   an artificially diminished level of consumption relative to a more robust baseline level. Too, community-based or tribally-conducted fish consumption studies often document broadly the subject group's fish consumption practices. Often, these studies include information about historic consumption and explore reasons for altered and diminished consumption practices.

Some of the available evidence documents suppression effects due to contamination. For example, as noted above, West, et al. recognized and named this effect in an early survey of Michigan sport anglers.[123] In a recent study of Lake Ontario anglers, Connelly, et al. cite recently altered health advisories that resulted in less Lake Ontario fishing as the reason that only 43% of anglers indicated that they had fished Lake Ontario in 1992.[124] A recent study of the Laotian communities in the San Francisco Bay area reports that 19.7% of survey respondents indicated that they had changed their fish consumption habits over the past five years, with 68.9% of these indicating that they eat less fish now.[125] Among the reasons cited for eating less fish: bay fish are "unsafe to eat."[126] Ken Jock, Director, Akwesasne Environment Program, provides an account of the effects of PCB contamination in the St. Lawrence River on the Mohawks at Akwesasne:

> *This all used to be a fishing village. That's all gone now. There's only one family that still fishes. . . . Our traditional lifestyle has been completely disrupted, and we have been forced to make choices to protect our future generations. . . . Many of the families used to eat 20-25 fish meals a month. It's now said that the traditional Mohawk diet is spaghetti.[127]*

Other available evidence documents suppression effects due to depletion or due to depletion *and* contamination. For example, as noted above, in the Pacific Northwest compromised aquatic ecosystems and depleted salmon and other fisheries mean that fish are no longer available for tribal members to take, as they are entitled to do in exercise of their treaty rights. According to Kelly Toy, Shellfish Biologist, Tulalip Tribes, with fewer fish available to be taken, many tribal members have been prevented from consuming fish at the level that they would

---

[123]Patrick West, et al., *Michigan Sports Anglers Fish Consumption Survey: Supplement I, Non-Response Bias and Consumption Suppression Effect Adjustments* (School of Natural Resources, University of Michigan, Ann Arbor; Natural Resource Sociology Research Lab, Technical Report No. 2 (1989).

[124]U.S. Environmental Protection Agency, Office of Water, *Ambient Water Quality Criteria Derivation Methodology Human Health: Technical Support Document* 97 (1998).

[125]Audrey Chiang, Asian Pacific Environmental Network, *A Seafood Consumption Survey of the Laotian Community in West Contra County, California* 18 (1998). Note that 31% of those who indicated that their consumption practices had changed indicated that they eat more fish now.

[126]Id.

[127]Winona LaDuke, *All Our Relations: Native Struggles for Land and Life* 17 (1999) (quoting Ken Jock, Director, Akwesasne Environment Program).

have were they able to exercise their treaty rights to the fullest extent.[128] Moses Squeochs, Director, Environmental Program, Fourteen Confederated Tribes and Bands of the Yakama Nation, confirms similarly depleted fisheries, diminished opportunities for catching and consuming fish, and compromised treaty rights.[129] A recent study of the Suquamish Tribe reports that approximately 2/3 of respondents (67%) indicated that their consumption patterns had changed over time, with 68% of these indicating that they ate less seafood (57%) or ate a different mix of species (11%) than twenty years ago.[130] "Most explanations for changes in consumption related to changes in family composition which affected harvesting patterns, accessibility/availability of finfish and shellfish, and restricted harvesting opportunities due to 'red tides' and increased pollution."[131] As one respondent elaborated:

> *We used to eat lingcod, sole, rockfish, flounder, and I caught Grunters for my grandfather. All of my brothers used to fish; now, only one of us can because the fish are diminishing in number . . . The water is not clean. Septics are malfunctioning . . . There's pollution from the Navy, and the filling at Keyport had a big effect . . . Beaches are dug out . . . We need to reseed and enhance our beaches in order to have the number of clams we need and are used to . . . We eat more geoduck now, because more are available to us, but we used to dry oysters and clams; they're good for teething . . .[132]*

Similarly, Hawaii's Thousand Friends relates:

> *Many shellfish and limu (seaweed) staples of Native Hawaiian diets are becoming harder to find or have disappeared due to pollution and/or destruction of habitat. Thus Native Hawaiians are unable to continue eating (healthy) foods traditional to their culture and lifestyle.[133]*

There is, however, a need to understand more fully the extent and causes of suppression effects. Among other things, the evidence presented here shows that people's responses to contamination and depletion are complex and varied. Further exploration of these effects would be useful. In particular, where consumption by communities of color, low-income communities, tribes, and other indigenous peoples seems relatively low, research is needed to ascertain whether a suppression effect is at work.

---

[128]Telephone Interview with Kelly Toy, Shellfish Biologist, Tulalip Tribes (November 9, 1999).

[129]Moses Squeochs, Director, Environmental Program, Fourteen Confederated Tribes and Bands of the Yakama Nation (Conference Call, Aug. 3, 2001).

[130]The Suquamish Tribe, *Fish Consumption Survey of the Suquamish Indian Tribe of the Port Madison Indian Reservation, Puget Sound* 2 (2001). Note that 31% of those who indicated that their consumption practices had changed indicated that they eat more fish now.

[131]Id.

[132]Id. at 68 (ellipses in original).

[133] Hawaii's Thousand Friends (Written Comments, March 11, 2002).

4. Implications

To the extent that people are prevented from consuming fish as they had or would due to contamination or depletion of the fish and aquatic ecosystems that support the fish, there are important implications for EPA's and other agencies' risk assessment, risk management, and risk communication approaches. As noted above, when environmental agencies set or approve water quality standards that rely on a picture of exposure that takes people to be eating smaller quantities of fish, agencies will permit relatively greater quantities of pollutants to remain in or be discharged to the waters and sediments. That is to say, agencies will set less protective standards. The downward spiral thus begins, as these aquatic environments and the fish they support will be permitted to become increasingly contaminated, and some individuals in turn might be expected to respond by reducing their fish consumption even further. Or some individuals in turn might find that there are fewer fish to be caught (and those that remain to be increasingly contaminated) or there are fewer places open for shellfish harvesting. In either case, studies would reflect even lower FCRs, and agencies would then set new standards assuming that little or no human exposure to contaminants occurs via fish consumption, and permit even greater quantities of pollutants in aquatic ecosystems.

In order to avoid this downward spiral, EPA should identify appropriate "baselines" that reflect the more robust levels of consumption and employ these baselines in setting and approving water quality criteria. There is, of course, the difficult question of what the appropriate baseline should be, and the answer will likely differ according to the circumstances surrounding and the group affected by the observed suppression effect. For example, as noted above, a tribe will often be able to cite a historical "point of reference" that would describe an appropriate baseline in terms of environmental quality, geographic delineation, and treaty rights.[134] In each case, there would be important questions of history, culture, and aspiration that would need to be considered in determining an appropriate baseline. An appropriate baseline might mean examination into what people *had* consumed as well as aspiration for what people *would* consume were there "fair access for all to a full range of resources,"[135] or were the conditions fulfilled for full exercise of treaty- and trust-protected rights and purposes. It is recognized that the resulting baseline would surely require EPA to depart from the then-current estimates of actual fish consumption by the relevant group. In so doing, EPA would need to shift its emphasis from a descriptive assessment to a normative assessment. This shift is not without precedent, however, and, importantly, would seem to be necessary in some cases to avoid the downward spiral noted here.

---

[134]Moses Squeochs, Director, Environmental Program, Fourteen Confederated Tribes and Bands of Yakama Nation (C3G Conference Call, August 3, 2001). For the Tribes and Bands of the Yakama Nation, for example, this point of reference would be 1855. Id.

[135]Principles of Environmental Justice, Proceedings of the First National People of Color Environmental Leadership Summit (1991) available at http://www.sccs.swarthmore.edu/org/speec/ejdef.html.

H. RESEARCH METHODS AND ISSUES

This part highlights two issues respecting EPA's current research methods and priorities: the importance of facilitating community-based or tribally-conducted research, and the need for research that seeks not only to describe affected groups' exposure but also to connect exposure to the sources of contaminants in aquatic environments.

1. Community-Based and Tribally-Conducted Research

It will often be crucial to the relevance, accuracy and acceptability of research in these areas that the affected community, group or tribe be central to the process throughout. In the case of consumption studies, for example, affected groups need to be involved from the earliest stages (e.g., project conception, group/subgroup identification, survey design) through implementation (e.g., survey administration, data interpretation) to utilization (e.g., community outreach regarding results, risk assessment, management and communication incorporating results). This is not only a matter of community access or tribal consultation, but importantly, a matter of scientific defensibility. There are currently sizeable gaps in the data and methods that are being used by EPA and other agencies to assess, manage, and communicate risk, and it is often the case that these gaps can only be filled by community- and tribally-based research. *Communities and tribes have expertise that is simply not going to be able to be replicated by non-member researchers.* This point is well supported by the large literature on "participatory research." Consider the following two examples of the importance of affected group involvement:

> Asian and Pacific Islanders in King County, Washington.[136] A study of the Asian and Pacific Islander communities (including members of Cambodian, Chinese, Filipino, Hmong, Japanese, Korean, Laotian, Mien, Samoan, and Vietnamese communities) in Seattle and King County, Washington was conducted by the Refugee Federation Service Center (the largest social aid organization for recent immigrants and refugees in King County) and the University of Washington. The study was funded by an Environmental Justice Community/University Partnership Grant through EPA Region 10. The community played a pivotal role in the study, from its initiation through the final report. A Community Steering Committee, comprised of members representing each of the ten affected ethnic groups, conducted the planning, design and development of the survey. They worked together with and received input from a Technical Committee (comprised of statisticians, toxicologists, epidemiologists, and other technical advisors) and an Advisory Committee (comprised of representatives from agencies, industry, and the medical profession). As the study authors note: "During the study period, the researchers had frequent interactions with the community because the researchers viewed the study as 'by the API community,' instead of 'for the API community.' This interaction and cooperation helped the study team in its understanding of community concerns and therefore gained the support of the community, which was vital for the completion of this

---

[136]Ruth Sechena, et al., *Asian and Pacific Islander Seafood Consumption Study* (1999).

study involving ten ethnic groups with diverse cultural backgrounds."[137] Among other things, the Community Steering Committee was instrumental to several aspects of the study design. It explained that the use of creel, mail, or telephone surveys would be culturally inappropriate, indicating that API community members would be unlikely to participate at all in a survey conducted by these methods; instead, a face-to-face questionnaire method was selected. It identified the seafood species and parts most often consumed by community members, and explained the usual preparation methods elements crucial to questionnaire design. It also suggested interviewers that would have the requisite cultural knowledge and fluency in both English and the various native languages of the study participants. Thus, for these and other reasons, this study likely produced more accurate data by (1) avoiding the non-response bias that likely plagues other studies attempting to gauge API consumption practices; (2) including quantities consumed where the species or part consumed might have been excluded altogether from other, more generalized studies (e.g., clam stomachs or the hepatopancreas of crabs); (3) identifying consumption and preparation practices that differ from the general population and so bear on risk assessment, risk management and risk communication decisions (e.g., consuming the "butter" as well as the meat of crabs). There are also other important advantages of a community-based study, including community education and empowerment. These issues will be taken up in Chapter Three.

The Suquamish Tribe.[138] A study of Suquamish tribal members (adults and children) living on and near the Port Madison Indian Reservation was conducted upon approval by the Suquamish Tribal Council. The study was conducted by the Suquamish Tribe and funded by the Agency for Toxic Substances and Disease Registry through a grant to the Washington State Department of Health . The stated purpose of the study was to determine seafood consumption rates, patterns, and habits of members of the tribe and, secondarily, to identify "cultural practices and attributes which affect consumption rates, patterns, and habits of members of the Suquamish Tribe."[139] A Project Support Team was established, comprised of two members of the Suquamish Tribal Council, the Director of Human Services, and the Self Governance Director, all of whom are enrolled Suquamish tribal members. The study manager from the Suquamish Tribe Fisheries Department worked together with individuals from the Washington Department of Health. Suquamish Elders were consulted concerning fish and shellfish important to tribal members for commercial, subsistence, and ceremonial purposes.[140] Additionally, transcripts of the Suquamish Tribe Oral History Project of 1982, anthropological and archeological literature were consulted to document cultural practices.[141] Tribal members were integral to the study design, survey administration, and data interpretation. The study was

---

[137]Id.

[138]The Suquamish Tribe, *Fish Consumption Survey of the Suquamish Indian Tribe of the Port Madison Indian Reservation, Puget Sound Region* (2000).

[139]Id. at 1.

[140]Id.

[141]Id. at 3.

designed to determine consumption rates by individual type of finfish and shellfish information of interest to the tribe and unavailable through other relevant fish consumption studies. Consumption data were gathered using a survey questionnaire and face-to-face interviews; these interviews were conducted by tribal members. These interviewers set up and conducted meetings with survey participants "in accordance with cultural norms."[142] The personal knowledge of those conducting the study enabled them to interpret the resulting data in a manner that ensured accuracy. For example, the data revealed some large fish consumption rates, which might be designated as "outliers" according to strictly numerical criteria. Because this designation often carries with it an assumption of error, reported consumption rates for outliers are often adjusted downward. In this case, however, "the study staff were familiar with a number of the individuals with large consumption rates and maintained that the reported rates were likely to reflect real consumption. Thus, no adjustment for potential outliers has been carried out."[143] Thus, for these and other reasons, this study likely produced more relevant, contextualized, and accurate information. Tribally-managed studies are also a manifestation of tribal self-governance and, in the case of the Washington treaty tribes, of their status as co-managers of the fish, shellfish and aquatic resources. Issues unique to tribes will be taken up at greater length in Chapter Four.

Other community-based or tribally-conducted studies have demonstrated similar advantages in terms of relevancy, accuracy, acceptability and appropriateness to the affected group. The community-based study team for the consumption survey of Laotian communities in West Contra County, for example, was able to identify and take advantage of important community festivals as a means of reaching survey participants;[144] to appreciate the existence and relevance of subgroups within the larger Laotian community;[145] and to interpret data in light of cultural, historical, social, economic and other relevant factors.[146] In the case of tribes, members have often lived their entire lives   and their families and ancestors have lived for generations   in the same place, about which they therefore have vast amounts of knowledge. In addition, many tribes today have developed extensive environment and resources management departments.

---

[142]Id. at 18-19.

[143]Id. at 23. The study authors note that, in the end, this inclusion had little influence on the reported percentiles, with all but one (the 95th percentile for "all finfish") being unaffected. Id. at 70-71.

[144]Audrey Chiang, Asian Pacific Environmental Network, *A Seafood Consumption Survey of the Laotian Community in West Contra Costa County, California* 6 (1998) (describing outreach conducted at the Laotian New Year's Festival, "one of the most well-attended community events in Richmond").

[145]Id. at 7-10 and 35-36 (discussing representation of the various ethnic groups within the Laotian community, including Mien (Christian), Mien (non-Christian), Lao, Khmu, Thaidum, Lue, Hmong, Lahu, and a Mien group from a different village in Laos than the Mien who are members of the first two groups).

[146]Id. at 36 (discussing likelihood that many respondents who fish in San Francisco Bay indicated that they did not, for fear that the survey was linked to law enforcement about fishing from the Bay, fear of losing disability benefits if they said they went fishing, or concern about "'losing the power to feed their family traditionally cooked meals'" and noting that the survey results therefore likely understated the extent of fishing in the Bay by community members).

Tribes and their members will thus be uniquely positioned to identify ecological changes,[147] suggests subjects for inquiry, and design and implement useful experiments, surveys and studies.

To the extent that research is conducted by and for communities and tribes, it can serve the additional important function of capacity building or, as Moses Squeochs, Fourteen Confederated Tribes and Bands of the Yakama Nation, perhaps more appropriately terms it, "capacity augmentation."[148] This goal is important and an issue of environmental justice in and of itself, for both communities and tribes. And, to the extent that communities and tribes see that their concerns are shaping the research to be conducted, that the information gathered will be relevant from their perspective, and that their members stand to enhance their skills, knowledge and capacity in the process   as opposed to merely providing information that enables others to enhance *their* skills, knowledge and capacity   participation and trust are likely to be increased, and accuracy thereby enhanced.[149]

Indeed, those affected are likely to have a unique and heightened interest in gathering relevant and accurate data. Given that they depend on the resource in question, they have an interest in determining precisely the nature and extent of the contamination, in producing a full and accurate picture of their exposure, and in addressing any resulting problems through risk management and risk communication.[150] It may be the case as well that affected communities and tribes are less likely than other governmental entities to be subject to the competing claims of multiple stakeholders   enabling them, among other things, to devote their full time and attention to the particular problem.

Funding is crucial to the ability of affected communities and tribes to be involved in research. Although community and tribal members have considerable expertise to offer, they

---

[147]See, e.g., Gerald Nicholia, Tanana, Interior Regional Meeting, Alaska Traditional Knowledge and Native Foods Database, available at www.nativeknowledge.org/db/concerns.asp ("But one thing I see is changes in the animals we live off of. The mining has affected us; mercury levels in our fish. I don't know what is in our moose. Few muskrats in our area. I don't know what happened to the whitefish in our area. It's hard to pinpoint. . . . But I know that there are a lot of changes in the Tanana area.").

[148] Moses Squeochs, *Testimony to National Environmental Justice Advisory Council* Vol III-97 (Annual Meeting Transcript) (Dec. 4, 2001) (observing "[I]n reference to a tribe, [I do not use the term capacity building,] but more so capacity augmentation. The capacity of the people that I'm from has been there for thousands of years. It's been along the Duwamish River for thousands of years. It's been in watersheds scattered across the country for thousands of years.")

[149]See, e.g., id. at 37 (noting that the survey planning team made connections with the Laotian Organizing Project's ongoing capacity building efforts regarding community health and safety, which motivated many community members to participate in the survey and explaining: "The planning team was originally hesitate about the perception commonly held by community members of outsiders taking information from the community without community people seeing the benefits of research. Linking the survey to a community based organization helped counter this perception.").

[150]Consider, e.g., the work of the Shoalwater Tribe to monitor shellfish in the Willapa Bay, described at greater length in Chapter 4. Electronic-mail Interview, Gary Burns, Environmental Programs Director, Shoalwater Bay Indian Tribe (Oct. 3, 2001).

often have minimal or no funding to support their work. *To a person*, community members, tribal members, inter-tribal organization staff, and state and local agency representatives who work with affected groups stressed the importance of adequate funding. Diana Lee, a research scientist with the California Department of Health Services who has worked extensively with communities as part of the Palos Verdes Fish Contamination Outreach and Education Project and other studies in the San Francisco Bay area, is emphatic:

> *I cannot underscore enough the need to provide funding to affected communities so that they can participate fully in every aspect of the research process, from needs assessment to dissemination of the results. Funding, moreover, needs to be provided on an on-going, rather than one-time, basis.*[151]

EPA, in particular, has to date helped fund several studies and projects that have contributed enormously to the advancement of research relevant to affected communities and tribes. The EPA has helped fund such important work as the fish consumption study of and by Asian and Pacific Islanders in King County, Washington; the fish consumption study of and by the four tribes who are members of the Columbia River Inter-Tribal Fish Commission; and the community-specific cumulative risk assessment for the Greenpoint/Williamsburg community in Brooklyn, New York. In addition, the EPA, together with the ATSDR, has recently announced relevant grant initiatives, including two programs: *Lifestyle and Cultural Practices of Tribal Populations and Risks from Toxic Substances in the Environment*[152] and *Superfund Minority Institutions Program: Hazardous Substance Research*.[153] Affected communities and tribes have commended EPA's past efforts to this end, and welcome EPA's new initiatives. However, those affected have noted that the need for funding to enable communities and tribes fully to be involved in research and decisions affecting risk assessment, management, and communication far outstrips the funding that has been so far made available.

2. Research Connecting Exposure to the Sources of Contamination

It is particularly important from the perspective of affected groups that research seeking to describe exposures more accurately be undertaken *as but one component of* research that presents

---

[151]Telephone Interview, Diana Lee, Research Scientist, California Department of Health Services (Oct. 26, 2001).

[152]U.S. Environmental Protection Agency, Office of Research and Development, *Lifestyle and Cultural Practices of Tribal Populations and Risks from Toxic Substances in the Environment* available at http://es.epa.gov/ncer/fra/02trib_risk.html (noting, importantly, that "It is expected that Tribal members and representatives will play a leading role in the planning, conduct, analysis, translation and dissemination of the research.").

[153] U.S. Environmental Protection Agency, Office of Research and Development, *Superfund Minority Institutions Program: Hazardous Substance Research* available at http://es/epa.gov/ncer/rfa/02minhazinst.html (listing as eligible program grant recipients "Minority institutions, including Historically Black Colleges and Universities (HBCUs), Hispanic Serving Institutions (HSIs), and Native American Tribal Colleges (TC) in the U.S.").

a fuller picture and seeks to connect affected groups' exposures to the sources of the contamination that gives rise to these exposures. As noted above, given their dependence on aquatic resources, communities of color, low-income communities, tribes, and other indigenous peoples have an acute interest in determining the nature, extent, and sources of such contamination, in producing a complete and accurate picture of their exposure, and in seeing that the contamination is addressed. Thus, while further research regarding various groups' exposure is important, it should not be undertaken at the expense of research that aims to identify the sources of the contamination and to understand that mechanisms by which substances that have been or are being emitted or discharged from these sources make their way to contact with humans (and other non-human components of aquatic ecosystems). Nor should research on exposure be undertaken in isolation of renewed efforts to *reduce* the resulting risks, a point echoed repeatedly by affected groups[154] and emphasized throughout this Report. As the Swinomish Indian Tribal Community stresses:

> *We urge [explicitly that EPA undertake and] support[] efforts to establish undeniable connections between contaminants found in harvested fish and shellfish and the sources of those contaminants. . . . [We believe that pinpointing the source of the pollution and mitigating it at the source will be the only successful strategy in accomplishing risk reduction.[155]*

I. REFINING AND REEVALUATING CURRENT RISK-BASED APPROACHES

Although quantitative risk assessment has increasingly, since the 1970s, been employed by environmental agencies to set health-based environmental standards, its use remains controversial.[156] Commentators have pointed out several serious concerns with quantitative risk assessment as currently practiced.[157] For example, they have taken issue with risk assessment's priorities and assumptions; they have noted that the considerable uncertainty and variability that characterizes health and environmental decisions means that risk assessment is a highly subjective process, requiring value judgments at numerous steps along the way;[158] and they have criticized the ways in which the use of risk assessment perpetuates and exacerbates the disproportionate

---

[154]See, e.g., Shawna Larson, Project Coordinator, Indigenous Environmental Network and Alaska Community Action on Toxics, Panelist, "Right to Toxic-Free Traditional Foods in Our Environment," Alaska Forum on the Environment (Feb. 4-8, 2002).

[155]Swinomish Indian Tribal Community, *Comments on the National Environmental Justice Advisory Council's Draft Fish Consumption Report* (Feb. 5, 2002).

[156]See, e.g., Mark Eliot Shere, *The Myth of Meaningful Environmental Risk Assessment*, 19 Harvard Environmental Law Review 409 (1995).

[157]See, e.g., Catherine A. O'Neill, *Variable Justice: Environmental Standards, Contaminated Fish, and "Acceptable" Risk to Native Peoples*, 19 Stanford Environmental Law Journal 3, 19-37 (2000).

[158]See, e.g., National Research Council, *Science and Judgment in Risk Assessment* (1994); O'Neill, *Variable Justice: Environmental Standards, Contaminated Fish, and "Acceptable" Risk to Native Peoples*, 19 Stanford Environmental Law Journal at 27-30.

burdens visited on communities of color, low-income communities, tribes, and other indigenous peoples.[159]

While quantitative risk assessment is not without attributes to recommend it, the continued presence of the concerns sketched above   and the observation that these concerns are often amplified when those who bear the risk are environmental justice communities   means that it would be inappropriate to embrace unexamined risk assessment as currently practiced. Reevaluation of the method, moreover, is particularly appropriate at this juncture in light of recent work elaborating risk assessment's limitations from the particular perspectives of various communities of color, low-income communities, tribes, and other indigenous peoples; in light of refinements developed by researchers in response to some of the limitations noted above; in light of alternatives envisioned by those whose objections are more fundamental in nature; and, more generally, in light of the lessons afforded by several decades of experience with what is, after all, a method of relatively recent origin in the environmental regulatory context. Reevaluation may also be useful given that the method is costly and time-consuming: "a single risk assessment on a single chemical might take up to five years and cost upwards of $5 million."[160]

This part identifies two categories of efforts that merit involvement by EPA and other health and environmental agencies: (1) efforts to refine current risk assessment methods; and (2) efforts to reevaluate risk assessment and employ alternative approaches, especially approaches that focus on prevention and precaution. This part does not aim to provide a complete account of the various efforts that might be undertaken in each category; rather, it discusses a few important examples and counsels further exploration by EPA and others, together with affected groups.

1. Refining Risk Assessment

As currently practiced, quantitative risk assessment focuses in the main on a finite set of adverse effects to human physical health, narrowly defined. From the perspectives of many of those affected, this understanding of the problem captures only part of what is at stake in decisions affecting the environment. Among other things, it fails to grasp the interrelated physical, psychological, social, and cultural nature of the harms that are visited on some groups when environments are contaminated. These concerns are to some extent outlined above, in Section A. The discussion here is meant to highlight current work suggesting refinements to risk assessment that may go some or all of the way to addressing these concerns, and to suggest that EPA look to these efforts and support similar work. Thus, to the extent that EPA continues to

---

[159]See, e.g., Robert R. Kuehn, *The Environmental Justice Implications of Quantitative Risk Assessment*, 1996 University of Illinois Law Review 103; Daniel C. Wigley & Kristin Schrader-Frechette, *Environmental Racism and Biased Methods of Risk Assessment*, 7 Risk: Health, Safety & Environment 55 (1996); O'Neill, *Variable Justice: Environmental Standards, Contaminated Fish, and "Acceptable" Risk to Native Peoples*, 19 Stanford Environmental Law Journal 3.

[160]*Protecting Public Health and the Environment: Implementing the Precautionary Principle,* "Introduction: To Foresee and Forestall" 1, 4 (Carolyn Raffensperger and Joel Tickner, eds. 1999). Note that "[t]his excludes the cost of the harm that may be caused by the activity under study." Id.

employ risk assessment as a tool for making environmental decisions, it should at least consider the following and other refinements.

It is possible to refine current risk assessment practices by expanding the risk assessment framework so that, from the outset, it includes social, cultural, and economic risks as well as physical and ecological risks. Stuart Harris, Confederated Tribes of the Umatilla Indian Reservation, and Barbara Harper, International Institute for Indigenous Resource Management, for example, have developed just such a framework for assessing and characterizing risks to tribal health and cultures.[161] This model not only takes a broader view of the components of risk assessment, incorporating all of the elements of an "overall eco-cultural system," including "human health (using appropriate exposure scenarios), ecological health, and socio-cultural/socio-economic health," but it does so in a way that is holistic in that it recognizes the interrelations among these components.[162] It employs the concept of "the natural-cultural resource dependency web based on cultural ecosystemic stories."[163] Among other things, it offers a risk assessment model that is more scientifically defensible in that it more completely and accurately captures the nature and extent of the risks than do conventional models.[164] A related point is that "risk" may be defined quite differently by different affected groups. It may be comprised of different components, or be differently understood. Therefore, it is important that the affected group itself be involved in determining the contours of "risk," i.e. describing what is at stake as well as involved in the subsequent step of determining what levels of risk are acceptable, in which contexts, and under which circumstances.[165]

It is also possible to refine current risk assessment practices by selectively employing the method. Thus, for example, risk assessment may be inappropriate where the contaminants to be regulated are persistent, bioaccumulative, and/or highly toxic or where the contaminants have particularly troubling effects (including not only human physical health, narrowly defined, but also human health and well-being along multiple dimensions including psychological, social, and cultural health; and including ecological health). The Columbia River Inter-Tribal Fish Commission offers just this perspective:

> CRITFC maintains that risk assessments have no useful purpose for making regulatory decisions for persistent, bioaccumulative toxics, known carcinogens, "probable human

---

[161]Stuart G. Harris & Barbara L. Harper, *Using Eco-cultural Dependency Webs in Risk Assessment and Characterization of Risks to Tribal Health and Cultures*, 2 Environmental Science & Pollut. Res. 91 (Special Issue, 2000).

[162]Id. at 92.

[163]Id.

[164]Id. Note, too, that the model suggested by Harris and Harper does not inherently contain any more uncertainty than conventional risk assessment models.

[165]Note that the answer may in some cases be that only "zero increased risk" is judged acceptable by those who must bear the risk.

carcinogens," and substances known to cause reproductive, developmental or neurological effects.[166]

Finally, it is possible to refine current risk assessment practices by incorporating, to a far greater extent, the precautionary principle (this principle is discussed below). Some commentators have begun to explore how this might be accomplished.[167]

2. Alternatives to Risk-Based Approaches

Quantitative risk assessment and related analytic approaches reflect one subjective set of priorities and assumptions for environmental policy. When agencies choose these tools, they choose to privilege certain values, at the expense of others. As commentators have recognized, these methods do not   and cannot   provide the neutral, bias-free bases for environmental decisions that some proponents have suggested. As currently practiced, for example, risk assessment assumes that some amount of risk from contamination is "acceptable," and that so long as this amount is not exceeded, there is no reason or relationship that would call upon humans to prevent or limit contamination. It excludes all experience or understanding that is not readily quantified, and accepts only certain kinds of knowledge as valid. It lends a false sense of precision and accuracy to decisions about enormously uncertain and highly variable events, and operates within a regulatory framework that, for the most part, places the burden of resolving uncertainties on risk-bearers rather than risk-producers. Many people of color, low-income people, tribes, and other indigenous people do not share some or all of these assumptions, and so have questioned methods based on these premises. As Moses Squeochs, Fourteen Confederated Tribes and Bands of the Yakama Nation, explains:

> *When I first began this work and I first learned about risk assessment, I took issue with it immediately and I still have issues with it today. That's been over 10 years now, and I have continually taken a position that risk assessment   or conventional risk assessment is based on an American experience, not an indigenous American experience. So there is a disparity there that needs to be recognized and it needs to be addressed.*[168]

---

[166]Columbia River Inter-Tribal Fish Commission, *Comments to Administrator Browner on the Draft Revisions to the Methodology for Deriving Ambient Water Quality Criteria for the Protection of Human Health* 3 (1999).

[167]See, e.g., Nicholas A. Ashford, *Protecting Public Health and the Environment: Implementing the Precautionary Principle* "A Conceptual Framework for the Use of the Precautionary Principle in Law"198 (Carolyn Raffensperger and Joel Tickner, eds. 1999); see also, Stuart G. Harris & Barbara L. Harper, *Using Eco-cultural Dependency Webs in Risk Assessment and Characterization of Risks to Tribal Health and Cultures*, 2 Environmental Science & Pollut. Res. 91, 92 (Special Issue, 2000) (noting that "[t]he Precautionary Principle is not the antithesis of risk-based decisionmaking, but complements it by allowing decisions to be made in the face of uncertainty that is inherent in all predictive and variable situations.")

[168]Moses Squeochs, Fourteen Confederated Tribes and Bands of the Yakama Nation, *Testimony to National Environmental Justice Advisory Council* Vol III-101 (Annual Meeting Transcript) (Dec. 4, 2001).

Affected groups and others have also worked to envision alternative approaches. Important among these is an approach guided by the *precautionary principle*. As Tom Goldtooth, Executive Director, Indigenous Environmental Network, observes:

> *[W]e are engaged in a clash of two competing paradigms. One is an aging model based upon quantitative risk assessment, assimilative capacities, and acceptable discharges for individual compounds, which has dominated chemical and environmental policy . . . The other is an emerging paradigm based upon prevention, precaution, and clean production processes; and this is what we've been calling precautionary action, or [the] precautionary principle.*[169]

In broad terms, the precautionary principle focuses on *preventing* environmental contamination in the first place. It views prevention as preferable to other approaches as a matter of efficiency, justice, and ethics. That is, prevention avoids the enormous monetary costs of having to cleanup contamination after it has been permitted (and, given the propensity of many pollutants to migrate, mingle and otherwise pose more severe   and more costly   problems once they are released into the environment, prevention will very often be cheaper than "cure" in this context)[170] and of having to care for the sick whose illnesses have resulted from exposure to contaminants. Prevention addresses the problem of irreversible and very long term effects, e.g., once someone has cancer, this cannot be reversed, only treated; once a species is extinct, it is gone forever; once the fishery on which the St. Regis Mohawk tribe relies is devastated, generations will come and go without being able to fish. These concerns simply cannot be addressed by after-the-fact cleanup or health care. Prevention also helps to alleviate the extraordinary burden from contamination that is currently borne by communities of color, low-income communities, tribes and other indigenous peoples. Finally, prevention does not discriminate against those whose spiritual or cultural traditions include an ethic of reciprocity.

Beyond this broad focus on prevention, what would be entailed by the precautionary principle has been more specifically elaborated. Although the precautionary principle has been defined somewhat differently in the various instruments and statements invoking it, at the heart of these definitions are several core concepts:

a. A judgment that something of great value is at stake (usually accompanied by a recognition that what is of value includes not only human but non-human components of ecosystems, and includes not only the well-being of present generations but of future generations);
b. An acknowledgment that the threat to what is of value is potentially serious and/or irreversible; and

---

[169]Tom Goldtooth, Executive Director, Indigenous Environmental Network, *Comments to the National Environmental Justice Advisory Council*, "Public Comment" Vol III-28 (Annual Meeting Transcript) (Dec. 4, 2001).
[170]*Protecting Public Health and the Environment: Implementing the Precautionary Principle*, "Introduction: To Foresee and Forestall" 1, 4 (Carolyn Raffensperger and Joel Tickner, eds. 1999).

c. A recognition, therefore, that action to prevent or reduce this threat is appropriate, and that uncertainty as to the existence or magnitude of the threat should not constitute a sufficient reason for refraining from action.

These concepts, in turn, have been taken to suggest further precepts, such as a shift in the burden of proof   such that those who propose to introduce or continue to produce toxic substances are required to demonstrate the non-existence of a threat; a preference for less toxic alternatives such that laws and policies that facilitate the search for less toxic substitutes are called for; and a "proportionality of response"   such that the appropriateness of actions taken to prevent or reduce the threat from contamination depends in part upon the seriousness or irreversibility of the threat relative to the costs of the action. Although these precepts, in particular, may not be present in every conception of the precautionary principle, the outline above gives some sense of the perspectives that underlie the principle.

The precautionary principle is a component of numerous international agreements, including several to which the United States is party.[171] Perhaps most prominent among these is Section 15 of the Rio Declaration of the United Nations Conference on Environment and Development, signed in 1992 by the United States and a host of other nation-states.[172] Not only is the precautionary approach a part of United States law as a result of its international commitments, but this approach is included in domestic law, in environmental statutes and elsewhere. Thus, for example, commentators have noted that the precautionary approach is embodied in aspects of the National Environmental Protection Act (NEPA), the Clean Water Act (CWA), the Toxic Substances Control Act (ToSCA), and the Pollution Prevention Act (PPA), among other federal, state, and tribal statutes.[173] And the U.S. President's Council on Sustainable Development, a multi-stakeholder presidential board, recently issued a statement invoking the precautionary approach.[174]

---

[171]For a list of these treaties and agreements, see Appendix B, in *Protecting Public Health and the Environment: Implementing the Precautionary Principle* 356 (Carolyn Raffensperger and Joel Tickner, eds. 1999).

[172]Section 15 provides: "In order to protect the environment, the precautionary approach shall be widely applied by states according to their capabilities. Where there are threats of serious or irreversible damage, lack of full scientific certainty shall not be used as a reason for postponing cost-effective measures to prevent environmental degradation." Rio Declaration on Environmental and Development, June 14, 1992, 31 International Legal Materials 874.

[173]See, e.g., *Protecting Public Health and the Environment: Implementing the Precautionary Principle*, "Introduction: To Foresee and Forestall" 1, 4-7 (Carolyn Raffensperger and Joel Tickner, eds. 1999).

[174]Principle number 12 provides: "We believe: even in the face of scientific uncertainty, society should take reasonable actions to avert risks where the potential harm to human health or the environment is thought to be serious or irreparable." President's Council on Sustainable Development, *Sustainable America: A New Consensus* (1996) (cited in *Protecting Public Health and the Environment: Implementing the Precautionary Principle,* "Appendix B" 356 (Carolyn Raffensperger and Joel Tickner, eds. 1999)).

Much work remains to be done to explore and specify the contours of the precautionary principle in various contexts; to identify and make use of opportunities for precautionary approaches within the existing legal structure in the United States; and to consider and advocate appropriate changes to existing laws. There is, nonetheless, a significant and growing body of recent work on which to build. For example, recent work by Carl F. Cranor contributes to efforts along each of these fronts.[175] First, he has sought to clarify and specify several aspects of the principle. He has suggested the clarification, among others, that whereas the lack of scientific certainty may not constitute a *sufficient* reason for refraining from action, it may nonetheless count *among* the reasons for choosing among actions or for refraining from action. Second, he has identified opportunities within existing environmental laws for EPA and other agencies to revisit interpretations that discourage precaution in favor of interpretations that incorporate precaution. He has pointed out that agencies may have latitude under statutes such as TOSCA to require manufacturers to make a greater pre-market showing of safety than is currently required before introducing substances (a) that are chemically similar to those known to be highly toxic or (b) that have certain characteristics, such as a tendency to persist, to bioaccumulate, or to be mutagenic. He has also argued that agencies may have the ability under various statutes to reinterpret the burdens and standards of proof that operate to permit such persistent, bioaccumulative, highly toxic substances to continue to be manufactured or produced as byproducts. Third, he has noted instances in which changes to existing laws might be warranted in order to implement the precautionary principle, and suggested models (e.g., particular aspects of the Swedish approach) for such changes. Other commentators, too, have contributed to the efforts to elaborate the precautionary principle. And an array of local efforts   ranging from community-led efforts to eliminate consumers' contributions to contamination to small businesses' undertakings to reduce their use of toxic inputs and as a result lower their costs   have devised creative ways to implement precaution in practice. EPA should draw on this body of work and support efforts further to develop it.

---

[175]Carl F. Cranor, *Protecting Public Health and the Environment: Implementing the Precautionary Principle,* "Asymmetric Information, the Precautionary Principle, and Burdens of Proof" 74 (Carolyn Raffensperger and Joel Tickner, eds. 1999).

CHAPTER II: USING EXISTING LEGAL AUTHORITIES

How might EPA's authority under federal environmental and other laws be implemented more effectively to sustain healthy aquatic ecosystems and to protect the health and safety of people consuming or using fish, aquatic plants, and wildlife?

RISK REDUCTION STRATEGIES AND PROBLEM POLLUTANTS

This chapter focuses on *risk reduction* strategies   that is, strategies by which agencies look to risk-producers to cleanup, limit, and prevent environmental contamination. In the case of contamination in aquatic ecosystems, these strategies have been developed under a variety of legal authorities, the Clean Water Act prominent among them. In addition to the authority provided by the Clean Water Act, this chapter considers how the authority of other relevant sources of law might be invoked more effectively to sustain healthy ecosystems and to protect the health and safety of people consuming or using fish, aquatic plants, and wildlife. This chapter begins by providing background on the contaminants of greatest concern to affected communities of color, low-income communities, tribes, and other indigenous peoples. Part A considers how EPA might better prevent and reduce contamination in the first place, focusing primarily on efforts under the Clean Water Act and secondarily on efforts under other legal authorities. Part B discusses how EPA might better cleanup and restore those aquatic ecosystems that are already contaminated, again focusing primarily on efforts under the Clean Water Act and secondarily on efforts under other legal authorities.

Access to water of sufficient quality and quantity is vital to tribal, state, and local governments, as well as to environmentalists, developers, industry, and the public including minority and low-income communities. Unquestionably, degradation of water quality threatens not only the viability of aquatic ecosystems, but also human health; subsistence, traditional, cultural, and spiritual practices; economies; sustainability of tribal homelands as contemplated by federal Indian treaties and other laws;[176] and ultimately all life itself. As Rachel Carson noted in her landmark book *Silent Spring:*

> *Water must also be thought of in terms of the chains of life it supports--from the small-as-dust green cells of the drifting plant plankton, though the minute water fleas to the fishes that strain plankton from the water and are in turn eaten by other fishes or by birds, mink, racoons--in an endless cyclic transfer of materials from life to life. We know that the necessary minerals in the water are so passed from link to link of the food chains. Can we suppose that poisons we introduce into water will not also enter into these cycles of nature?*[177]

Quite simply, poisoning the aquatic food chain ultimately poisons the Earth's entire food web.

The pollutants enumerated below are believed to result in harm to aquatic ecosystems and to pose the greatest risks to the health of people consuming or using fish, aquatic plants and wildlife for traditional, cultural and religious purposes. These pollutants have been identified by federal, tribal, state, and territorial governments as well as by affected groups and independent researchers. While numerous contaminants are potentially a basis for concern,[178] available data indicate that the following contaminants are currently the source of greatest concern.

---

[176]Often, pursuant to explicit treaties, tribes bargained with the with federal government for the terms of vast land cessions and the retention of certain other lands for Indian use and occupation. Through express treaty terms or by virtue of retained aboriginal title, tribes reserved every incident of ownership not expressly relinquished to the federal government or abrogated by Congress. United States v. Winans, 198 U.S. 371, 381 (1905). These reserved rights include a recognized right to water sufficient to fulfill the purposes of the reservation. Winters v. United States, 207 U.S. 564, 577 (1908). Among other things, reserved rights have been understood to include water to maintain a permanent homeland, to preserve, produce, or sustain food and other reservation resources, and to maintain the tribe's way of life. See, e.g. Winters v. United States, 143 F. 740, 742 (1906); Colville Confederated Tribes v. Walton, 647 F.2d 42, 49 (1981 9th Cir.), cert. denied, 454 U.S. 1092 (1981); Felix S. Cohen, *Handbook of Federal Indian Law* 588-89 (1982 ed.). Frequently, treaties expressly retained a tribe's right to hunt, fish, and gather both on a reservation and off-reservation in all usual and accustomed places. United States v. Winans, 198 U.S. 371, 381 (1905); United States v. Adair, 723 F.2d 1394, 1410, 1417-18 (9th Cir. 1983), cert. denied, Oregon v. United States, 467 U.S. 1252 (1984).

[177]Rachel Carson, *Silent Spring* at 46 *(1962).*

[178]There are more than 70,000 chemicals currently in use; yet for the vast majority of these, comprehensive data about human and environmental health effects is sorely lacking. Of these chemicals, those that are highly toxic, that persist in the environment for relatively long periods, and that bioaccumulate are likely to be of particular concern here. The Washington State Department of Ecology, for example, has identified 64 highly toxic, persistent and bioaccumulative contaminants to be screened and prioritized (of these, nine have been slated for immediate action) as part of its initiative to address persistent, bioaccumlative toxins. See Washington State Department of Ecology, *Proposed Strategy to Continually Reduce Persistent, Bioaccumulative Toxins (PBTs) in Washington State* (No. 00-03-054) (Dec. 2000) available at http://www.ecy.wa.gov/pubs/0003054.pdf.

Five contaminants — mercury, PCBs, dioxins, DDT, and chlordane — are responsible for the majority of fish and wildlife consumption advisories issued by federal, tribal, state, or territorial governments.[179] These five contaminants are often also among the contaminants of greatest concern according to those affected. For example, David Ludder, of the Legal Environmental Assistance Foundation in Tallahassee reports that affected communities in Florida, Alabama, and Georgia are concerned in the main with these five contaminants and toxaphene.[180] Similarly, the Asian Pacific Environmental Network cites evidence of the presence of these five chemicals and dieldrin at levels of concern for those consuming fish from San Francisco Bay, particularly members of the Laotian community in West Contra Costa County.[181] In addition to these five contaminants, there are approximately 40 different chemicals or chemical groups that give rise to at least one fish and wildlife consumption advisory.[182]

While the existence of a consumption advisory provides one useful gauge as to which contaminants are the basis for concern, there are limitations to this measure. Importantly, the absence of a consumption advisory does not necessarily mean the absence of contamination. In some cases, the necessary assessments of fish and wildlife tissues have not yet been undertaken, often for lack of resources.[183] In other cases, states or tribes might decline to issue fish consumption advisories for a variety of reasons, including economic, health and cultural

------

[179] According to the EPA Office of Water, most advisories are triggered by one or more of five primary contaminants: mercury, PCBs, dioxins, DDT, and chlordane. See U.S. Environmental Protection Agency, Office of Water, *Update: National Listing of Fish and Wildlife Advisories* 5 (April 2001) available at www.epa.gov/ost/fish.

[180] Telephone Interview with David Ludder, Legal Environmental Assistance Foundation, Tallahassee, Florida (Aug. 22, 2001). Ludder noted, however, that this concern was premised primarily on the existence of fish consumption advisories and so indicated that this was a preliminary list.

[181] Audrey Chiang, Asian Pacific Environmental Network, *A Seafood Consumption Survey of the Laotian Community of West Contra Costa County, California* App. 1 (1998) (citing San Francisco Bay Regional Water Quality Control Board, Office of Health Hazard Assessment, *Chemical Contamination in Fish from San Francisco Bay: Study Results* (1995)).

[182] These include Arsenic, Cadmium, Chlorinated Benzene, Chlorinated Pesticides, Chromium, Copper, Creosote, Dichloroethane, Gasoline, Hexachlorobutadiene, Industrial & Municipal Discharge, Kepone, Lead, Lindane, Metals, Organo-metallics, PAHs, PBBs, Pentachlorobenzene, Pentachloroethylene, Photomirex, Phthalate Esters, Selenium, Tetrachlorobenzene, Tetrachloroethane, Tetrachloroethylene, Tributyltin, Trichloroethane, Trichloromethane, Vinyl Chloride, VOCs, Zinc.

[183] The trend to date has been for advisories to increase as assessments are completed. Thus, EPA notes that the number of advisories in 2000 represents a 7% increase over the number reported in 1999 and a 124% increase over the number reported in 1993 and observes that "[t]he increase in advisories issued by the states [territories and tribes] generally reflects an increase in the number of assessments of chemical contaminants in fish and wildlife tissues." U.S. Environmental Protection Agency, Office of Water, *Update: National Listing of Fish and Wildlife Advisories* 2 (April 2001) available at www.epa.gov/ost/fish. The need for additional funding to address a shortfall in resources for tissue and environmental assessments is particularly acute for many tribes.

reasons.[184] The Fond du Lac Environmental Program, for example, is in the process of issuing "tribal consumption guidelines."[185] Contrary to "advisories," these guidelines do not warn *against* consumption of fish or wildlife; rather, they provide guidelines for healthy consumption, consistent with tribal traditions and practices.[186] In addition, fish and wildlife advisories generally arise from one exposure scenario (consuming contaminated fish or wildlife), and so do not account for other routes or sources of exposure to those consuming or using fish, aquatic plants and wildlife for traditional, cultural and religious purposes. (e.g., consuming contaminated aquatic plants; consuming or otherwise being exposed to contaminated waters, etc.). And, fish and wildlife advisories focus on the problem of the contamination of fish and wildlife, and leave unaddressed the problem of the availability of fish, aquatic plants, and wildlife for consumption and use.

Thus, in addition to the five contaminants that have given rise to the bulk of fish and wildlife consumption advisories, there are other contaminants of concern. Chief among these are contaminants that are highly toxic, bioaccumulative, and persistent. The Convention on Persistent Organic Pollutants (POPs) initially targets twelve POPs of concern: in addition to PCBs, dioxins, DDT and chlordane, the Convention identifies aldrin, dieldrin, endrin, helptachlor, hexachlorobenzene, mirex, toxaphene, and furans as being of primary concern.[187] The EPA has also identified these same twelve contaminants as part of its Persistent Bioaccumulative Toxin

---

[184]See, generally, Stuart Harris, *Impacts of Fish Contamination on Native American Culture* (talk delivered to the Annual National Forum on Contaminants in Fish, May 9, 2001) Neither Wyoming nor Alaska have issued fish or wildlife consumption advisories. Briefing by Rich Healy, U.S. Environmental Protection Agency, Office of Water to Fish Consumption Workgroup (Jun. 26, 2001). But see the recently issued *Statement from the Alaska Division of Public Health*, expressly denouncing the applicability of the general mercury advisories in Alaska and recommending "unrestricted consumption of fish from Alaskan waters" for all, given their independent review of mercury levels in Alaska fish, the known health benefits of fish consumption, and the fact that "the subsistence lifestyle and diet are of great importance to the self-determination, cultural, spiritual, social, and overall health and well being of Alaska Natives." *Mercury and National Fish Advisories Statement* from Alaska Division of Public Health: Recommendations for Fish Consumption in Alaska (Bulletin no. 6) (Jun. 15, 2001) (endorsed by the Alaska Department of Environmental Conservation, Alaska Department of Health and Social Services, Alaska Native Health Board; Alaska Native Science Commission; Alaska Native Tribal Health Consortium; Aleutian/Pribilof Islands Association, Inc.; Institute for Circumpolar Health Studies; University of Alaska Anchorage; North Slope Borough; University of Alaska Fairbanks; and Yukpm Kuskokwim Health Corporation) available at www.epi.hss.state.ak.us/bulletins/docs/b2001_06.htm
[185]Telephone Interview with Nancy Costa, Fond du Lac Environmental Program (Jul. 31, 2001).
[186]Id. Costa explains that the Fond du Lac Environmental Program is careful *not* to use the word "advisory," because "the last thing we want to do is discourage tribal and band members from eating their native diet, given the serious health effects that we've seen of getting away from a native diet." Id.; see also, Great Lakes Indian Fish & Wildlife Commission, *Masinaigan Supplement: How to Enjoy Fish Safely* (Fall 2000).
[187]Convention on Persistent Organic Pollutants (POPs). The United States is a signatory to this Convention, although it awaits the advice and consent of the Senate available at http://www.unece.org/env/lrtap/protocol/98pop.htm.

(PBT) Initiative. Each of these POPs or PBTs is also the source of at least one fish or wildlife consumption advisory.[188]

A variety of pesticides[189] have emerged as particular sources of concern for various affected communities, groups and tribes. The Shoalwater Bay Indian Reservation is concerned with the health of tribal members and the flourishing of the shellfish resource in Willapa Bay, on which members of the tribe depend for commercial, subsistence, and ceremonial uses. Although tribal studies are only recently underway (such that there is no evidence at this time that these pesticides are in fact harming shellfisheries), potential sources of contamination include pesticides such as diazinon, lorsban, and guthion, all of which are used by nearby commercial cranberry bog farmers; carbaryl and glyphosate, applied to the oyster beds and tideflats; and various organochlorine herbicides, sprayed in surrounding and upland areas by the U.S. Forest Service as it seeks to kill "nuisance" species, typically after clear-cut logging.[190] The Louisiana Environmental Action Network is concerned with the high levels of pesticides (among other contaminants), particularly atrazine and cyanazine, that a recent study revealed to be present in the Mississippi River between New Orleans and Baton Rouge: "As would be expected, the pesticides appeared in early spring and persisted throughout the summer, coinciding with the southern and midwestern growing seasons."[191] The study focused on the Mississippi River as a source of drinking water, noting that "[p]esticides presented the largest health hazard, where maximum levels were found to be 60 to 360 times the EPA's Maximum Contamination Level (MCL) for drinking water."[192] Various community and fishing groups have identified 48 pesticides commonly used in the Pacific Northwest that have been determined by either EPA or the United States Geological Survey (USGS) to threaten salmon and salmon habitat.[193]

Lead is a source of concern for those consuming fish from the Spokane River from the Idaho state line to the Seven Mile Bridge in Washington, given recent studies revealing elevated

---

[188]See U.S. Environmental Protection Agency, Office of Water, *National Fish and Wildlife Contamination Program.* available at www.epa.gov/ost/fish.

[189]The term "pesticides", as used throughout this report, is meant to encompass all pesticides, including rodenticides, insecticides, herbicides, and fungicides, unless the context indicates a different usage.

[190]E-mail Correspondence with Gary Burns, Environmental Programs Director, Shoalwater Bay Indian Tribe (Oct. 3, 2001); E-mail Correspondence with Chetana Acharya, Community Outreach and Education Program Manager, NIEHS Center for Ecogenetics and Environmental Health, University of Washington (Oct. 2, 2001); Paul Shukovsky, *Tribe Sounds Alarm Over Fetal Deaths: 13 Pregnancies in 2 years; 1 Baby Survives*, Seattle Post-Intelligencer (Feb. 22, 1999).

[191]Louisiana Environmental Action Network, *Final Report on the Riverkeeper Project* (1998) available at www.leanweb.org/rivkeep.html.

[192]Id.

[193]"Groups Uncover Government Documents Showing Pesticides Can Harm Salmon," (May 7, 2001) available at www.pesticide.org/MSJnewsrelease.html (joint press release by Washington Toxics Coalition; Northwest Coalition for Alternatives to Pesticides; Pacific Coast Federation of Fishermen's Associations; Institute for Fisheries Resources; and Earthjustice Legal Defense Fund in course of litigation against EPA for Endangered Species Act violations).

lead levels (along with elevated levels of other metals), particularly for children (given that lead causes adverse developmental effects) and for those, such as Russian immigrants, who consume the whole fish (given that lead concentrates in the bones and brains of fish).[194]   Lead is also a source of concern for the Coeur d'Alene Tribe, given its presence (along with cadmium) in and on water potatoes, a staple of the Coeur d'Alene diet.[195]

Fecal coliform, marine biotoxins (e.g., saxitoxin and domoic acid released by algal blooms), and various other bacterial and viral contaminants are sources of concern for those communities, groups and tribes that rely on shellfish for commercial, subsistence, and/or ceremonial purposes. Thus, these contaminants are a source of concern for tribal resource managers in the Puget Sound and coastal regions of Washington,[196] among them the Shoalwater Tribe,[197] the Suquamish Tribe,[198] the Lower Elwha Klallam Tribe,[199] and the Tulalip Tribes.[200] These contaminants are a source of concern for various communities of color and low-income communities in Southern California.[201] And they are a source of concern for Alaskan Natives. For example, at a southeast regional meeting called to discuss Alaskan Natives' concerns with contaminants in native foods, Dangel Helen, Douglas, observes:

> There is in North Douglas a development not served by a sewer line. A lot of the mud flats are contaminated. The shellfish aren't good to eat.[202]

Finally, these and several additional pollutants are of particular concern to one or more affected groups or tribes. For example, the Fond du Lac Environmental Program is concerned with contamination from metals, given the negative effects of several metals (aluminum, cadmium, copper, lead, and zinc, in addition to mercury) on the growth of wild rice.[203] The Tulalip Tribes

---

[194]Karen Dorn Steele, *Agencies Warn of Lead in River's Fish; Advisory Targets Consumption of Contaminated Fish Caught in Stretch of Spokane River* A1 The Spokesman Review (Jun. 21, 2000).

[195]Telephone Interview with Marc Stifelman, Environmental Protection Agency (Region X)(Oct. 30, 2001).

[196]See, generally, Northwest Indian Fisheries Commission, *Tribal Shellfish Management* available at www.nwifc.wa.gov/ctnrm/2001_shellfish.htm.

[197]E-mail Correspondence with Gary Burns, Environmental Programs Director, Shoalwater Bay Indian Tribe (Oct. 3, 2001); E-mail Correspondence with Chetana Acharya, Community Outreach and Education Program Manager, NIEHS Center for Ecogenetics and Environmental Health, University of Washington (Oct. 2, 2001).

[198]Telephone Interview with Jay Zischke, Marine Fish Program Manager, Suquamish Tribe Fisheries Department (Oct. 17, 2001).

[199]Telephone Interview with Russ Busch, Attorney, Legal Counsel for the Lower Elwha Klallam Tribe. (Oct. 4, 2001).

[200]Terry Williams, Commissioner, Tulalip Tribes, Fisheries and Natural Resources (C3G Conference Call, Jul. 20, 2001).

[201]Telephone Interview with Marianne Yamaguchi, Santa Monica Bay Restoration Project.

[202]Alaska Traditional Knowledge and Native Foods Database, *Native Concerns.* Available at www.nativeknowledge.org/db/concerns/asp.

[203]Telephone Interview with Larry Schwarzkopf, Fond du Lac Resources Program (Jul. 12, 2001).

are concerned with sediment and silt loadings, given their contribution to degradation of salmon habitat and, ultimately, to the depletion of the salmon fishery.[204] The various communities that fish the Devil's Swamp, Devil's Swamp Lake, Bayou Baton Rouge, and Capitol Lake in East Baton Rouge Parish face contamination from lead and arsenic, in addition to hexachlorobenzene, hexachloro-1,3-butadiene, PCBs and mercury.[205] The Fourteen Confederated Tribes of the Yakama Indian Nation and the Confederated Tribes of the Umatilla Indian Reservation are concerned with a host of contaminants in the Columbia River, which is "heavily laden with heavy metals from mining, agricultural chemicals from intensive orchards and vineyards, radionuclides from Hanford, runoff from dairy farms, and PCBs from a variety of sources."[206] As Chief Johnny Jackson elaborates:

> *I'm from the Columbia River. I've lived there all my life. I was born and raised there. I'm a fisherman. My family have all been fishermen . . . Many of my people today are dying of cancer as well as diabetes . . . and we talk about cleaning up the area and cleaning up the water and the air, but nobody talks about what is happening up at Hanford and what's happening to the soil and the water at Hanford, and what it's doing to our river. . . We're fishing people. Fishing is our life and fish is our food, but we don't know what they're swimming through when they are going back up that river. I think it's a great injustice until somebody does something about it and cleans that river up and stops pollution at Hanford.[207]*

In addition, there is concern that the health of aquatic ecosystems is being compromised by temperature changes; changes in pH and dissolved oxygen content; introduction of exotic species; dams, diversions, and other alterations; and numerous other affronts.

The discussion below elaborates the health effects and sources of mercury, PCBs, dioxins, DDT, chlordane, and, to a lesser extent, the remaining POPs/PBTs, and other contaminants of concern.

---

[204]Terry Williams, Commissioner, Tulalip Tribes, Fisheries and Natural Resources (C3G Conference Call, Jul. 20, 2001).

[205]See Louisiana Department of Health and Hospitals, under cooperative agreement with The Agency for Toxic Substance and Disease Registry, *Public Health Assessment: Petro-Processors of Louisiana Incorporate Baton Rouge, East Baton Rouge Parish, Louisiana* (Jan. 16, 1996). Available at atsdr1.atsdr.cdc.gov/HAC/PHA/petro/pet toc.htm.

[206]Barbara Harper and Stuart Harris, *Proceedings of the American Fisheries Society: Forum on Contaminants in Fish*, "Tribal Technical Issues in Risk Reduction Through Fish Advisories" 17 (1999).

[207]Chief Johnny Jackson, *Comment to the National Environmental Justice Advisory Council* Vol III-4-6 (Annual meeting transcript) (Dec. 4, 2001).

Mercury

Background

Mercury is responsible, at least in part, for nearly 79% of all fish and shellfish advisories issued in the United States; as of December, 2000, it was the basis for 2,242 advisories issued by 41 states, territories or tribes.[208] Thirteen states have issued statewide advisories for mercury in the freshwater lakes and/or rivers within their boundaries; another nine states have issued statewide mercury advisories for their coastal marine waters.[209] Mercury is also responsible for the first ever issuance of a national fish consumption advisory: in January, 2001, the EPA (together with ATSDR) and the FDA each independently issued advisories cautioning various populations against consuming fish due to mercury contamination.[210]

Mercury has been identified as a major pollutant of concern by the Great Lakes Indian Fish and Wildlife Commission (GLIFWC) and the Fond du Lac Environmental Program, given its deleterious effects on both fish and wild rice.[211] Mercury has been identified as a pollutant of concern by the St. Regis Mohawk Tribe Environment Division (although of less significance than PCBs).[212] Hawaii's Thousand Friends observes that mercury has been identified as the major contaminant in fish eaten in Hawai'i.[213] Mercury has been identified as a major concern by the Grand Cal Task Force, given its significant contribution to the contamination of the Grand Calumet River and the Indian Harbor Ship Canal, where "virtually all fish tested in Indiana show levels of mercury and all streams are considered impaired."[214] Mercury has been identified as a source of significant concern in Louisiana, particularly in the heavily contaminated parishes along the Mississippi River between New Orleans and Baton Rouge by the Louisiana Environmental

---

[208]See U.S. Environmental Protection Agency, Office of Water, *Mercury Update: Impact on Fish Advisories* 4 (June 2001) available at www.epa.gov/ost/fish/chemfacts.html. [hereinafter "EPA. Mercury Fact Sheet"]

[209]Id.

[210]U.S. Environmental Protection Agency advisories are available at www.epa.gov/ost/fish. U.S. Food and Drug Administration advisories are available at www.cfsan.fda.gov/~dms/admehg.html. Briefing by Rich Healy, U.S. Environmental Protection Agency, Office of Water to Fish Consumption Workgroup (Jun. 26, 2001).

[211]Great Lakes Indian Fish & Wildlife Commission, *Masinaigan Supplement: How to Enjoy Fish Safely* (Fall 2000) available at www.glifwc.org. Telephone Interview with Larry Schwarzkopf, Fond du Lac Resources Program (Jul. 12, 2001).

[212]Telephone Interview with Shawn Martin, Clean Water Manager, St. Regis Mohawk Tribe Environment Division (Jul. 12, 2001).

[213]Hawaii's Thousand Friends (Written Comments, March 11, 2002).

[214]Telephone Interview with Bowden Quinn, Executive Director, Grand Cal Task Force (Oct. 10, 2001); Grand Calumet Task Force, *Mercury and the Grand Calumet River* available at www.igc.apc.org/gctf/newsletter002.htm..

Action Network and by Dr. Barry Kohl, Department of Geology, Tulane University.[215] Mercury is a source of concern for the Passamaquoddy tribe, who rely on both saltwater and freshwater fish, given that all lakes in the state of Maine are under a state-issued fish advisory for mercury.[216] At an interior regional meeting called to discuss Alaskan Natives' concerns with contaminants in native foods, Orville Huntington, Huslia, observes:

> *Around home, I think it's an accumulation. All those poisons dumped in the river are in the fish and they accumulate in your body. . . . The pike around Hog River I won't eat anymore because there's too much mercury in there.[217]*

Health Effects[218]

Methylmercury is rapidly and nearly completely absorbed by humans from the gastrointestinal tract. It readily crosses the placental and blood/brain barriers. The National Research Council (NRC) of the National Academy of Sciences observes: "[Methylmercury (MeHg)] is highly toxic. Exposure to MeHg can result in adverse effects in several organ systems throughout the life span of humans and animals. There are extensive data on the effects of MeHg on the development of the brain (neurodevelopmental effects) in humans and animals. . . . Effects [at high doses] included mental retardation, cerebral palsy, deafness, blindness, and dysarthria in individuals exposed in utero and sensory and motor impairment in exposed adults. Chronic, low-dose prenatal MeHg exposure from maternal consumption of fish has been associated with more subtle end points of neurotoxicity in children. Those end points include poor performance on neurobehavioral tests, particularly on tests of attention, fine-motor function, language, visual-spatial abilities (e.g., drawing), and verbal memory."[219] There is also evidence of adverse effects on developing and adult cardiovascular systems in both humans and animals.[220] Some studies have demonstrated an association between methylmercury and cancer, but, according to the NRC, these studies are inconclusive.[221] EPA concurs and does not regulate methylmercury as a carcinogen.

---

[215]Telephone Interview with Marylee Orr, Louisiana Environmental Action Network (Oct. 17, 2001); Telephone Interview with Dr. Barry Kohl, Department of Geology, Tulane University (Oct. 17, 2001).

[216]See Paul Kuehnert, *Health Status and Needs Assessment of Native Americans in Maine: Final Report* (Jan. 15, 2000) available at www.state.me.us/dhs/boh/files/nar/nar.htm.. U.S. Environmental Protection Agency fish advisories available at www.epa.gov/ost/fish.

[217]Alaska Traditional Knowledge and Native Foods Database, *Native Concerns* available at www.nativeknowledge.org/db/concerns.asp.

[218]Unless otherwise noted, health effects information is taken from the EPA Mercury Fact Sheet.

[219]National Research Council, National Academy of Sciences, *Toxicological Effects of Methymercury* 4 (2000).

[220]Id.

[221]Id.

Sources of Mercury in the Environment[222]

Overview: Nearly 80% of the mercury contamination in surface waters comes from mercury emissions to the air. Mercury contamination also comes from direct discharges to the water, from releases to soils, and from naturally occurring mercury in the environment.

Mercury exists in the environment as elemental mercury (metallic mercury), and in inorganic and organic mercury compounds (primarily methylmercury).

Air: Mercury is released to the air by solid waste incineration and fossil fuel combustion, especially coal-fired power plants (in combination, these sources account for approximately 87% of mercury emissions in the United States); mining and smelting operations; industrial operations involving the use of mercury such as chlor-alkali production facilities; cement production; medical waste incineration (accounts for approximately 10% of mercury emissions in the United States),[223] and non-industrial combustion (e.g., wildfires and open burning).

Water/Sediments: Mercury is released to surface waters from naturally occurring mercury in rocks and from industrial processes, including pulp and paper mills, leather tanning, electroplating, and chemical manufacturing, and from some wastewater treatment facilities. Mercury emissions to the air are an important indirect source of mercury in surface waters: mercury is deposited from rain and other processes to water surfaces and to soils. Sediments contaminated with mercury also contribute mercury to surface waters upon being disturbed (e.g., by flooding or dredging).

Soils: Mercury is released to soils through the direct application of fertilizers, fungicides, and sludge or "recycled" industrial waste containing mercury to soils and crops. Mercury is also released to soils when solid waste, including batteries and thermometers, and municipal incinerator ash is disposed in landfills.

Notes

Unlike many other contaminants that are the source of fish consumption advisories, mercury does not accumulate primarily in the fatty tissue of fish but in the muscle (i.e., the portion of fish that comprises a fillet). Thus, skinning and trimming the fish do not reduce the amount of mercury in a fillet, nor is mercury removed by cooking processes.[224]

---

[222]Unless otherwise noted, sources information is taken from the EPA Mercury Fact Sheet.

[223]U.S. Environmental Protection Agency, *Mercury Study Report to Congress*, "Vol. 1: Executive Summary" (No. EPA-452/R-97-003) (December 1997) available at www.epa.gov/oar/mercury.html.

[224]U.S. Environmental Protection Agency Mercury Fact Sheet; Great Lakes Indian Fish & Wildlife Commission, *Masinaigan Supplement: How to Enjoy Fish Safely* (Fall 2000) available at www.glifwc.org.

PCBs[225]

Background

PCBs are responsible, at least in part, for nearly 27% of all fish and shellfish advisories issued in the United States; as of December, 1998, PCBs were the basis for 679 advisories issued by 37 states, territories or tribes.[226] Three states have issued statewide advisories for PCBs in the freshwater lakes and/or rivers within their boundaries; another six states have issued statewide PCBs advisories for their coastal marine waters.[227]

PCBs have been identified as a major pollutant of concern by the St. Regis Mohawk Tribe Environment Division.[228] PCBs have been cited by the Village of Savoonga and other Alaska Native villages as "[posing] special problems for Alaska Tribes who live near PCB contaminated former U.S. military sites."[229] PCBs have been identified by the Arbor Hill Environmental Justice Corporation as impacting the health of inner city communities, many of whose members subsistence fish along the Hudson River in upstate New York.[230] PCBs have been cited as a source of significant "community concern" given the number of anglers fishing along the contaminated Lower Fox River in the Green Bay area of Wisconsin (including Caucasians, Hmong, Laotian, Native American, and African-American anglers).[231] PCBs have been identified as among the issues of concern in Alabama by Project AWAKE, given that recent fish tissue monitoring by the Alabama Department of Environmental Management has revealed levels of PCBS exceeding FDA guidelines in striped bass from upper Lay Reservoir and channel catfish from upper Neely Henry Reservoir.[232]

---

[225]"PCBs" is a shorthand for a group of 209 individual cogeners – members of a group of structurally similar chemicals with different configurations. PCBs generally occur as a complex mixture of some assortment of these cogeners.

[226]U.S. Environmental Protection Agency, Office of Water, *Polychlorinated Biphenyls (PCBs) Update: Impact on Fish Advisories* 3-4 (September 1999) available at www.epa.gov/ost/fish/chemfacts.html. [hereinafter EPA PCBs Fact Sheet]

[227]Id.

[228]Telephone Interview with Shawn Martin, Clean Water Manager, St. Regis Mohawk Tribe Environment Division (Jul. 12, 2001).

[229]See, e.g., Native Village of Savoonga, Resolution # 00-10.

[230] *"Fishing for Justice – May 13, 2000 Island Creek Park on the Hudson River"* available at www.ejcr.cau.edu/fishingforjust.htm (citing Arbor Hill Environmental Justice Corporation President Aaron Mair's call for increased awareness of the issue and for "GE to do the right thing and clean up the PCB's they dumped into the River").

[231]Dyan M. Steenport, et al., *Fish Consumption Habits and Advisory Awareness Among Fox River Anglers*, Wisconsin Medical Journal (November 2000) available at www.wismed.org/wmj/nov2000/fish.html.

[232]Facsimile Communication, Daisy Carter, Project AWAKE (Oct. 25, 2001); Alabama Department of Environmental Management, *ADEM Announces Results of Fiscal Year 2001 Fish Tissue Monitoring Effort* (Apr. 25, 2001) available at www.adem.state.al.us/EduInfo/PressReleases/4fish01.htm..

Health Effects[233]

PCBs have been classified by EPA as "probable human carcinogens." Studies have suggested that PCBs may play a role in inducing breast cancer. Studies have linked PCBs to increased risk of several other cancers as well, including: liver, biliary tract, gall bladder, gastrointestinal tract, pancreas, melanoma, and non-Hodgkin's lymphoma. PCBs may also cause non-carcinogenic effects, including reproductive effects and developmental effects (primarily to the nervous system). PCBs tend to accumulate in the human body in the liver, adipose tissue (fat), skin, and breast milk; PCBs have also been found in plasma, follicular fluid, and sperm fluid. Fetuses may be exposed to PCBs in utero, and babies may be exposed to PCBs during breastfeeding. According to EPA, "[s]ome human studies have suggested that PCB exposure may cause adverse effects in children and developing fetuses while other studies have not shown effects. Reported effects include lower IQ scores, low birth weight, and lower behavior assessment scores."[234]

Sources of PCBs in the Environment[235]

Overview: The manufacture of PCBs was banned in the United States in 1979. However, items containing PCBs that were still in service at the time of the ban were "grandfathered" in and not required to be removed from use; some remain in use today. For example, electrical transformers containing PCBs are still in use and have a life expectancy of 30 years. The major source of PCBs in the environment is from past releases that have not been cleaned up; most PCBs are contained in sediments and are released from sediments over long periods of time to the waters, air, and soil.

There are no naturally occurring sources of PCBs; all PCBs in the environment are therefore of human origin.

Air: PCBs from past releases to soils and surface waters evaporate or volatilize to the air over long periods of time. From the air, they are redeposited back to the land and to surface waters.

Water/Sediments: Most PCBs from past releases are contained in sediments. PCBs are extremely persistent in the environment: they have half-lives in sediments ranging from months to years; they have very low solubility in water and low volatility. Because of these characteristics, PCBs continue to be released from sediments to surface waters over long periods of time. PCBs may also be mobilized to surface waters if they are disturbed (e.g. flooding, dredging). In addition to evaporation or revolatization, PCBs may be transferred from surface waters by adsorption to sediments.

---

[233]Unless otherwise noted, health effects information is taken from EPA PCBs Fact Sheet.
[234]EPA PCBs Fact Sheet at 5.
[235]Unless noted, sources information is taken from EPA PCBs Fact Sheet.

Soils: PCBs from past releases may also be contained in soils. PCBs have long half-lives in soils and are released over long periods by evaporation or volatilization to air, and are in turn redeposited to soils and surface waters.

Dioxins[236]

Background

Dioxins/furans are responsible, at least in part, for approximately 2% of all fish and shellfish advisories issued in the United States; as of December, 1998, dioxins/furans were the basis for 59 advisories issued by 19 states, territories or tribes.[237] Three states, Maine, New Jersey, and New York, have issued statewide dioxins/furans advisories for their coastal marine waters.[238] Dioxins are the source of advisories on all of the Great Lakes.[239] Dioxins are also the source of advisories for the Potomac River and numerous National Estuary Program and National Estuarine Research Reserve System sites, including Casco Bay (ME), Wells (ME), Long Island Sound, Peconic Bay (NY), the Hudson River, New York/New Jersey Harbor, Barnegat Bay (NJ), Jacques Cousteau-Great Bay and Mullica River (NJ), Delware Estuary, Albemarle-Pamlico Sounds (NC), Galveston Bay (TX), Puget Sound (WA), and the Columbia River.[240]

Dioxins are a major source of concern for the Penobscot Indian Nation.[241] Although recent changes in rules affecting pulp and paper mills in Maine that use chlorine in their bleaching process (requiring a switch from the use of elemental chlorine to chlorine dioxide) may be reducing dioxin levels in the Penobscot River and sediments, the use of chlorine dioxide still leads to discharges that result in small amounts of dioxins in the water, and historical discharges, among

---

[236]"Dioxins" is a shorthand for a group of synthetic organic chemicals, comprised of 210 structurally related chlorinated dibenzo-p-dioxins (CDDs) and chlorinated dibenzofurans (CDFs). This group of compounds ranges in toxicity, with 2,3,7,8-TCDD being the most toxic.

[237]U.S. Environmental Protection Agency, Office of Water, *Polychlorinated Dibenzo-p-dioxins and Related Compounds Update: Impact of Fish Advisories* 3 (Sept. 1999). Available at www.epa.gov/ost/fish/chemfacts.html. [hereinafter EPA Dioxins Fact Sheet]

[238]Id.; U.S. Environmental Protection Agency, *Update: National Listing of Fish and Wildlife Advisories* 3-5 (2001) available at www.epa.gov/ost.

[239]Id.

[240]Id.

[241]Dawn Gagnon, *Spiritual Keepers of the Penobscot*, Bangor Daily News (Oct. 6, 1995); Andrew Kekacs, *Penobscots Oppose Mill Permit; Any Discharge of Dioxin in River Detrimental, Tribal Member Says*, Bangor Daily News (Mar. 4, 1997); Mary Anne Lagasse, *Indians, People's Alliance Take Fish Advisories to Task; King Critics Say Dioxin Problem Downplayed*, Bangor Daily News (Apr. 2, 1997); Dieter Bradbury, *Contamination in Fish Weakens Cultural Link for Maine Tribe: Catching and Eating Fish is a Tradition No Longer Passed on to Many Penobscot Children*, Portland Press Herald (Sept. 30, 1997).

other sources, still likely contribute to the presence of dioxins in the sediments.[242] Given dioxins' persistence in the environment, its propensity to bioaccumulate (concentrations of dioxins in aquatic organisms may be hundreds to thousands of times higher than the concentrations found in surrounding waters or sediments), and its extreme toxicity even small amounts of discharge are reason for the Penobscot Nation Department of Natural Resources to be concerned.[243]

Health Effects[244]

Studies suggest a wide variety of adverse effects from dioxin, although there is still debate about the extent of these effects in humans. Among these are adverse effects on hepatic, gastrointestinal, hematological, dermal, endocrine, immunological, neurological, reproductive, and developmental systems. A recent report concluded more than a decade of study on dioxin's cancer-causing potential, identifying TCDD as a "human carcinogen" and the "mixture of dioxins to which people are exposed" as a "likely human carcinogen."[245] Even very small amounts of dioxins may be toxic to humans.

Sources of Dioxins in the Environment[246]

Overview: Dioxins in the environment are primarily the unintended by-products of industrial and other processes that use or burn chlorine. The major source of dioxins in the environment is incineration. Other sources of dioxins include direct discharges to water from industrial processes, resuspension of contaminated sediments, and releases from soils.

---

[242]As a result of recent regulations, EPA projects considerable reductions in *discharges* of dioxins to waters; however, there is little or no data characterizing the *levels* of dioxins in the waters and sediments, resulting from historic discharges and the cycling of dioxins through the environment. See, generally, U.S. Environmental Protection Agency, *Exposure and Human Health Reassessment of 2,3,7,8-Tetrachlorodibenzo-p-Dioxin (TCDD) and Related Compounds* (Draft, 2000)[hereinafter "Draft Dioxin Reassessment"]; U.S. Environmental Protection Agency, Office of Research and Development, *Information Sheet 4, Dioxin: Summary of Major EPA Control Efforts* (June 12, 2000); Telephone Interview with Dwain Winters, U.S. Environmental Protection Agency (March 29, 2002). See, also, Andrew Kekacs, *Penobscots Oppose Mill Permit; Any Discharge of Dioxin in River Detrimental, Tribal Member Says*, Bangor Daily News (Mar. 4, 1997); Mary Anne Lagasse, *Indians, People's Alliance Take Fish Advisories to Task; King Critics Say Dioxin Problem Downplayed*, Bangor Daily News (Apr. 2, 1997).

[243]See, generally, Draft Dioxin Reassessment; accord, Dawn Gagnon, *Spiritual Keepers of the Penobscot*, Bangor Daily News (Oct. 6, 1995) (quoting Director John Banks: "Dioxin is suspected of being the most toxic compound that the EPA has ever evaluated.").

[244]Unless otherwise noted, health effects information is taken from EPA Dioxins Fact Sheet.

[245]National Institute of Health, *Ninth Report on Carcinogens*. The National Institute of Health is a part of the U.S. Department of Health and Human Services. Available at ehis.niehs.nih.gov/roc/ninth/rahc/tcddsticker.pdf. Dioxin was listed as "Known to be a Human Carcinogen in the January 2001 addendum to the Ninth Report on Carcinogens." Id. See, also, Draft Dioxin Reassessment.

[246]Unless otherwise noted, sources information is taken from EPA Dioxins Fact Sheet.

Air: Most dioxins are introduced into the environment as emissions to the air. Incineration is a major source of dioxins (including incineration of municipal solid waste, medical waste, sewage sludge, and hazardous waste), although the relative contribution of incineration is projected to decline over the next several years, as regulations require reductions.[247] Dioxins are also emitted from backyard burning, metal smelting, cement kilns, land-applied sewage sludge, residential and industrial wood burning, coal-fired utilities, diesel trucks, and pulp and paper mills.[248] Dioxins released into the air may be suspended for a long time and travel great distances before being deposited to soils and surface waters.

Water/Sediments: Dioxins are discharged directly to surface waters from pulp and paper mills that use chlorine compounds in bleaching processes.[249] Dioxins are also discharged to waters from the industrial production of chlorinated organic chemicals, such as chlorinated phenols. Most dioxins are contained in sediments, where they persist for long periods because of half-lives ranging from months to years. Particles resuspended from sediments to surface waters are an important source of dioxin in surface waters.

Soils: Dioxins enter the soils when industrial wastes and municipal sludge contaminated with dioxins are applied as fertilizer to crops or grazing lands. Dioxins that have been emitted to the air are also deposited to soils. Dioxins in the soils may in turn be released into surface waters through run-off or leaching.

Chlordane[250]

Background

Chlordane is responsible for advisories on Lake Superior, Lake Michigan, and Lake Huron.[251] It is the source of advisories for several National Estuary Program and National Estuarine Research Reserve System sites, including the Potomac, Black and Anacostia Rivers (all of which connect to Chesapeake Bay).[252] The Baltimore Harbor is under advisory for chlordane, as is the New York/New Jersey Harbor, Barnegat Bay (NJ), Jacques Cousteau-Great Bay and

_____

[247]U.S. Environmental Protection Agency, *Inventory of Sources of Dioxin in the United States* (1998; updated 2000)(Draft); accord, Chlorine Chemistry Council (untitled and undated fact sheet)
[248]Id.
[249]Id.
[250]"Chlordane" is a manufactured mixture of more than 26 compounds. Chlordane is used here to refer to chlordane and to the multiple breakdown products of chlordane, which themselves are persistent and bioaccumulative.
[251]U.S. Environmental Protection Agency, *Update: National Listing of Fish and Wildlife Advisories* 3-5 (2001) available at www.epa.gov/ost.
[252]Id.

Mullica River (NJ), and Delaware Estuary.[253] Chlordane is the source of a statewide advisory for lakes and rivers in New York[254].

According to a recent study of the Greenpoint/Williamsburg community in the Borough of Brooklyn in New York City, fish are a major source of chlordane exposure for African-Americans and Hasidic Jews, and shellfish are a major source of chlordane exposure for Hispanics/Caribbean Americans.[255]

Health Effects

Chlordane is associated with cancer in some but not all studies; it is classified by EPA as a probable human carcinogen.[256] Chlordane also has adverse effects on the central nervous system, the digestive system, and the liver at higher doses. Chlordane metabolites may reside in human breast milk, and may be passed on to infants through breastfeeding.

Sources of Chlordane in the Environment

Overview: The manufacture and use of chlordane has been banned in the United States since 1988. It was once used as an agricultural pesticide (on crops including corn and citrus), and on home lawns and gardens. One of chlordane's most common uses was for treatment of termites. Once chlordane is released into the environment, it may evaporate or it may bind itself to soil particles (particularly in the upper layers of soil) or to sediments in water. The breakdown of chlordane once it is bound to soil particles or sediment is very slow. According to the National Resources Defense Council, "[s]o persistent is the residue, that a recent study showed that detectable levels of chlordane are still present in some food grown in the United States, even though it has been decades since chlordane was used in agriculture."[257]

Air: Chlordane from past applications to agricultural soils, soils near houses treated for termite control, or soils near waste sites and landfills may be present in the air in small amounts.

Water/Sediments: Chlordane from past releases is contained in surface waters and especially in sediments. It is highly persistent, and may be present in sediments for years.

---

[253]Id.

[254]Id.

[255]Industrial Economics, Inc., *Community-Specific Cumulative Exposure Assessment for Greenpoint/Williamsburg New York* 2-19 (1999).

[256]Washington State Department of Ecology, *Proposed Strategy to Continually Reduce Persistent, Bioaccumulative Toxins (PBTs) in Washington State* 44 (No. 00-03-054) (Dec. 2000) available at http://www.ecy.wa.gov/pubs/0003054.pdf.

[257]Natural Resources Defense Council, *Healthy Milk, Healthy Baby: Chemical Pollution in Mother's Milk; Chemicals: Chlordane* available at www.nrdc.org/breastmilk/chem1.asp.

Soils: Chlordane from past releases is also contained in soils, where it is highly persistent. Chlordane has been found in some cases to be present in soil up to 20 years after application.[258]

DDT[259]

Background

DDT is the source of a statewide advisory for lakes and rivers in New York, as well as advisories in California, Texas, and Maine.[260] The total number of advisories for DDT increased from 40 in 1999 to 44 in 2000.[261]

DDT is a contaminant of concern for the Fourteen Confederated Tribes of the Yakama Nation, given that the Yakama River, which forms a reservation boundary and is a tributary to the Columbia River, is contaminated with DDT and currently under a state-issued advisory.[262]

Health Effects

DDT, together with DDD and DDE, is classified by EPA as a probable human carcinogen. DDT may cause damage to the central nervous system at high doses, leading to tremors and seizures.[263]

Sources of DDT in the Environment

Overview: DDT was one of the most widely used pesticides in the United States from 1946 to 1972. Its use has been banned in the United States, except for "public health emergencies."[264]

Other Persistent Organic Pollutants (POPs)/Persistent Bioaccumulative Toxins (PBTs)

Several other contaminants are sources of concern because they are bioaccumulative and persistent. That is, these contaminants accumulate in aquatic organisms at concentrations many times higher than the concentrations present in surrounding waters. They also persist for long

---

[258]Id.

[259]"DDT' here refers not only to DDT, but also to its breakdown products, DDD and DDE.

[260]U.S. Environmental Protection Agency, *Update: National Listing of Fish and Wildlife Advisories* 3-5 (2001) available at www.epa.gov/ost.

[261]Id.

[262]Barbara Harper and Stuart Harris, *Proceedings of the American Fisheries Society: Forum on Contaminants in Fish*, "Tribal Technical Issues in Risk Reduction Through Fish Advisories" 17 (1999).

[263]Washington State Department of Ecology, *Proposed Strategy to Continually Reduce Persistent, Bioaccumulative Toxins (PBTs) in Washington State* 44-45 (No. 00-03-054) (December 2000) available at http://www.ecy.wa.gov/pubs/0003054.pdf.

[264]Id.

periods of time in the environment, particularly in the sediments where bottom-dwelling aquatic species can accumulate them and pass them up the food chain to fish, other predatory species, and, ultimately, humans. The contaminants are also highly toxic. In addition to the five contaminants canvassed above, the Convention on Persistent Organic Pollutants and the EPA's Persistent Bioaccumulative Toxin Initiative each include among the POPs or PBTs of concern the following seven pesticides: Aldrin, Dieldrin, Endrin, Heptachlor, Hexachlorobenzene, Mirex, and Toxaphene;[265] and the industrial chemical Hexachlorobenzene. Note that this list is likely not exhaustive; these contaminants are merely those that have been identified as being of the very highest priority. Some groups have argued, for example, the lead belongs on this list, given that it is persistent, it builds up in bone tissue, it is toxic even in minute concentrations, and its effects on exposed children are particularly troubling.[266] In some cases, governments and agencies are in the process of studying whether additions are appropriate. The Washington State Department of Ecology, for example, has identified more than 60 additional candidates for screening and prioritization, based on initial evaluations demonstrating their persistence, propensity to bioaccumulate and toxicity.[267]

Exposure to these POPs or PBTs has been linked to a wide range of toxic effects in fish, wildlife, and humans, including cancer, adverse developmental effects and adverse effects on the nervous, reproductive, immune and endocrine systems.[268] POPs or PBTs are contaminants of concern for many affected communities, groups and tribes.[269] The Indigenous Environmental Network, for example, explains some of their concerns:

> *Indigenous Peoples have special cultural and spiritual relationships to traditional foods that create increased consumption patterns compared to non-Indigenous populations.*

---

[265]See U.S. Environmental Protection Agency, Office of Water, *Toxaphene Update: Impact on Fish Advisories* (September 1999) available at www.epa.gov/ost/fish/chemfacts.html.

[266]Washington Toxics Coalition, *Comments on Ecology's Draft Strategy Addressing Persistent Pollutants* available at www.watoxics.org/uaPBTcomments.htm.

[267]Washington State Department of Ecology, *Proposed Strategy to Continually Reduce Persistent, Bioaccumulative Toxins (PBTs) in Washington State* 60-61 (No. 00-03-054) (December 2000) available at http://www.ecy.wa.gov/pubs/0003054.pdf.

[268]Id. at 5.

[269]Numerous tribes and indigenous peoples' organizations passed resolutions to this effect during the negotiating process for the International Treaty on Persistent Organic Pollutants, urging the "elimination, phase-out, or reduction wit the aim to eliminate toxic substances that are persistent and bioaccumulate in the environment and in the bodies of American Indian/Alaska Native populations." See, e.g., The National Congress of American Indians, *Resolution # PSC-99-054*; Great Lakes Indian Fish & Wildlife Commission, *Resolution No. 8-16-89-01*; Alaska Inter-tribal Council, *Resolution 99-27*; Qawalangin Tribe of Unalaska, *Resolution # 00-05*; Tanana Chiefs Conference, Inc., *Resolution No. 2000-38*; Traditional Council of Togiak, *Resolution 00-30*; Native Village of Wales, *Resolution 00-09*; Algaaciq Tribal Government, *Resolution 00-19*; Native Village of Fort Yukon, *Resolution No. 00-21*; Native Village of Elim, *Resolution 00-11*; Chickaloon Village Traditional Council, *Resolution # 000801-01*; Bill Moore's Slough Elder's Council, *Resolution # 2000-09*; Chenega I.R.A. Council, *Resolution # 00-26*; Native Village of Savoonga, *Resolution # 00-10*.

Unfortunately, the main way POPs enter our bodies is through food. POPs have been found in eagles, cormorants, ducks, geese, caribou, reindeer, raccoons, rabbits, quail, deer, moose, bison, turtles, crocodiles, sheep, cows, polar bears, seals, whales, and fish. . . . Advisories prohibiting or discouraging the consumption of traditional foods affect Indigenous Peoples' right to practice our cultural and spiritual ways.[270]

Similarly, Faith Gemmill, Arctic Village, Alaska, explains:

I speak before you today as a young Gwichin woman with an infant daughter and with a deep commitment to ensuring her future and the continuation of the Indigenous way of life. . . . One cannot separate the health of the environment from the health of our peoples. . . . As Indigenous peoples we are greatly concerned when we realize evidence which suggests that women, infants, and children are very vulnerable to POPs. This threatens the very existence of our peoples and cultures. The multigenerational impacts threaten our hope of healthy, thriving, and productive future generations.[271]

A. PREVENTION AND REDUCTION

How might EPA better prevent contamination in the first place in order to protect the aquatic ecosystems and the health of people consuming or using fish, aquatic plants, and wildlife for subsistence, traditional, cultural, or religious purposes?

Efforts to prevent or reduce contamination in the first place are vital to protecting the health of communities of color, low-income communities, tribes, and other indigenous peoples. These efforts are especially important given that members of these groups are among the most highly-exposed to environmental contaminants (as discussed in Chapter One) and given that for many of these groups, risk avoidance   eating less fish, using a different preparation method, fishing in a different location   is simply not a realistic or culturally appropriate option (as will be discussed in Chapter Three). Thus, these groups will disproportionately bear the burden of sources of ongoing contamination that are not adequately addressed. Prevention and reduction efforts will need to be directed at those contaminants of concern that are still being used or produced, including mercury, dioxins, and others.

---

[270]Indigenous Environmental Network, *Drum Beat for Mother Earth: Persistent Organic Pollutants (POPs)* available at www.ienearth/org/pops threat-p2.html.

[271]Faith Gemmill, Gwichin, Arctic Village, Alaska, Oral and Written Testimony at the Third Session of the United Nations Environment program Intergovernmental Negotiating Committee for and International Legally Binding Instrument for Implementing International Action on Certain Persistent Organic Pollutants (POPs) (Sept. 8, 1999).

1. Clean Water Act

Enacted in 1972, the Clean Water Act[272] (CWA) and its complex implementing regulations and guidelines focus on protecting public natural resources and welfare and improving water quality through the control of discharges of pollutants into national waters. The statutory objective of the CWA is "to restore and maintain the chemical, physical, and biological integrity of the Nation's waters."[273] As stated in the CWA, national goals provide that: (1) the discharge of pollution into navigable waters be eliminated by 1985; (2) an interim goal of water quality that provides for the protection and propagation of fish, shellfish, and wildlife and for recreation be achieved by July 1, 1983; (3) the discharge of toxic pollutants in toxic amounts be prohibited; (4) federal financial assistance be provided to construct publicly owned waste treatment works; (5) areawide waste treatment management planning processes be developed to assure adequate control of pollution sources in each state; (6) major research and demonstration efforts be undertaken to eliminate the discharge of pollutants into national waters; and (7) programs to control point and nonpoint discharges be developed expeditiously to meet the goals of the CWA.[274] Water quality standards are key to implementing the framework of the CWA and are necessary for regulatory and enforcement actions to protect water quality where existing controls like technology-based limitations may be insufficient to maintain or restore water quality.

Generally, the CWA requires that the U.S. Environmental Protection Agency (EPA) set standards for various sources of pollution, to enforce those standards through permitting systems, and, where a state so requests to delegate primary enforcement authority to that state. As originally enacted, the CWA, as well as many other federal environmental laws, did not mention tribes or Indian reservations or provide for direct participation by tribal governments. Because the jurisdictional rules applicable to Indian country left EPA unable to pursue its usual practice of delegating primary enforcement responsibility to states, EPA was forced to develop special rules and practices concerning environmental regulation on Indian reservations and the role to be played by tribal governments. In November 1984, EPA issued the EPA Policy for the Administration of Environmental Programs on Indian Reservations (Indian Policy) to address tribal participation and the unique circumstances presented by Indian country.[275] Each EPA Administrator, including most recently Administrator Christine Todd Whitman, has reaffirmed the principles enumerated in the Indian Policy.[276] In 1987, Congress amended the CWA to allow federally-recognized tribes to be treated as states for certain purposes under the Act. As of

---

[272]33 U.S.C. §§ 1251-1387.

[273]33 U.S.C. § 1251(a).

[274]33 U.S.C. § 1251(a).

[275]U.S. Environmental Protection Agency, *Policy for the Administration of Environmental Programs on Indian Reservations* (Nov. 8, 1984).

[276]On July 11, 2001, Administrator Whitman issued a Memorandum on EPA Indian Policy to all EPA Employees recognizing the right of tribes as sovereign governments to self-determination and acknowledging the federal government's trust responsibility owed to tribes. The Administrator also reaffirmed EPA's commitment to the long-established Indian Policy and "in building a stronger partnership with tribal governments to protect the human health and environment of Indian communities."

December 2000, only eighteen tribes (of the approximately 565 total federally recognized tribes) have received treatment as a state status and adopted standards for purposes of the water quality standards effective under the CWA, and EPA has promulgated standards for one additional tribe.[277] As a result, a large gap exists in water quality standards coverage in Indian country. For example, tribal lands lacking approved water quality standards constitute an area approximating the size of all of New England plus New Jersey and as many reservation residents as the populations of Wyoming, Alaska, and Vermont combined.[278] Where tribes have not yet received treatment as a state status and assumed responsibility for CWA on their reservations and lands, EPA is responsible for implementing and enforcing the CWA within Indian country pursuant to the CWA and the federal trust responsibility owed to tribes.[279] Toward that end, EPA recently has been considering a proposal to develop core federal water quality standards for certain waters in Indian country that do not have water quality standards under the CWA.[280] The Core Standards currently call for a four-part hierarchy for selecting a fish consumption rate for use in setting water quality standards in Indian country. This hierarchy sets up a preference for using "the results of any existing fish consumption surveys of local Indian country watersheds to establish fish intake provisions that are representative of the populations being addressed."[281] While this preference for local data is appropriate, the reality, as discussed in Chapter 1, is that many tribes have not gathered this data   often for lack of resources. In the absence of such data, the proposed Core Standards would look to EPA's default fish consumption rates, and perhaps to a rate as low as 17.5 grams/day.[282] As noted in Chapter 1, this number grossly underestimates consumption for many tribes.

As discussed in Chapter One, EPA has recently updated its default values for fish consumption rates, as part of its revisions to the Ambient Water Quality Criteria Methodology for the Protection of Human Health, pursuant to CWA 304(a). The EPA has indicated that the revised values will likely guide water quality standard-setting and policy for years to come (the former values were in place for roughly 20 years). This may be problematic from the perspective of affected groups whose members consume fish at the highest levels, and whose practices are therefore not adequately accounted for or protected by even the revised AWQC Methodology. Moreover, as noted in Chapter One, to the extent that the revised AWQC Methodology

---

[277]*EPA Fact Sheet: Water Quality Standards for Indian Country* (April 2001) (available online at http://www.epa.gov/ost/standards/tribal/tribalfact.html). Note, we need the Office of Water or the AIEO to verify this figure officially at the time of the report.

[278]Id.

[279]The courts have long recognized that the United States has a trust relationship with Indian tribes. See, e.g. Worcester v. Georgia, 31 U.S. 515 (1832); Cherokee Nation v. Georgia, 30 U.S. 1 (1831).

[280]On January 19, 2001, EPA's Administrator signed the proposed Federal Water Quality Standards for Indian Country and Other Provisions Regarding Federal Water Quality Standards, which were withdrawn from the Federal Register on January 20, 2001 to allow regulatory review by the Administrator. 66 Fed. Reg. 7701 (Jan. 24, 2001).

[281]U.S. Environmental Protection Agency, Office of Water, *Federal Water quality Standards for Indian Country and Other Provisions Regarding Federal Water Quality Standards* (unofficial prepublication copy, Jan.19, 2001) available at www.epa.gov/ost/standards/tribal/ .

[282]Id. at 17.

recommends that states and tribes prefer local data, EPA will need to provide funding to enable this preference to exist as a meaningful option. And, to the extent that EPA's revised AWQC Methodology proposes that "acceptable" risk for the general population be defined as an incremental cancer risk of 1 in 100,000 to 1 in 1,000,000, but deems a greater level of risk "acceptable" for "more highly exposed subgroups," including subsistence fishers, i.e., up to 1 in 10,000, this is a troubling potential source of environmental injustice.[283] EPA should decline to exercise this option to provide lower levels of protection to communities of color, low-income communities, tribes, and other indigenous peoples as it sets and approves water quality standards. Additionally, as a general matter, EPA needs to take into account the differences in fish consumption rates, practices, and context, as outlined in Chapter One, as it undertakes triennial reviews of state and tribal water quality standards under CWA 303(c)(1).

Additionally, the CWA provides some authority for addressing non-point sources of water pollution (including through TMDLs). Given that non-point sources are major contributors of numerous contaminants of concern, this authority should be interpreted broadly to enable EPA to prevent and reduce contamination from these sources. Non-point sources, moreover, are of particular concern to some affected groups. In Hawai'i, for example, there is a need for further studies on the effect of non-point sources on fish and other aquatic resources on which Native Hawaiians and other communities of color in Hawai'i depend, and for more extensive efforts to prevent and reduce pollution from these sources. As explained by Hawaii's Thousand Friends:

> When it rains, Hawaii's short watersheds create immediate impacts to coastal areas from non-point source pollution. Studies so far have concentrated on impacts to estuaries, receiving ocean waters and coral, but not on impacts to fish and cru stations.

Commentators have noted, moreover, the inefficiencies and unfairness, from the perspective of point sources, of failing to recognize and address as well the considerable relative contributions of non-point sources.

Neither the CWA nor its regulations alone will accomplish the objective and goals of the CWA. EPA, and authorized state and tribal governments, simply must ensure strict and widespread compliance with the CWA. Without such enforcement, polluters have absolutely no incentive to comply with the CWA as "noncompliance results in economic benefits (the free use of public waterways for waste disposal), while compliance exacts a financial cost (the construction and operation of expensive pollution removal facilities)."[284]

Water quantity is also of serious concern given, among other things, its recognized connections to and implications for water quality and integrity. For example, congressional goals and policies under the Clean Water Act direct federal agencies to "co-operate with State and local agencies to develop comprehensive solutions to prevent, reduce and eliminate pollution in concert

---

[283]Draft AWQC Methodology at 43,762.
[284]John Cronin and Robert F. Kennedy, Jr., *The Riverkeepers* 178 (1997).

with programs for managing water resources."[285] And the U.S. Supreme Court has recognized the connection between water quantity and quality, upholding a state's imposition of minimum instream flows as part of a Section 401 determination.[286] Wetlands, which provide essential wildlife habitats, are also recognized as an integral and natural way of removing pollutants from water bodies, and the Clean Water Act's Section 404 permitting program as well as EPA's "no net loss" strategy for wetlands preserves both the quality and quantity of these waters. Additionally, reduction in water quality affects surface flows and may increase the concentration of pollutants and other chemicals.[287]

2. Other Authorities

The Clean Air Act (CAA) is an important source of authority for addressing contamination of aquatic environments that results in part from the deposition of toxic contaminants emitted into the air. For example, it is estimated that air emissions account for some 80% of mercury contamination in water. Most dioxins released into the environment also come from emissions to air; as noted above, dioxins emitted into the air may be suspended for a long time and travel great distances before being deposited to surface waters. Among other things, the CAA Section 112 addresses certain "hazardous air pollutants;" the 1990 amendments to the CAA direct EPA to develop rules for categories of sources that emit these hazardous air pollutants, and to do so over the next ten years. EPA has promulgated many of these rules, although there are some source categories for which EPA is still in the process of rule development. Because mercury compounds and dioxin are among the hazardous air pollutants regulated under CAA Section 112, this provides an important basis for preventing and reducing these contaminants. Moreover, EPA has several upcoming opportunities under Section 112 (e.g., upcoming rule for coal-fired power plants, the single largest source of mercury emissions nationwide; upcoming rule for chlor-alkali plants, a significant source of mercury, particularly in some locales, such as Louisiana;[288] upcoming rule for industrial boilers, another important source of mercury) to address these concerns as it develops these rules. In addition, whether under CAA authority and/or other authorities, the EPA needs to attend to sources of toxic air pollutants that are currently un- or under-regulated (e.g., dioxin emissions from backyard burning). The relative contribution to dioxin emissions from these sources has increased as industrial and other sources of dioxins have been required to control their emissions; as such, addressing these un- and under-regulated sources will be a challenge for the near future.[289] Again, commentators have noted that where this

---

[285]33 U.S.C. § 1251(g).

[286]PUD No. 1 v. Washington Dep't of Ecology, 511 U.S. 700 (1994).

[287]See, e.g., United States v. Gila Valley Irrigation Dist., 920 F. Supp. 1444 (D. Ariz. 1996) (finding that upstream water uses reduced surface flows and increased saline levels in water reaching an Indian reservation to the extent that traditional agricultural activities were impaired and recognizing that the tribe was entitled to surface water of adequate quantity as well as quality).

[288]Telephone Interview with Dr. Barry Kohl, Department of Geology, Tulane University (Oct. 17, 2001).

[289]U.S. Environmental Protection Agency, *Inventory of Sources of Dioxin in the United States* (1998; updated 2000)(Draft); accord, Chlorine Chemistry Council (untitled and undated fact sheet).

is the case, issues of inefficiency and unfairness, from the perspective of regulated sources, mean that agencies should also look to un- and under-regulated sources for reductions. And while some community groups have recently taken it upon themselves to get community members to reduce backyard burning,[290] EPA should not rely on ad hoc, voluntary efforts but should work to coordinate, facilitate, and, where appropriate, require reduction from these and other un- and under-regulated sources.

The CAA also provides authority to address other air-related sources of contaminated waters. For example, the CAA regulates oxides of nitrogen (NOx) through a variety of provisions. NOx causes acidification and euthrophication (a process in which an overabundance of nutrients causes some algae to multiply exponentially causing oxygen depletion that limits the ability of some species to thrive and survive), a potential problem for shellfisheries and other aquatic resources. Among these, the New Source Review program, which decides controls for NOx on new or modified facilities on a case-by-case basis, is under review pursuant to the National Energy Policy. In addition, implementation of the new Ozone National Ambient Air Quality Standard (NAAQS) may affect NOx emissions as NOx is an important ozone precursor.

Other statutory and regulatory authorities similarly provide authority useful for preventing and reducing contamination of fish and aquatic environments. Several statutes and regulations pertaining to hazardous waste may provide authority to address more thoroughly the use of "recycled" wastes from various industrial processes as fertilizer   which is then applied to crops, grazing lands, and gardens, and may contribute to run-off of dioxins, lead, mercury, cadmium, and other contaminants of concern to surface waters and contamination of groundwater, including drinking water. Although current regulations address this practice, they contain a loophole exempting steel mill waste and may still permit unacceptable levels of these contaminants in fertilizer.

The Federal Insecticide, Fungicide, and Rodenticide Control Act (FIFRA) may provide authority to address the fact that "[w]ell over a billion pounds of pesticides are applied annually in the United States, at least 50 million pounds in the Great Lakes Watershed alone."[291] Also authority under FIFRA is limited, there may well be opportunities for EPA to use the available tools more aggressively, e.g., prominent advisories on pesticide labels, prohibitions on use within a specified distances from wells (well set-backs), prohibitions on use in designated geographic areas, and restricting pesticides' use to certified applicators.[292]

---

[290]Shawna Larson, Project Coordinator, Indigenous Environmental Network and Alaska Community Action on Toxics, Panelist, "Food, Toxic Chemicals & Health: An Environmental Justice Forum," Anchorage, AK (Feb. 6, 2002).

[291]U.S. General Accounting Office, *Issues Concerning Pesticides Used in the Great Lakes Watershed* (1993).

[292]Zygmunt J. B. Plater, et al., *Environmental Law and Policy: Nature, Law, and Society* 728 (2d ed. 1998).

The Pollution Prevention Act (PPA), enacted in 1990, might similarly be mined for tools that EPA might employ more aggressively to prevent pollution from entering aquatic environments in the first place.

Finally, a variety of sources of authority and EPA offices have been gathered in EPA's recent Contaminated Sediment Management Strategy. Given that in terms of volume, some 10% of the sediments underlying the nation's waters are contaminated, that 96 of the watersheds tested indicate contamination at levels of serious concern, and that the contaminants that most frequently contributed to this concern were mercury, PCBs, pesticides (especially DDT), and PAHs, addressing sediment contamination should indeed be a priority.[293]

B. CLEANUP AND RESTORATION

How might EPA enhance restoration efforts in order to rehabilitate aquatic ecosystems and thereby protect the health of people consuming or using fish, aquatic plants, and wildlife for subsistence, traditional, cultural, or religious purposes?

Many aquatic environments remain degraded such that they require restoration in order to ensure the viability of the ecosystem; the health of people consuming or using fish, aquatic plants, and wildlife for subsistence, traditional, cultural, or religious purposes; the ability to support economies dependent on aquatic resources; and the sustainability of tribal homelands. Efforts to cleanup and restore contaminated aquatic environments are vital to protecting the health of communities of color, low-income communities, tribes, and other indigenous peoples. These efforts are especially important given that members of these groups are among the most highly-exposed to environmental contaminants (as discussed in Chapter One) and given that for many of these groups, risk avoidance   eating less fish, using a different preparation method, fishing in a different location   is simply not a realistic or culturally appropriate option (as will be discussed in Chapter Three). Thus, these groups will disproportionately bear the burden of existing contamination that is not adequately addressed. Moreover, because production (and, in many cases, use) in the United States has been banned for several of the contaminants of greatest concern   for example, PCBs, DDT, chlordane, and toxaphene   the presence of these contaminants in the environment can only be reduced through cleanup and restoration efforts.

"Restoration" has been taken by different people to mean different things.[294] Restoration has sometimes been defined somewhat narrowly, to the exclusion of the historical, cultural, legal, and social contexts within which restoration takes place. Thus, for example, the National Research Council has defined restoration of aquatic ecosystems as "the reestablishment of

---

[293]U.S. Environmental Protection Agency, Office of Science and Technology, *The Incidence and Severity of Sediment Contamination in Surface Waters of the United States, Volume 1: National Contaminant Survey* (1997).

[294]For several examples relevant to the restoration of aquatic environments, see U.S. Environmental Protection Agency, Office of Water, *River Corridor and Wetland Restoration*, "What is Restoration?" at www.epa.gov/owow/wetlands/restore/defs.html.

predisturbance aquatic functions and related physical, chemical and biological characteristics."[295] Others define restoration more broadly and suggest that the ends and means of restoration can only be contemplated *in context*, i.e. in light of the particular historical, cultural, legal, and social circumstances of a place. The Society for Ecological Restoration, for example, observes that restoration should attend to "regional and historical context," and must take into account the need to sustain cultural activities, especially the cultural practices of indigenous peoples.[296] Similarly, among the Principles of Environmental Justice articulated by the First National People of Color Environmental Leadership Summit, is that "[e]nvironmental justice affirms the need for urban and rural ecological policies to clean up and rebuild our cities and rural areas in balance with nature, honoring the cultural integrity of our communities and providing fair access for all to a full range of resources."[297]

In the case of restoration affecting tribal homelands (including tribal resources and culturally-important resources whether located on- or off-reservation), tribes and commentators have noted that the ends or "point of reference" for restorative efforts cannot be considered separately from the obligations that the United States has undertaken in treaties and as part of its trust responsibility.[298] Restoration here must attend to the purposes for which tribal lands and resources have been reserved under treaties and protected in furtherance of the federal trust responsibility.[299] As noted above, arguably the primary purpose of all reservations is the creation of a permanent tribal homeland where the tribe can maintain its traditional subsistence activities including the exercise of treaty rights to hunt, fish, and gather. Water of sufficient quality and quantity for this purpose is essential.[300] Thus, for example, in introducing their plan for restoring salmon and other anadromous fish in the Columbia River Basin, *Wy-Kan-Ush-Mi Wa-Kish-Wit*,

---

[295]National Research Council, *Restoration of Aquatic Ecosystems* 18 (1992).

[296]See, generally, The Society for Ecological Restoration at www.ser.org.

[297]*Proceedings of the First National People of Color Environmental Leadership Summit*, "Principles of Environmental Justice" xiii (1991).

[298]Moses Squeochs, Director, Environmental Program, Fourteen Confederated Tribes and Bands of the Yakama Nation (Aug. 3, 2001 conference call).

[299]Jana Walker, Attorney, Law Offices of Jana L. Walker (Aug. 3, 2001 conference call); Mary Christina Wood, *Indian Land and the Promise of Native Sovereignty: The Trust Doctrine Revisited*, 1994 Utah Law Review 1471; Mary Christina Wood, *Fulfilling the Executive's Trust Responsibility Toward Native Nations on Environmental Issues: A Partial Critique of the Clinton administration's Promises and Performances*, 25 Environmental Law 733 (1995); Mary Christina Wood, *Protecting the Attributes of Native Sovereignty: A New Trust Paradigm for Federal Actions Affecting Tribal Lands and Resources*, 1995 Utah Law Review 109.

[300]See, e.g. Winters v. United States, 143 F. 740, 742 (1906); Colville Confederated Tribes v. Walton, 647 F.2d 42, 49 (9th Cir.1981), *cert. denied*, 454 U.S. 1092 (1981); Felix S. Cohen, *Handbook of Federal Indian Law*, 588-89 (1982 ed.); see also Mary Christina Wood *Indian Land and the Promise of Native Sovereignty: The Trust Doctrine Revisited*, 1994 Utah Law Review 1471; Mary Christina Wood, *Fulfilling the Executive's Trust Responsibility Toward Native Nations on Environmental Issues: A Partial Critique of the Clinton administration's Promises and Performances*, 25 Environmental Law 733 (1995); Mary Christina Wood, *Protecting the Attributes of Native Sovereignty: A New Trust Paradigm for Federal Actions Affecting Tribal Lands and Resources*, 1995 Utah Law Review 109.

the Columbia River treaty tribes explain that "[u]nlike other plans, this plan establishes a foundation for the United States and its citizens to honor their treaty and trust obligations to the four tribes. If implemented, it would at least begin to meet ceremonial, subsistence, and commercial needs of tribal members and to return fish to many of the tribes' usual and accustomed fishing places, as guaranteed in the 1855 treaties."[301]   Restoration affecting tribal lands and resources, moreover, must attend to the related matters of cultural flourishing and tribal sovereignty.[302] As John LaVelle observes in the context of restoration plans for *Paha Sapa* or the Black Hills, those pursuing plans "must embrace the restoration of tribal sovereignty and cultural integrity as an indispensable remedial norm to be realized through the proposal's development and implementation."[303]

EPA's Watershed Ecology Team has set forth Principles for the Ecological Restoration of Aquatic Resources.[304] These "Guiding Principles" include (1) preserve and protect aquatic resources; (2) restore ecological integrity; (3) restore natural structure; (4) restore natural function; (5) work within the watershed and broader landscape context; (6) understand the natural potential of the watershed; (7) address ongoing causes of degradation; (8) develop clear, achievable, and measurable goals; (9) focus on feasibility; (10) use a reference site; (11) anticipate future changes; (12) involve the skills and insights of a multi-disciplinary team; (13) design for self-sustainability; (14) use passive restoration, when appropriate; (15) restore native species and avoid non-native species; (16) use natural fixes and bioengineering techniques, where possible; and (17) monitor and adopt where changes are necessary.

1. Clean Water Act

As noted above, the statutory objective of the CWA is "to *restore* and maintain the chemical, physical, and biological integrity of the Nation's waters."[305] In addition to the efforts discussed above in conjunction with prevention and reduction, EPA should read its authority under the CWA consonant with this stated objective and look creatively and aggressively for restoration opportunities.

---

[301]Columbia River Inter-Tribal Fish Commission, 1 Wy-Kan-Ush-Mi Wa-Kish-Wit: Spirit of the Salmon, iv (1995).

[302]See, e.g., id. at v ("protect tribal sovereignty" among goals of restoration); *Chairman's Corner: The Exercise of Tribal Sovereignty Lies at the Heart of Healthy Ecosystems.* Fort Apache Scout 2 (May 24, 1996); see, generally, Winona LaDuke, *All Our Relations: Native Struggles for Land and Life* (1999).

[303]John P. LaVelle, *Rescuing Paha Sapa: Achieving Environmental Justice by Restoring the Great Grasslands and Returning the Sacred Black Hills to the Great Sioux Nation*, 5 Great Plains Natural Resources Journal 40, 78 (Spr./Sum. 2001) (italics omitted).

[304]U.S. Environmental Protection Agency, *Principles for the Ecological Restoration of Aquatic Resources* (2000) available at www.epa.gov/owow/wetlands/restore/principles.html.

[305]33 U.S.C. § 1251(a).

2. Other Authorities

Clearly, the focus of CERCLA or "Superfund" is on cleanup and restoration of contaminated environments, including aquatic environments. Under CERCLA and its implementing regulations, once contaminated sites have been identified as potential priorities for cleanup action, EPA investigates the nature and extent of the threat posed by the contamination (the "remedial investigation" or "RI") and develops alternative approaches for responding to the contamination at that site (the "feasibility study" or "FS"). EPA uses a screening process to evaluate the alternatives identified during the RI/FS, which includes, among other criteria, whether the alternatives comply with all "applicable, relevant, and appropriate requirements," whether they achieve overall protection of human health and the environment, whether they reduce the toxicity, mobility or volume of the contamination through treatment, whether they are effective in the short-term as well as the long-term, whether they are implementable and how much they cost, and whether they are acceptable to the state and to the community. Note that these criteria provide EPA with considerable latitude to choose a more or a less protective alternative as the "remedy" for the contamination. EPA's work in this regard could be improved in several ways relevant to communities of color, low-income communities, tribes, and other indigenous peoples. First, EPA needs to set cleanup levels and determine appropriate remedies in light of the considerations discussed in Chapter 1. Specifically, when EPA sets cleanup levels for contaminated sediments and surfaces waters, it needs to take into account the different fish consumption rates, practices and contexts of affected groups and set levels sufficiently protective of these groups. EPA site managers need to consider matters of aggregate or multiple exposures and cumulative risks, and delineate sites, goal, and remedies accordingly. EPA needs to refrain from falling back on "institutional controls" (e.g., put a fence around the site and post "No Fishing" signs) and undertake aggressive cleanups where the sites are past or present locations for fishing and other activities that expose communities of color, low-income communities, tribes, and other indigenous peoples to contamination. Second, EPA needs to take seriously the requirement of "community acceptance" as it chooses among alternatives. In order to do so, it needs to ensure that participation by affected communities (and co-management by affected tribes) takes place from the outset and at every point in the decision-making process. To accomplish this, EPA should be ready to provide financial and technical support. These issues of affected group involvement are also taken up in Chapter One and Chapter Three. Finally, to the extent that the Natural Resource Damage provisions of CERCLA (or other statutes) are invoked, involved agencies should work with the community to ensure that efforts are undertaken with an eye toward making the community whole. Community involvement here, of course, will be critical; tribes may well be involved in their roles as Natural Resource Damage trustees. The discussion above regarding restoration is also relevant here.

Other statutory and regulatory authorities similarly provide authority useful for cleaning up and restoring contaminated aquatic environments. Among these, as discussed above in the context of prevention and reduction, a variety of sources of authority and EPA offices have been gathered in EPA's recent Contaminated Sediment Management Strategy.

CHAPTER III: FISH CONSUMPTION ADVISORIES

What role should fish consumption advisories play in efforts to protect more effectively the health and safety of people consuming or using fish, aquatic plants, and wildlife?

Whereas Chapter Two focused on issues surrounding *risk reduction* strategies, this chapter focuses on issues surrounding a *risk avoidance* strategy: fish and wildlife consumption advisories. Rather than looking, as risk reduction strategies do, to the risk-producers to cleanup, limit, and prevent environmental contamination, risk avoidance strategies look to *risk-bearers* — those who bear the risks of contamination — to change their lives and practices in order to avoid exposure to harmful contaminants. They do this by encouraging or requiring individuals to change the way they live, specifically, to alter or refrain from certain pursuits or practices that, once a place has been allowed to become contaminated, expose them to risk.

It is important to note that with risk avoidance strategies such as fish consumption advisories, the *responsibility* for addressing environmental contamination and its harmful human health effects is allocated to those who are made to bear the risks of contamination rather than to the sources of that contamination. Furthermore, because risk avoidance strategies place this responsibility on those who are exposed to environmental contaminants, they will necessarily impose a greater burden on communities of color, low-income communities, tribes, and other indigenous peoples. As has been amply demonstrated, it is members of these groups who are among the most exposed.

In light of these and other considerations, and in view of the reality of the harmful health effects of consuming fish from seriously contaminated environments, Part A of this chapter will take up the question: what role should fish consumption advisories play in efforts to protect more effectively the health and safety of people consuming or using fish, aquatic plants, and wildlife? *It is important to note that the answer to this question is likely to be different for different communities, groups, or tribes, and should be determined by or together with the affected group.*

Parts B, C and D will examine the related matter of fish consumption advisories' "effectiveness." The concept of "effectiveness" itself raises a host of issues, the first of which is definitional: what is meant by an "effective" advisory? Again, the answer to this question may be different for different agencies and for different communities, groups, or tribes. This question will be discussed in Part B. Part C will canvas the current state of research regarding how those to whom advisories are directed respond to this information, focusing on what is known about awareness and responses among communities of color, low-income communities, tribes, and other indigenous peoples. Part D will then explore ways in which to improve the effectiveness of risk communication and fish consumption advisories. Throughout, this chapter will seek to address the question: how can EPA better meet the needs of all people, including communities of color, low-income communities, tribes, and other indigenous peoples, as it works to address degradation of aquatic ecosystems and to protect the health and safety of people consuming or using fish, aquatic plants, and wildlife?

A. FISH CONSUMPTION ADVISORIES' ROLE

Risk avoidance strategies such as fish consumption advisories shift the responsibility for addressing environmental contamination's harmful health effects to risk-bearers, as opposed to allocating this responsibility to risk-producers. In the case of fish consumption advisories, this choice disproportionately burdens communities of color, low-income communities, tribes, and other indigenous peoples, given that these groups consume fish at higher rates and according to different practices than the general population, as discussed in Chapter One. When agencies employ fish consumption advisories, moreover, they assume that there are adequate substitutes in the lives of those to whom the advisories are directed for fishing and fish consumption. Although consumption advisories issued by federal or state agencies typically do not state as much explicitly, they rely implicitly on the assumption that there are ready substitutes for being able to fish at the same place, in the same manner, and for the same fish as one had traditionally or would today were the fish not contaminated. This assumption requires a judgment on the part of the agencies that such a substitution (1) is possible, and (2) will not occasion great loss.[306] This is a value judgment that is likely to reflect the understandings of the dominant society that fishing and fish consumption are expendable "habits," "activities," or "behaviors," for which, at the very least, substitutes can be readily obtained; and, that various groups' particular fishing and fish consumption practices can be altered without great anguish (or that this anguish and loss does not matter).[307]

However, this value judgment does not reflect the understandings of many of those who are affected those who are being asked to change their lives and practices. First, it is often unrealistic as a practical matter to think that there are substitutes ready at hand for fishing, preparing fish, and eating fish in the manner currently practiced by affected individuals. This may be so for economic, geographic, historical, cultural, and/or other reasons. It is often difficult if not impossible to fish at a different bay, river, lake, or bayou how would one get there if it is too far to walk, or if the bus doesn't go there, or if there isn't any money to put enough gas in the car? how would one learn what it takes to catch fish at a new place, and how would one put food on the table in the meantime? what if all of the waters nearby were also contaminated, as is likely to be the case when the sources of the contaminants are air emissions (e.g., mercury) or the entire area is heavily industrialized (e.g., the Mississippi River Corridor between New Orleans and Baton Rouge) or the entire area is plagued by pesticide runoff from farms? It is often difficult if not impossible to fish for different species or to fish for younger fish as some advisories suggest what does one do for dinner when the only fish that are biting that day are old and the "wrong" species? It is often difficult if not impossible to stop eating fish altogether and to obtain nutrition benefits similar to fish from other sources what if one cannot afford to pay for substitute sources of protein, such as beef, which is often more expensive? how does one account for the fact that fish are unequaled in regard to some nutrition benefits: for example, fish are an especially efficient source of protein inasmuch as fish are low in fat relative to other protein sources? Consider, for example, the obstacles and concerns identified by the following.

---

[306]Catherine A. O'Neill, *Risk Avoidance and Environmental Justice* (forthcoming).
[307]Id.

Raymond Moseley, a fisher along the Columbia Slough in Portland, Oregon, explains:

> *We have caught big fish down there, between them two posts. Plenty catfish in there. Ain't too many other places to fish   except way out of town.*[308]

A low-income, African American fisher along the Detroit River, explains:

> *Yes, income affects everything. A fishing license is expensive   or outrageous is more like it. You need money for everything. To fish is expensive and what happens when you are poor? . . . You even have to spend money on gas so that you can get to the water and if you can't get there then you can't get food.*[309]

According to an account of the response of Alaskan Natives on Nelson Island to an unusual year marked by reduced numbers of herring and a prevalence of fatty herring:

> *Several families did not fish for herring at all, resulting in the lowest overall household involvement in herring production in the years of survey. Instead, they diverted efforts to increase halibut, Pacific cod, and salmon harvests, filling drying racks and freezers with these welcome, but less preferred, alternatives. Local residents do not consider halibut and Pacific cod adequate, or even improved, substitutes for herring, as non-local people may, but these species certainly are preferred by Nelson Island families to non-local, imported foods. Herring is the traditional winter food for Nelson Island families. Changing subsistence fishing strategies often means purchasing new gear and more gasoline, adjusting processing and drying facilities, investing more time fishing for other species, and altering subsistence production roles in the family*[310]

Yin Ling Leung, Executive Director of Asians and Pacific Islanders for Reproductive Health, California, explains:

> *To our communities, being able to fish means being able to either put food on the table, or basically eat a much less nutritious meal. I think that's a non-choice.*[311]

---

[308]Videotape: The Water in Our Backyard (City of Portland, Bureau of Environmental Services).

[309]Patrick C. West and Brunilda Vargus, *A Subsistence-Culture Model for High Toxic Fish Consumption by Low-Income Afro-Americans from the Detroit River* 15 (forthcoming).

[310]Mary C. Pete, *Subsistence Herring Fishing in the Nelson Island and Nunivak Island Districts* (1991) available at www.nativeknowledge.org/db/files/tp196.htm.

[311]Audrey Chiang, Asian Pacific Environmental Network, *A Seafood Consumption Survey of the Laotian Community in West Contra Costa County, California* 1 (1998).

As Daisy Carter, Project AWAKE, Coatopa, Alabama, summarizes,

When it comes to people, their health and survival, EPA must become real. It is not about formality, but reality.[312]

Second, even if those affected in some senses could as a practical matter alter their fishing and fish consumption practices, to be asked or required to do so might be *unthinkable* in the sense of occasioning profound loss or anguish. This may be so for traditional, cultural, religious, historical, and/or other reasons. For some communities or peoples, fish and fishing are a way of life, a way to be who they are. For these groups it is *necessary* to fish in traditional places, and to catch, prepare and eat fish in accordance with traditional ways. From their perspective, these are not expendable "habits," "activities," or "behaviors;" they are crucial for survival of the individual, the community or people, and, in some cases, the entirety of the earth.

Barbara Harper, Fourteen Confederated Tribes and Bands of the Yakama Nation, and Stuart Harris, Confederated Tribes of the Umatilla Indian Reservation, explain:

There are many issues relating to the evaluation of tribal health risk and, even more importantly, the health of people as they exist within their eco-cultural communities. . . . We need to think not only about human people as receptors, but about the culture itself as a receptor. We should be very uncomfortable about having to write a fish advisory in the first place. . . Really, there is just a single cultural community that is comprised of human and fish peoples and their rules for behaving and mutually surviving. It has been explained that the fish community existed first, and accepted people as community members, but only if human people follow certain rules of participating in the ecology, including a nutritionally adequate level of respectful consumption (a sacrament), and protecting the fish members from contamination and habitat degradation in return for being protected from starvation. Writing a fish advisory to protect some community members from other members is very disquieting, and causes many consequences on its own.[313]

Similarly, the Swinomish Indian Tribal Community explains:

In the Swinomish Tribal Community, fish and shellfish represent vital subsistence and commercial resources for the Tribe as well as an important point of cultural association for the Tribe's identity. Employed in cultural and religious ceremonies, incorporated into the common diet, and sold to support families on the Reservation, the current ecological status and fate of these species is of utmost interest to the Tribe. . . . [We believe that risk reduction exemplifies a much more effective answer to addressing the risk [from contamination] than does risk avoidance. . . . [O]ptions such as closing

---

[312]Daisy Carter, Project AWAKE (Written Comments to FCW, undated).

[313]Barbara Harper and Stuart Harris, *Proceedings of the American Fisheries Society: Contaminants in Fish,* "Tribal Technical Issues in Risk Reduction Through Fish Advisories"17 (1999).

harvesting sites, substituting with other sources of food, and posting "no fishing" signs are not viable considerations for reducing risk.[314]

And, as Hawaii's Thousand Friends emphasizes:

> *For the Native Hawaiian, the proposal of not eating fish because of contamination is unimaginable and unacceptable.*[315]

Thus, it is often impossible to conceive of fishing at a different bay, river, lake, or stream   what if it belongs to someone else traditionally, historically and/or legally? This is an issue, in particular, for many tribes, especially the fishing tribes (e.g., of the Pacific Northwest or of the Great Lakes), whose rights to hunt, fish, and gather are tied to particular places and protected by treaties   these place-based rights are not transferable. Nor can many tribal fishers imagine going "somewhere else" to fish, even if they could. Margaret Palmer, a Yakama tribal fisher, elaborates:

> *I don't feel like it's within our rights, as the tribe that we are, to go to a different area and live off of something that maybe God has blessed them with. This is our blessing. This is the way we see it. This is where we should stay. I don't believe that I would leave the area. I believe I would stay where I'm at   by the water. It's our lineage.*[316]

Moreover, the particularized skills and knowledge that tribal peoples have developed over centuries are place-specific and comprise a part of their intergenerational heritage, to be passed from generation to generation. It is often impossible to fish for, hunt for, or gather different species or to fish for younger fish as some advisories suggest   what if a particular species is bound up with one's cultural identity and with every aspect of who one is, as in the case of salmon and the Native peoples of the Pacific Northwest or in the case of wild rice and the Native peoples of Northern Minnesota?

Winona LaDuke, Mississippi Band of Anishinaabeg, explains:

> *It's mid-September in northern Minnesota. Somewhere on one of the many lakes Lennie Butcher and his wife Cleo are making wild rice. Mamoominikewag. That is what they do.*

> *It's a misty morning on Big Chippewa Lake. The Anishinaabeg couple drag their canoe toward the water's edge. The woman boards in the front and sits on her haunches. The man pushes the canoe offshore and jumps in the boat behind her. As they pole toward the wild rice beds, they can feel the crisp dampness of September on their faces. The man rises to stand, his head visible just above the tall sticks of rice. The woman pulls the*

---

[314]Swinomish Indian Tribal Community, *Comments on the NEJAC Draft Fish Consumption Report* (Feb. 5, 2002).

[315]Hawaii's Thousand Friends (Written Comments, March 11, 2002).

[316]Videotape: My Strength is From the Fish (Columbia River Inter-Tribal Fish Commission 1994).

rice over her lap with a stick and gently raps it with another one. This is a thousand-year-old scene on Big Chippewa Lake. And there is a community that intends to carry it on for another thousand years.

There are many wild rice lakes on the White Earth reservation in northern Minnesota; my community, the Anishinaabeg, calls the rice Manoomin, *or a gift from the Creator. Every year, half our people harvest the wild rice, the fortunate ones generating a large chunk of their income from it. But wild rice is not just about money and food. It's about feeding the soul.*[317]

Or what if a particular preparation method is an important component of traditional, cultural, or ceremonial use?

A majority of respondents [to the Seafood Consumption Survey of the Laotian Community in West Contra Costa County, California] (76.1%) said they always eat the skin of the fish. Some respondents also report regularly consuming the head and organs of the fish. Many chemicals are concentrated in the fat, which is just underneath the skin, and in the organs of the fish. Consumption of these parts of the fish exposes a person to higher amounts of chemical contaminants than consumption of only the fillet.

Cooking methods often determine which parts of the fish are eaten. The California Environmental Protection Agency (Cal EPA) health advisory recommends that people eat only fillet portions of fish, and bake, broil, steam or grill fish on a rack so that juices from the fat drip off during cooking. This survey shows that frying, baking, steaming, grilling, and making "fish pudding" are the most common ways of preparing fish in the Laotian community. According to the survey staff, the whole fish, including the head, skin, and organs, is frequently cooked when frying, baking, steaming and grilling fish. . . . "Fish pudding" or lap is also made out of the whole fish, and is oftentimes made from raw fish. When making lap, the organs of the fish are commonly removed, cooked separately, chopped up and then included in the mixture. According to the survey staff, striped bass is a popular fish for lap. Sauces and pastes made from whole and raw fish, shrimp or crab are also popular traditional Laotian condiments. The health advisory's recommendations for methods of cooking fish to lower one's risk of taking in harmful chemicals clearly are at odds with traditional ways of preparing fish and other seafoods.[318]

---

[317]Winona LaDuke, *All Our Relations: Native Struggles for Land and Life* 115 (1999).

[318]Audrey Chiang, Asian Pacific Environmental Network, *A Seafood Consumption Survey of the Laotian Community in West Contra Costa County, California* 35 (1998).

According to a recent study of African American fishers on the Detroit River, frying is "a firmly rooted cultural tradition amongst African Americans" and is either the only method or the preferred method of preparing fish; as one fisher summarized:

> It's cultural. Blacks fry. It's simple.[319]

It is often simply impossible to stop eating fish altogether and to obtain nutrition benefits similar to fish from other sources. For some communities and peoples, there are simply no replacements that equal the nutritional and health benefits   in the broadest sense of these terms   of the fish, aquatic plants, and wildlife that they have traditionally consumed. Yvonne Smith and Laura Berg explain in *Wana Chinook Tymoo*, in a sidebar entitled "Declining Fish, Declining Health:"

> *The shortage of salmon and other fish has necessitated dramatic changed in the diet of the Indian people of the Columbia River Basin. They have experienced a steady decline in health as a result.*
>
> *Researchers worldwide state what Indians have known all along, that there are health benefits to consuming fish. . . .*
>
> *Ted Strong reported that when his relatives, many now deceased, spoke of those that came before them, they talked about people who lived long lives, into their 90's and beyond. "Those ancestors ate the traditional foods," he said. . . .*
>
> *Whatever other factors have contributed to the shortened lives and high death rate among the Indian people of the basin, there is little doubt dietary changes have had a significant impact.*
>
> *Joanna Meninick has watched the health of her people decline as the scarcity of salmon has increased, "diabetes, cancer, heart disease. All of these are on the increase."*
>
> *Many traditional foods are gone, or have become inaccessible. C'lày (pronounced chu-lie) is an example. Made from dried salmon, berries, and other oils and foods, the powdery preparation has multiple uses. "It is good medicine, said Bill Yal-lup, Sr. "You can mix it with certain roots, certain foods . . . very good for the heart."*
>
> *But c'lày is in short supply. It takes many pounds of dried salmon to make. Whole salmon, needed for ceremonies and subsistence, comes first.*

---

[319]Katharine J. Hornbarger, et al., *Targeted Audience Analysis: Recommendations for Effectively Communicating Toxic Fish Consumption Advisories to Anglers on the Detroit River* 26 (1994) (noting that anglers described several ways of frying: "pan frying, deep fat frying, and the most often cited method, coating the fish with cornmeal and then frying.").

Pierson Mitchell noted that he had salmon for lunch at home sometimes, when it was available, but he missed the c'làr. Getting it occasionally in the Christmas basket was a treat. "If our people had remained on the diet of the salmon, our health would be better today," he said.[320]

Similarly, Silas Whitman, Nez Perce, explains:

One thing I have noticed over the years is that the Nez Perce people are highly susceptible to minute changes in diet, especially those that revolve around fish. If we supplant native foods with other foods, often times the nutritive values of that supplanted product cannot be ingested or stay in the system to the degree that our bodies as Nez Perce people can use them. From that come health problems that are eroding our mortality. So as we help the salmon and other fish to recover we help ourselves.[321]

And it is no less a source of profound loss and anguish for those whose have already been forced to give up fish because of the gross contamination of their fishing places. It is no less *necessary* for these communities or peoples to fish in traditional places, and to catch, prepare and eat fish in accordance with traditional ways. They have been made to suspend or alter their practices, but they cannot be viewed as having "chosen" to abandon these practices. The strength and resilience of these affected communities and peoples cannot now be taken to justify a claim that fish are no longer important to their survival as individuals and peoples, such that it would be permissible to allow the contamination to continue and remain. Winona LaDuke recounts:

"This is a classic environmental justice site," says Ken Jock, a director of the Akwesasene Environment Program. A slight man, with soft eyes and a quiet manner, he spends much of his time arguing with agencies about implementation of the law. His huge office is full of reports and photos documenting the extent of the [PCB contamination at Akwesasne, on the St. Lawrence River]. The reports, photos, and sheer size of the Akwesasne Environment Program dwarf the infrastructure of most Indian nations in the country. Yet it seems that even with reams of paper, the action taken by federal agencies is minimal. "This all used to be a fishing village. That's all gone now. There's only one family that still fishes," Jock says. "We can't farm here because of all of those air emissions. Industry has pretty much taken the entire traditional lifestyle away from the community here."

Today 65 percent of the Mohawks on Akwesasne reservation have diabetes, says Jock. Henry Lickers, director of the environmental health branch of the Mohawk Council of Akwesasne echoes Jock: "Our traditional lifestyle has been completely disrupted, and we have been forced to make choices to protect our future generations," says Lickers.

---

[320]Yvonne Smith and Laura Berg, *Ancient Tradition, Modern Reality: Is There a Future for a Salmon-Based Culture?* 1 Wana Chinook Tymoo 14 (1998).

[321]Dan Landeen and Allen Pinkham, *Salmon and His People: Fish and Fishing in Nez Perce Culture* 21 (1999).

"Many of the families used to eat 20-25 fish meals a month. It's now said that the traditional Mohawk diet is spaghetti."[322]

Thus, it may be impractical or impossible for those who are affected by contaminated aquatic environments to give up or alter their fish consumption practices. This may be so for economic, geographic, historical, traditional, cultural, religious, and/or legal reasons. Yet, the reality of gross contamination means that these practices may expose members of affected communities, groups and tribes to serious health risks   some of the contaminants contained in the fish, aquatic plants, and wildlife cause cancer, some wreak neurological damage, some are linked to reproductive and developmental damage, some disrupt endocrine functions, and some cause a range of these and other harms to humans. This poses a sad and dire dilemma.

What role should fish consumption advisories play in agencies' response? Broadly speaking, there are three possible policy options. These might be thought of as occupying a continuum. On the one end, agencies might rely exclusively on fish consumption advisories to address this dilemma. This option might reflect the view that it is cheaper and easier to address affected communities' and tribes' exposure by getting them to stop eating fish than it is to require risk-producers to prevent, reduce, and cleanup contamination. And, assuming the fish consumption advisories were effective (a question taken up in the next part of this chapter), affected communities would be protected from the harms of cancer and the like. There would, of course, be some losses   any substitute food sources might not be of equal nutritional quality or might not be what members of these communities would prefer to eat   but these losses would have to have been judged to be worth the benefits of not being exposed to the host of contaminants contained in the fish.

On the other end, agencies might abandon the use of fish consumption advisories altogether, and instead push aggressively for pollution prevention and cleanup. With this option, agencies' time and financial resources would be devoted entirely to preventing, reducing, and cleaning up contamination, such that aquatic environments would be returned to health and would be able to sustain fish, aquatic plants, and wildlife that were safe for humans to consume and use at the earliest possible time. This option might reflect the view that the only real way to protect health and safety of humans who consume or use these resources is to address the source of the health risk, i.e., the contamination. This option might reflect the view that it would be a misdirection of scarce agency time and money to continue to try to use and improve fish advisories   that this time and money would be better spent on prevention, reduction, and cleanup. Or it might reflect the view that even advising affected communities, groups, or tribes to alter their fish consumption practices is inappropriate, given the discrimination against and potential affront to those for whom these practices have cultural, traditional, or religious dimensions.

In the middle are a range of policy options that recognize some temporary role for fish consumption advisories but emphasize that they not become agencies' primary policy response to

---

[322]Winona LaDuke, *All Our Relations: Native Struggles for Land and Life* 17 (1999).

the adverse health effects of contaminated aquatic environments. These middle options would grow out of a sense that neither the first nor second options actually addressed the concerns of at least some communities of color, low-income communities, tribes, and other indigenous peoples. The first option would shift the burdens of contamination entirely from those who have produced the risks to those who bear them. This is unjust and unacceptable. It would also give continued license to real and grave harms   among them nutritional deficits, other health detriments, and cultural discrimination. It would stand idly by as aquatic food sources were ultimately allowed to remain or become poisoned and forever "off limits" to those groups that formerly relied on these resources. The second option would address some of these long-term concerns, but would fail to inform affected groups in the short term. This, too, is unjust and unacceptable. The second option would, as Daisy Carter puts it, withhold from those most affected precisely what they need and are entitled to: *the information and knowledge to help themselves.*[323] It would turn its back to the reality that fish are already contaminated   and will remain contaminated for some time, even given the most ambitious cleanup schedules   and real people will suffer when they eat or use this fish. Finally, the options that chart a middle course recognize that there may be ways to address at least some of the concerns of those affected by fashioning *appropriate* advisories (e.g., appropriate in terms of language, cultural, and other group- and place-specific considerations).

Moreover, the range of options here might enable agencies to be attentive to and respectful of the different concerns of different communities, groups, and tribes.   That is to say, a particular community or tribe could choose one of the other options as most appropriate for its needs. *This brings up the crucial point that it is for the affected group to determine what will be appropriate from its perspective.*

Note that tribes' particular circumstances need to be taken into account. Tribes are sovereign nations, and in their governmental capacities are in the position of deciding for themselves what role fish consumption advisories should play in their efforts to protect the health and safety of tribal people consuming or using fish, aquatic plants, and wildlife.[324] Some tribes have decided to issue fish advisories to protect their members from contamination   often contamination that was permitted not by the tribes themselves but by state and federal agencies.[325] Some tribes or groups of tribes have opted not to issue fish consumption advisories but instead to develop "tribal consumption guidelines." [326] These guidelines tend to focus on the first and third functions of the typical advisory, i.e., providing information and suggesting alternative ways to continue consuming fish, rather than on the second function, i.e., discouraging fish consumption

[323]Daisy Carter, Project AWAKE (Written Comments to FCW, undated).

[324]See, e.g., Swinomish Indian Tribal Community, *Comments on NEJAC Draft Fish Consumption Report* (Feb. 5, 2002).

[325]See, e.g., James Ransom, Director, Haudenosuanee Environmental Task Force, *Proceedings of the American Fisheries Society: Contaminants in Fish* 25 (1999) (describing fish advisory issued by St. Regis Mohawk Health Services).

[326]Telephone Interview with Nancy Costa, Fond du Lac Environmental Program (Jul. 31, 2001); Great Lakes Indian Fish & Wildlife Commission, Masinaigan Supplement: How to Enjoy Fish Safely (Fall 2000).

altogether. Tribal consumption guidelines may also offer information that the typical federal- or state-issued advisory doesn't about the health benefits to tribal members of eating a "Native diet" and the health risks of turning to a "western diet."[327] Nancy Costa, of Fond du Lac Environment Program, explains:

> *"The last thing we want to do is to discourage tribal members from eating fish given (among other things) the serious health effects we have seen for those who have gotten away from a Native diet."*[328]

Similarly, Elaine Abraham, a Tlingit elder from Yakutat, notes efforts to enhance appreciation of the cultural and nutritional value of Native foods, and cautions against focusing only on the potential health risks without acknowledging the important, multi-faceted benefits:

> *Why are you starting with talk about concerns? I have enough trouble getting my granddaughter to eat Native foods!*[329]

Tribal consumption guidelines may employ the indigenous language and artwork of those affected.[330] It is important to note that several tribes have indicated that they would like to be able to examine the question what role advisories or guidelines should play in their efforts to protect the health and safety of tribal people consuming or using fish, aquatic plants, and wildlife, and, potentially to fashion appropriate advisories or guidelines, but that they do not have sufficient technical and/or financial resources to do so. These tribes have stated that additional resources would, therefore, be crucial.

But tribes and tribal members are also affected by the environmental management decisions of federal and state agencies. In the Pacific Northwest, for example, federal and state agencies make numerous decisions that have permitted the contamination and depletion of the salmon and other culturally significant, treaty-protected tribal resources. Here, federal and state policy choices regarding the role of fish consumption advisories will have an impact on tribal members exercising their treaty-guaranteed rights to fish in all "usual and accustomed" areas, many of which are managed in whole or in part by federal and state agencies. To the extent that these agencies look to risk avoidance rather than risk reduction measures, they may risk running afoul of treaty obligations. Further, when these agencies issue fish consumption advisories that affect tribal members and resources, they have sometimes failed to communicate their actions to tribes as they should in accordance with tribes' status as sovereign nations and, for federal agencies, in compliance with the Executive Order on maintaining the appropriate "government-to-

---

[327]Telephone Interview with Nancy Costa, Fond du Lac Environmental Program (Jul. 31, 2001).
[328]Id.
[329]Alaska Traditional Knowledge and Native Foods Database, *Resource Guide for Mini-Grants* available at www.iser.uaa.alaska.edu/projects/contam/ResourceGuide/index.htm
[330]Telephone Interview with Nancy Costa, Fond du Lac Environmental Program (Jul. 31, 2001); see also, Great Lakes Indian Fish & Wildlife Commission, *Masinaigan Supplement: How to Enjoy Safely* (Fall 2000).

government" relationship with tribes. Issues particular to American Indian tribes and Alaskan Native villages are discussed further in Chapter Four.

Finally, even where agencies, together with affected groups, opt to continue to issue advisories, they need to redouble their efforts to prevent and reduce new sources of contamination and to cleanup and restore environments and fisheries that are already contaminated. *This caveat was strongly emphasized by affected groups everywhere.* Agency representatives acknowledge this need. For example, Elizabeth Southerland, Standards and Applied Science Division, Office of Science and Technology, Office of Water, opened this year's National Forum on Contaminants in Fish by describing "how water quality-based programs at both the federal and state levels seek not only to advise people on ways to minimize public health risks, but also to implement management measures to reduce the pollution problems so that measures like fish consumption advisories can be rescinded. No one wants consumption advisories in place any longer than necessary."[331] Yet, advisories have been in effect in some places since the 1970s and EPA has created a separate advisory program, which has been in place for about a decade. Furthermore, EPA appears to anticipate continued efforts to issue advisories and to ensure that those affected "comply" with them. In its Strategic Plan, for example, EPA states among its objectives: "[by 2005, consumption of contaminated fish will be reduced."[332] EPA's commitment to ensuring that advisories remain a temporary, second-best response to contamination and its effects on human health needs to be backed up by a reprioritization of goals   prevention, reduction and cleanup first and foremost   and by a redoubling of resources allocated to returning aquatic environments and fisheries to a state where it is safe for people to fish.

B. EFFECTIVENESS: BACKGROUND AND DEFINITION

1. Advisories' Components and Functions

In order to facilitate deliberation about this middle course, it seems useful to examine more closely the components and functions of a typical fish consumption advisory. A typical advisory might be thought of as comprised of three functional parts: (1) provide information about the nature and extent of the contamination and its adverse health effects (e.g., which waters are affected? which species? what are the contaminants of concern? what are the adverse health effects from these contaminants? which subgroups are affected?); (2) encourage avoidance by one or more of several means (e.g., refraining from eating fish altogether; reducing amount of fish consumed); and, sometimes, (3) suggest alternative means to continue eating fish (e.g., altering frequency of fish meals; altering preparation methods; fishing at other sites; fishing for and eating other species). These functions sometimes overlap. In addition, there are functions that advisories could usefully serve but that the typical advisory does not attempt to serve, e.g., capacity-building or empowerment in the affected group.

---

[331] *Proceedings of the National Forum on Contaminants in Fish* I-10 (May 6 and 9, 2001).

[332] U.S. Environmental Protection Agency, Office of the Chief Financial Officer, *Strategic Plan* 29-30 (No. 190-R-97-002) (September 1997) available at www.epa.gov/ocfopage/plan/epastrat.pdf.

Consider this excerpt for the current advisory for organic contamination in Louisiana:

Water body	Causative pollutants	Recommendations	Approximate size affected
Devil's Swamp, Devil's Swamp Lake and Bayou Baton Rouge (Parish: East Baton Rouge)	Hexachlorobenzene, Hexachloro- 1,3-butadiene, PCBs, Lead, Mercury, Arsenic	Avoid swimming, limit fish consumption to TWO MEALS PER MONTH.	7.0 square miles
Capitol Lake (Parish: East Baton Rouge)	Priority organics (PCBs)	No fish consumption.	0.12 mile

This advisory provides information identifying the relevant contaminants, the affected waterbodies, the approximate geographical extent of the contamination, and, given that the recommendations apply to all "fish," the species covered. This information all serves the first function. Do the recommendations "limit fish consumption to two meals per month" and "no fish consumption" serve mainly to translate information about the nature and extent of the contamination and its health effects into a form that is readily usable by those who would otherwise consume these fish (an extension of the first function)? Or do they serve mainly to discourage fish consumption (the second function) with all of the pros and cons of doing so, as discussed above in Part A? This information may serve both the first and second functions (and may be perceived to serve different functions by different communities, groups or tribes).

Note that this advisory's recommendations are not accompanied by suggestions of alternative means that would allow the continued consumption of fish, albeit of different species or according to different practices the third function.

Finally, without more information about the process of fashioning and disseminating this advisory, it is difficult to determine to what extent it serves the additional functions of capacity-building and empowerment from the perspective of the affected groups. To highlight but one aspect of these additional functions: although this advisory identifies the "causative pollutants," it does not go on to provide information about the sources of those pollutants (e.g., particular industrial or other facilities) nor about upcoming risk assessment and risk management decisions relevant to the pollutants and sources of concern.

2. Defining "Effectiveness"

There are likely to be differences in how one defines "effective"in this context differences among agencies and the various affected communities, groups and tribes. The first function of advisories to provide information is the least controversial. There is likely widespread agreement that an effective advisory is one that successfully *communicates* information about the nature and extent of the contamination and about the relevant adverse health effects. Advisories' first function is important to securing environmental justice. Although questions remain about whether current advisories actually communicate this information in understandable and appropriate ways (these will be taken up below, in Parts C and D), there seems to be little question that advisories or something akin to advisories *should* serve this function. As Ticiang Diangson, Supervising Planning and Development Specialist and Environmental Justice Advocate, Seattle Public Utilities, explains:

Although prevention would be the ideal solution, the essential question after contamination is, how can the harmed community be made "whole?" First and foremost, the community needs to be truly __informed__ about the range of harm/risk it has been exposed to. . . .

Communication, of course, requires that information be conveyed in a language, via a medium, in accordance with cultural considerations, and generally in a way that will enable it to reach and be understood by those affected   these issues are the focus of Part D.

The second function of advisories   to discourage fish consumption   is more problematic. Given the grave losses along myriad dimensions that are occasioned by not fishing and consuming fish, "success" here comes at a considerable price. To the extent that agencies judge advisories' effectiveness according to whether they elicit a decrease in fish consumption, agencies may misfocus their efforts from the perspectives of at least some affected groups. A measure of success that focuses on getting people to reduce their fish consumption may fail to appreciate the traditional, cultural, or religious reasons that make reducing consumption inappropriate, and in so doing, perpetuate cultural discrimination. In these cases, affected people may well have access to, understand, and "believe" the relevant advisories, they may simply decline to "comply" with them. As Hawaii's Thousand Friends observes:

> *A barrier to making fish consumption advisories work in Hawai'i is that no one will listen because eating fish is part of the culture.*[333]

The third function that advisories sometimes serve   to suggest alternative means (e.g., alternative fishing sites, alternative species, alternative preparation methods) to continue eating fish   is also problematic. To the extent that agencies judge advisories' effectiveness according to whether they convince people to switch to these alternative practices, agencies may again misfocus their efforts in a way that is an affront to the traditions, cultures, or religious beliefs of some of those affected. Consider, for example, the observations of the Asian Pacific Environmental Network:

> *The California Environmental Protection Agency (Cal EPA) health advisory recommends that people eat only fillet portions of fish, and bake, broil, steam or grill fish on a rack so that juices from the fat drip off during cooking. . . . The health advisory's recommendations for methods of cooking fish to lower one's risk of taking in harmful chemicals clearly are at odds with traditional ways of preparing fish and other seafoods.*[334]

To the extent that agencies judge advisories' effectiveness according to whether they convince people to switch to alternative practices that haven't been identified as appropriate *by* the affected

---

[333]Hawaii's Thousand Friends (Written Comments, March 11, 2002).

[334]Audrey Chiang, Asian Pacific Environmental Network, *A Seafood Consumption Survey of the Laotian Community in West Contra Costa County, California* 35 (1998).

group, agencies may fail to appreciate the economic, geographic, social, and other practical realities facing the affected group.

The fourth function that advisories might serve – capacity-building and empowerment – are important to securing environmental justice. It is crucial that those affected play central roles in developing and disseminating the information that they deem appropriate to their needs. Such efforts – *led* by those in the community, and *supported* by the EPA and other agencies – can contribute to the larger goals of what the Laotian Organizing Project calls *"participatory learning and culturally-appropriate organizing."*[335] EPA and other agencies should view this as an opportunity to work with communities on the ground as they work to empower themselves. As Daisy Carter, Project AWAKE, observes:

> *The question is does the federal government (EPA) want to educate, inform, and enlighten citizens to become active in making decisions for themselves? The answer is no. Companies and the government would not be able to exploit these citizens who are at risk if this was done. Citizens would ask questions and become involved in their own destiny. However, without knowledge, communities who are at risk are prey. . . .*

> *One of the major roles of NEJAC is to find a way to empower local citizens who are in impacted areas to set up lines of communication and data bases to acquire information related to their needs.*

And, as noted above, advisories enhance their effectiveness in this regard when they provide information that enables affected communities and tribes to become educated about and involved in risk assessment and risk management decisions – that is, information that does not merely instruct "Do Not Eat the Fish," but that identifies the sources of contamination as well as relevant upcoming decisions about preventing, reducing, and cleaning up contamination for these sources.

Additionally, it seems that agencies' views of effectiveness are sometimes preoccupied by concerns that may bear little on effectiveness for communities of color, low-income communities, tribes, and other indigenous peoples. For example, state and federal agencies have devoted considerable effort to achieving "national consistency" in fish advisory programs. This effort was an "important objective" of the 1999 American Fisheries Society Forum on Contaminants in Fish (attended by 41 states, 7 federal agencies, and others). Yet few dividends from such efforts may accrue to communities of color, low-income communities, tribes, and other indigenous peoples: an affluent recreational fisher who lives in Ohio but vacations in Michigan might be confused by the differing approaches to fish consumption advisories taken by these two states, and so might benefit from consistency between them.[336] Fishers from environmental justice communities are

---

[335]Maria Kong and Pamela Chiang, Laotian Organizing Project & Asian Pacific Environmental Network, *Fighting Fire with Fire* 5 (2001).

[336]Hugh F. MacDonald and Kevin J. Boyle, *Effect of a Statewide Sport Fish Consumption Advisory on Open-Water Fishing in Maine*, 17 Journal of Fisheries Management 687 (1997). Note, however, that consistency might be relevant to environmental justice communities where jurisdiction over a

less likely to be traveling about, fishing in multiple states   this may be so for historic, geographical, cultural, economic, or legal reasons, or some combination of these.   These individuals are thus less likely to benefit from consistency among states.

In sum, "effectiveness" from the perspective of communities of color, low-income communities, tribes, and other indigenous peoples is likely to focus on the first and fourth functions, while for some affected groups, it is likely to include the second and third functions. However, definitions of effectiveness and appropriateness will likely vary with varying local and cultural contexts. Thus, it will be important to determine the perspective of the particular affected group on this question, and to look to this perspective to guide every aspect of any advisory process, including evaluation of its success.

C. EFFECTIVENESS: AVAILABLE EVIDENCE

Before discussing to what extent advisories are effective from the perspectives of communities of color, low-income communities, tribes, and other indigenous peoples, it is useful to canvass the available evidence on responses to the fish consumption advisories that have been issued. As a general matter, although advisories have been in effect in some places since the early 1970s, relatively little is known about how they affect humans' behavior.[337] Again, there is more evidence based on anecdote or local knowledge than based on formal study. For example, the California Department of Health Services notes that health advisories extending from Malibu to Newport Beach have been in place for many years, but that:

> [O]utreach and education about the advisories has been difficult to accomplish. Of particular concern are the non-English speaking populations who may have difficulty obtaining and understanding health information.[338]

To the extent that empirical data have been gathered, they tend to provide two kinds of information (1) whether people are aware of an advisory; and/or (2) whether people have altered their consumption practices as a result. "Awareness," in turn, includes (a) whether people are aware that an advisory exists, and (b) whether people are aware of an advisory's content and recommendations. Sometimes these data are gathered alongside studies of fish consumption rates and practices. These data-gathering efforts vary in the extent to which they gather socioeconomic and other data relevant to environmental justice communities.

According to one survey designed to gauge the effectiveness of Great Lakes sport fish consumption advisories, for example, "half the sport fish consumers were unaware of the fish advisory for PCBs in the Great Lakes. The lowest awareness was among women, minority

---

single estuary, river or other waterway fished by these groups is shared by neighboring states.
    [337]Id.
    [338]California Department of Health, Environmental Health Investigations Branch, *Palos Verdes Shelf Outreach and Education Project on Fish Contamination Issues* (fact sheet available from California Department of Health Services).

groups, and persons with no high school degree."[339] Another survey of fish consumption patterns and advisory awareness among anglers on the Fox River in Wisconsin found that 95% of anglers who ate fish were unaware of Wisconsin's fish advisory pamphlet and 50% of anglers who ate fish had neither heard nor read about the health risks of eating Fox River fish. Asians (primarily Hmong and Laotians) represented 70% of the anglers who had not heard about the health risks (although they represented only 19% of the total anglers surveyed).[340] The survey found further that most of the anglers surveyed did not eat the fish they caught in the Fox River (83%)and that of these, 75% said they did not eat the fish because they were concerned about the contaminants. Of those anglers who ate the fish they caught, Asians made up the largest group, comprising 59% of fish eaters. The survey's authors observed:

> *Eating fish forms a regular part of the diet and culture for the Asians (Hmong and Laotians) living in the Green Bay area. White Bass, listed in the advisory as "Do Not Eat," appears to be their fish of choice. Although the number of Asian anglers fishing along the Fox River decreased after being informed by an interpreter that White Bass is not safe to eat, there is concern that some of these anglers still may be eating White Bass caught from other nearby contaminated waters. Many Asian anglers may not understand the fish advisory because of the language barrier or may not believe the fish advisory because no immediate physical ill effects have been observed from eating contaminated fish.*[341]

A third survey, of Maine open-water anglers, examined the effect of a 1994 statewide fish consumption advisory.[342] 63% of all anglers knew about the issuance of a mercury advisory regarding covering fish from all lakes and ponds in Maine. All socioeconomic characteristics (here: gender, age, fishing "effort") except education and income were the same for the groups who were aware of the advisory and those who were not. Of the anglers who were aware of the advisory, 22% of Maine residents and 23% of non-residents altered their fishing behavior, indicating that but for the advisory they *would* have consumed more fish, fished more days, or fished more or different waters.[343] A fourth survey, of fish consumption patterns and advisory awareness among the Laotian communities in West Contra Costa County, California, found that 48.5% of survey respondents had heard of a health advisory about eating fish and shellfish from the San Francisco Bay. Only a fraction of these (59.5%), however, could recall what the advisory

---

[339]John Tilden et. al, *Health Advisories for Consumers of Great Lakes Sport-Fish: Is the Message Being Received?*, 105 Environmental Health Perspective 1360 (December 1997).

[340]Dyan M. Steenport, et al., *Fish Consumption Habits and Advisory Awareness Among Fox River Anglers*, Wisconsin Medical Journal (November 2000) available at www.wismed.org/wmj/nov2000/fish.html.

[341]Dyan M. Steenport, et al., *Fish Consumption Habits and Advisory Awareness Among Fox River Anglers*, Wisconsin Medical Journal (November 2000) available at www.wismed.org/wmj/nov2000/fish.html.

[342]Hugh F. MacDonald and Kevin J. Boyle, *Effect of a Statewide Sport Fish Consumption Advisory on Open-Water Fishing in Maine*, 17 Journal of Fisheries Management 687 (1997).

[343]Id.

said and none could recall an advisory more specific than "pregnant women should not eat large amounts of Bay fish," or "Bay fish are not safe to eat."[344] The survey found a statistically significant difference in awareness of the health advisory among ethnic groups within the larger Laotian community, with Khmu respondents being more likely to have heard of the advisory.[345] Of those who were aware of the health advisory, 60.3% said that it had influenced a change in their fishing or fish consumption habits. Of those whose habits were influenced, 62.7% said they no longer eat fish from the Bay or eat less fish from the Bay and 29.9% said they no longer eat fish from any source or eat less fish from all sources.[346] An account of a fifth survey, by the Environmental Health Investigations Branch of the California Department of Health, concludes:

> *Although the health advisory has been in place since 1994, outreach and education about the advisory to different fishing populations has been difficult to accomplish. The recently completed San Francisco Bay Seafood Consumption Study indicates that about two thirds of people fishing have no awareness or limited understanding of the advisory.*[347]

With this and other available evidence to go on, it appears that people of color and people with low incomes, limited English proficiency, or relatively little education are less likely to be aware of fish consumption advisories; that some portion of the people of color who are aware of advisories alters their consumption patterns as a result, but that a significant portion does not alter their consumption patterns; that there are differences among various ethnic groups in these respects; and that while contamination and advisories are not influencing all individuals to reduce their fish consumption, they are influencing individuals at sufficient rates to contribute to suppression effects (discussed in Chapter 1). Additionally, here as elsewhere, there is a need to gather further information especially about those groups and subgroups about which less is known.

D. EFFECTIVENESS: RISK COMMUNICATION AND CONSUMPTION ADVISORIES

The discussion in this Part tracks the components of risk communication as identified in the EPA's *Guidance for Assessing Chemical Contaminant Data for Use in Fish Advisories, Volume IV: Risk Communication*,[348] by the organizers of the 2001 National Risk Communication

---

[344]Audrey Chiang, Asian Pacific Environmental Network, *A Seafood Consumption Survey of the Laotian Community in West Contra Costa County, California* 29 (1998).

[345]Id. at 31.

[346]Id. at 30; Great Lakes Indian Fish & Wildlife Commission, *Masinaigan Supplement: How to Enjoy Fish Safely* (Fall 2000) available at www.glifwc.org.

[347]California Department of Health, Environmental Health Investigations Branch, *San Francisco Bay Fish Consumption Outreach and Education Project* (fact sheet available from California Department of Health Services).

[348]U.S. Environmental Protection Agency, Office of Water, *Guidance for Assessing Chemical Contaminant Data for Use in Fish Advisories, Volume IV: Risk Communication* 3 (1995).

Conference,[349] and in the risk communication literature more generally. That is, after discussing general risk communication issues in Section 1, issues of "audience identification" and "needs assessment" are examined in Section 2; issues of message content are explored in Section 3; issues of media choice are taken up in Section 4; issues of implementation are discussed in Section 5; and issues of evaluation are addressed in Section 6. In addition, the matters of funding and capacity-building are explored in Section 7.

1. Risk Communication – Overarching Issues

"Risk communication is a two-way street." This phrase is often repeated, but less often honored in practice with the result that communication may not actually occur. How can the risk communication process be rehabilitated?

As a preliminary matter, EPA and other agencies should reexamine the terms conventionally used to describe the various participants in the risk communication process. Agencies often refer to the "public," the "community," or the "audience," on one hand, and agency and other "experts" on the other.[350] These terms set up a dichotomy that denies that members of affected groups are themselves "experts," with knowledge crucial to successful risk communication including effective fish consumption advisories. A more appropriate terminology would recognize affected groups' expertise, and not withhold from them the appellation "expert." In a similar vein, agencies often refer to "target audiences," who are affected groups that receive messages, and distinguish these from "risk communicators," who are agencies that generate and disseminate messages.[351] These terms indicate a one-way flow of information (*from* agencies *to* affected groups) rather than a two-way process; and these terms may also carry the connotation of agencies as being active in the process whereas affected groups are passive. A more appropriate terminology might use words such as "partners" or (particularly in the case of tribes) "co-managers." While these may seem small quibbles over a few words, these words frame the relationship among the various participants in the risk communication process, and may serve to undermine successful, two-way communication before the process even gets off the ground.

Then, it is necessary to put into practice the concept of "partnership" or of "co-management." *Affected groups must be involved as partners or co-managers at every point in*

---

[349]Proceedings from the National Risk Communication Conference. May 6-8, 2001. Chicago, IL. Sponsored by the Minnesota Department of Health, US. EPA and the Society Risk Analysis. EPA Cooperative Agreement Grant #X-82825101-0. August 2001. Available on line at http://www.epa.gov/ost/fish/forum/riskconf.pdf.

[350]U.S. Environmental Protection Agency, *Guidance for Assessing Chemical Contaminant Data for Use in Fish Advisories*, *Volume IV: Risk Communication* 3 and throughout (1995).
[351]Id; see also, *National Risk Communication Conference, Proceedings Document* I-5 (2001)(describing "Risk Communicator Presentation session, which described "getting to know the audience from the risk communicator's point of view.")

the risk communication process. This is the single most important lesson that EPA and other agencies should take away from this discussion of effective fish consumption advisories. All of the elements of effective fish consumption advisories will fall into place if agencies and affected communities or tribes consider together the questions and answers. That is to say, communities and tribes will articulate their needs; affected groups and agencies will each share their respective concerns; affected groups will help ensure that the content and medium of advisories are appropriate to their membership (e.g., in terms of language, literacy, culture, practice); affected groups will be able to contribute creative implementation strategies appropriate to their membership; and affected groups will have knowledge indispensable to the evaluation process. As in the case of research in general (discussed in Chapter One), communities and tribes have expertise relevant to risk communication that is simply not going to be able to be replicated by non-member researchers. This is supported by the large body of literature on "participatory research." Members of these affected groups ought to be recognized as the experts they are, and their work ought to be supported financially (whether though dispensing grants to community groups, tribes, and partnerships formed by affected groups, through hiring affected group members as expert consultants, or through other means). EPA and other agencies should recognize the difficulty of achieving full involvement   and thus actual risk communication   in the absence of financial support. This issue of funding is taken up at greater length below.

EPA and other agencies should work to reconceptualize risk communication approaches from large-scale, abstracted, one-time efforts to develop and disseminate various communication "products" (e.g, developing and posting fish consumption advisory signs) to local, contextualized, ongoing efforts to establish and maintain relationships with a particular affected community or tribe.[352] While this reconceptualization may be necessitated to a greater degree for some groups and contexts than others, the existence of an ongoing relationship will enhance communication regardless. And, while building and maintaining a relationship will likely require more time and resources than agencies have typically been able to devote to risk communication,[353] the dividends would seem to be worth it. For example, representatives of agencies and affected groups alike have suggested that a lack of familiarity or trust has been a barrier to effective fish consumption advisories in the past (resulting, e.g., in a reluctance by affected group members to participate in baseline consumption rate studies or other information-gathering efforts; or in a scepticism on the

---

[352]See, e.g., Telephone Interview, Diana Lee, Research Scientist, California Department of Health Services (Oct. 26, 2001)

[353]See, e.g., Ed Horn, Bureau of Toxic Substance Assessment, New York State Department of Health, National Risk Communication Conference II-25 (2001) ("The most effective ways of communicating with hard-to-reach populations are extremely labor intensive. They are going to require someone in the target community who has the respect of the community and an understanding of the community. It requires constant work; it's not just a matter of sending a brochure out. We can send 20,000 brochures out fairly easily and inexpensively, but if we have to travel to meet with the target population in small groups, then this requires additional staff.").

part of affected groups regarding the intent behind or the accuracy of agencies' messages).[354] To the extent this is the case, the existence of an ongoing, regular relationship would go far toward dismantling this barrier.[355] The importance of gaining trust and building a good relationship bears emphasis. Affected groups often cite agencies' lack of "follow through" as a source of mistrust. Chee Choy, Project Manager for the Columbia Slough Sediment Project, Bureau of Environmental Services, Portland, Oregon, elaborates:

> *After an agency has made a commitment to addressing environmental justice by committing the necessary resources, the next step perhaps is to work on gaining trust and credibility with ethnic minority, immigrant, and low-income communities. . . . Among these communities, there is a severe lack of trust that government will listen to or take care of their concerns.*
>
> *Many immigrant and low-income communities place a strong emphasis on quality relationships. They need to know you care, are sincere, have their interests in mind (as opposed to your agency's interest) and there is follow-through on your commitments. These relationship features do not come about in a short term, but rather must be developed over time. So, if your agency's outreach staff visits a community group only when you need their help, your commitment to that community may be seen as tokenism or serving your needs. One way to develop and maintain a long-term relationship is to have regular   perhaps once a month or a quarter   meetings (these could be over coffee, breakfast or lunch) or to pay routine visits to [a community group's] office, even when there is nothing you need their help on. During these visits, once must show genuine interest in the community group's activities, and where appropriate, find out if there are ways you can help them in some of their activities, even if those activities do not directly pertain to your project's objectives.[356]*

To this end, several affected groups have recommended partnering with existing community groups and local service providers. For example, Hawaii's Thousand Friends urges:

---

[354]See, e.g., Ed Horn, Bureau of Toxic Substance Assessment, New York State Department of Health, National Risk Communication Conference II-23-25 (2001); Telephone Interview, Chee Choy, Portland Bureau of Environmental Services (Oct. 26, 2001); Audrey Chiang, Asian Pacific Environmental Network, *A Seafood Consumption Survey of the Laotian Community in West Contra Costa County, California* 36 (1998).

[355]See, e.g., Telephone Interview, Chee Choy, Portland Bureau of Environmental Services (Oct. 26, 2001); Telephone Interview, Diana Lee, Research Scientist, California Department of Health Services (Oct. 26, 2001).

[356]Chee Choy, Project Manager, Columbia Slough Sediment Project, Bureau of Environmental Services, City of Portland, Oregon, *Comments on the NEJAC Draft Fish Consumption Report* 4 (Feb. 1, 2002) (The commenter notes that the comments are "based on my personal experiences and opinions as a first-generation immigrant working as a Project Manager for the Bureau of Environmental Services, City of Portland, on the Columbia Slough Sediment Project in Portland, Oregon. This statement does not necessarily reflect the opinions of the City of Portland.").

To best reach Hawaii's diverse multi-ethnic and indigenous Native Hawaiian populations about the risk of fish consumption, we recommend the following: Work through existing community health centers since they have existing outreach infrastructure. This is especially true for health centers in communities with a predominantly Native Hawaiian population and Hawaiian homestead communities; . . . Form partnerships with organizations that work with the same nationality and culture as those targeted, using grants and technical assistance . . . [357]

Again, this relationship cannot happen without the involvement of communities and tribes; to facilitate this involvement, financial support will often by critical.

In order to realize actual communication — that is, a *process* of respectful information *exchange* — agencies, in particular, need to work to enhance their skills as active, flexible, and open listeners. Relevant information may come in unexpected or non-conventional forms — in anecdote rather than empirical study, in a conversation rather than in an article in a peer-reviewed journal, in a narrative (such as the narratives gathered in this Report) rather than in a table or chart, or in an indirect or non-verbal form, rather than bluntly and directly. In many cases, these may indeed be the sources of the most valuable information.[358] Chee Choy, Project Manager for the Columbia Slough Sediment Project, Bureau of Environmental Services, Portland, Oregon, offers one such example:

In some traditional Asian cultures, and perhaps in other cultures as well, feedback may be communicated in indirect ways (e.g., reading between the lines, so to speak) because it is seen as impolite to disagree with you, or that giving you an honest but negative comment may mean a loss of face for you. This is where having built a relationship with a community will help you to identify verbal and non-verbal cues about an indirect comment and to seek an honest comment that you can understand. [359]

---

[357]Hawaii's Thousand Friends (Written Comments, March 11, 2002); accord, id. (noting that "the City of Portland has been contracting with the International Refugee Center of Oregon (IRCO) and the Hispanic Access Center to hire people who are from the Russian, Southeast Asian, and Hispanic communities to conduct fish advisory outreach to their respective communities.").

[358]See, e.g., Katharine J. Hornbarger, et al., *Targeted Audience Analysis: Recommendations for Effectively Communicating Toxic Fish Consumption Advisories to Anglers on the Detroit River* 14-18 (June, 1994) (discussing considerable benefits of "conversational interviewing" techniques).

[359]Chee Choy, Project Manager, Columbia Slough Sediment Project, Bureau of Environmental Services, City of Portland, Oregon, *Comments on the NEJAC Draft Fish Consumption Report* 5 (Feb. 1, 2002) (The commenter notes that the comments are "based on my personal experiences and opinions as a first-generation immigrant working as a Project Manager for the Bureau of Environmental Services, City of Portland, on the Columbia Slough Sediment Project in Portland, Oregon. This statement does not necessarily reflect the opinions of the City of Portland.").

Often, this approach will not be easy. Not only will it take time — time to sit down and visit, time to ask further questions in order to understand — but also real work.[360] There may be language barriers to hurdle, differences in communication styles to decipher and address, large cultural differences to bridge. "Public comment periods" or "breakout sessions" may not provide useful avenues for conversation from everybody's perspective. Similarly, public meetings held in hotels or convention centers may not provide a very familiar, welcoming or accessible (e.g., by walking or using public transportation) site for many from affected groups.[361] Sometimes, where the participants in a conversation come from radically different cultures or start with radically incompatible worldviews, there may never be complete understanding. But even if there are glimpses of understanding, the process itself is important (e.g., to building good relationships). Moreover, if the conversations are ongoing, understanding is likely to increase over time. For example, Josee Cung, Program Manager, Southeast Asian Program, Minnesota Department of Natural Resources, describes a collaborative effort with the Minnesota Department of Health and community leaders to design and implement culturally appropriate education regarding consumption of contaminated fish, which includes "education delivery" methods such as:

* *[Sessions in] anglers' homes, as a version of the storytelling tradition and often involving elders*

* *Day field trips that include bus travel to fishing sites, the education component followed by a hands-on session of actual fishing and fish cutting and preparation*

* *Several sessions have ended with a communal meal of the caught fish prepared jointly by instructors and students*

* *All activities are planned and take place under community sponsorship. Heads of community organizations promote and publicize the educational sessions and work with [the Department of Natural Resources] to recruit and enroll participants*[362]

Agencies not only need to hear information that comes to them in unexpected forms, but also need to be open to information that provides unexpected substance. Agencies should work

---

[360]See, e.g., Kerry Kirk Pflugh, Bureau Chief, Raritan Watershed, Division of Watershed Management, New Jersey Department of Environmental Protection, *National Risk Communication Conference, Proceedings Document*, "Community Outreach to At-Risk Urban Anglers: A Case Study in Risk Communication of Fish Consumption Advisories" II-36 (2001) (noting, among the "lessons learned:" "Be flexible, take time to visit, listen, and learn.").

[361]See, e.g., Chee Choy, Project Manager, Columbia Slough Sediment Project, Bureau of Environmental Services, City of Portland, Oregon, *Comments on the NEJAC Draft Fish Consumption Report* 5 (Feb. 1, 2002) (The commenter notes that the comments are "based on my personal experiences and opinions as a first-generation immigrant working as a Project Manager for the Bureau of Environmental Services, City of Portland, on the Columbia Slough Sediment Project in Portland, Oregon. This statement does not necessarily reflect the opinions of the City of Portland.").

[362]Josee N. Cung, Program Manager, Southeast Asian Program, Minnesota Department of Natural Resources, National Risk Communication Conference, Proceedings Document, II-52-53 (2001).

to accept information they don't (yet) know they need   e.g., the answer to the question that the member of an affected group *wishes* the agency had asked (because this is what is most important from her perspective), the community- or tribally- developed research agenda that frames the issues differently than the agency would. Agencies should work to take in (and redirect if necessary) information that appears to pertain to a related but different program or agency. Thus, in the context of fish consumption advisories, those in environmental agencies' fish advisory programs should work together with those in their water quality standards and clean up programs to ensure that the comments they hear   e.g., "clean up existing contamination so that advisories can be lifted"   get registered with those in relevant programs *as well as with those setting priorities among programs and efforts.* Similarly, those in health agencies should work together with those in environmental agencies to ensure that such comments get passed along and that there is a connection between relevant staff working to address the issues.[363]   While it is never easy to hear information that may require one to reevaluate current priorities, methods, or approaches, this reevaluation may be the key to efforts that are defensible as a matter of science and social science, acceptable from the perspective of communities and tribes, and, ultimately, effective as a matter of risk communication.

Involvement by affected groups is necessary as well because they, ultimately, are the ones who will bear the brunt of harms from contamination not addressed and communication not achieved. They, among all "stakeholders," are the ones who face the most immediate and often irreversible losses   it is not just a matter of being out a few dollars on the profit side of the ledger but a matter of their health and the health of their children, a matter of their culture, traditions, and deeply-held beliefs. Given what is at stake for affected communities and tribes, they should be among the first to learn about contamination and its possible effects for them, and they should be among the first involved in determining how to respond. Richard Brown, Coordinator, Black United Front explains, in the context of the low-income and largely African American community in Northeast Portland, Oregon that fishes in, swims in, and is affected by the contaminated Columbia Slough:

> *The things that happen to people are devastating. You know you don't recover from a lot of these things because we don't find out about them until they've really taken its toll. Those are concerns I've always had about the way people in low-income communities have been treated as fare as environmental issues go.*[364]

---

[363]Richard Greene, Delaware Department of Natural Resources and Environmental Control, for example, notes that Delaware is undertaking efforts to link fish advisories and water quality standards under the CWA's TMDL program, but comments that "state [water quality standards] program participants need to acquaint themselves with their fish advisory program counterparts and start a serious dialogue. They also need to establish common goals; improving water quality and lifting advisories can result from agency cooperation." *Proceedings of the National Forum on Contaminants in Fish* I-13 (2001).

[364]Videotape: The Water in Our Backyard (City of Portland, Bureau of Environmental Services).

Ticiang Diangson, Supervising Planning and Development Specialist and Environmental Justice Advocate, Seattle Public Utilities, observes:

> [I]t takes inordinate effort on the part of harmed communities to gain acknowledgment of the impact of the contamination and to get real-life implementation to solutions to the impact.

To the extent that research is conducted by and for communities and tribes, it can serve the additional important function of capacity building. This goal is important and an issue of environmental justice in and of itself, for both communities and tribes. And, to the extent that communities and tribes see that their concerns are shaping the research to be conducted, that the information gathered will be relevant from their perspective, and that their members stand to enhance their skills, knowledge and capacity in the process as opposed to merely providing information that enables others to enhance *their* skills, knowledge and capacity participation and trust are likely to be increased, and accuracy thereby enhanced.[365]

As noted in Chapter One in the context of research in general, funding is crucial to the ability of affected communities and tribes to be involved in research, including research about risk communication. This point is elaborated below, in Section 7.

Finally, it is important to note that there are considerable resources on which EPA and other agencies interested in improving risk communication with affected groups can draw resources that have been developed by or with the involvement of communities of color, low-income communities, tribes, and other indigenous peoples. Rather than attempt to repeat their work here, this Report refers to several of these sources: the National Environmental Justice Advisory Council Public Participation Plan; the National Environmental Justice Advisory Council Indigenous Peoples' Subcommittee, Recommendation on Environmental Health and Research Needs Within Indian Country and Alaska Native Villages; the Outreach Strategy developed as a part of EPA's Asian American and Pacific Islander Initiative; and the (Draft) Strategy on Limited English Proficiency.

2. Different Communities and Tribes, Differing Concerns and Needs

The term "affected groups" here includes a large and diverse array of groups, each of which consumes and uses fish, aquatic plants, and wildlife in differing cultural, traditional, religious, historical, economic, and legal contexts. It will be crucial for any risk communication effort to recognize, therefore, the diverse contexts, interests, and needs that characterize affected

---

[365]See, e.g., id. at 37 (noting that the survey planning team made connections with the Laotian Organizing Project's ongoing capacity building efforts regarding community health and safety, which motivated many community members to participate in the survey and explaining: "The planning team was originally hesitate about the perception commonly held by community members of outsiders taking information from the community without community people seeing the benefits of research. Linking the survey to a community based organization helped counter this perception.").

groups, including but not limited to groups with limited English proficiency; groups with limited or no literacy; low-income communities; immigrant and refugee communities; African-American communities, various Asian and Pacific Islander communities and subcommunities (e.g., Mien, Lao, Khmu, and Thaidum communities within the Laotian community in West Contra Costa, CA); various Hispanic communities and subcommunities (e.g., Caribbean-American communities in the Greenpoint/Williamsburg area of Brooklyn, NY); various Native Americans, Native Hawaiians, and Alaskan Natives (including members of tribes and villages, members of non-federally recognized tribes, and urban Native people). "Affected groups" also refers to subgroups within these larger groups, including but not limited to nursing infants; children; pregnant women and women of childbearing age; elders; traditionalists versus modernists in terms of practices that implicate fish consumption; and subgroups defined by geographical region.

EPA and other agencies have increasingly recognized this diversity and its relevance to fish consumption advisories and other risk communication efforts. For example, EPA, in particular, has recognized the diversity of Asian and Pacific Islander communities, and provides an "Asian American and Pacific Islander Primer" on its Asian American and Pacific Islander Initiative website.[366] This primer identifies Asian Americans as those with origins in one or more of 28 Asian nations, and Pacific Islanders as those with origins in one or more of 19 island nations.[367] EPA has undertaken a number of efforts as part of this initiative that attend to the diversity of this group.[368] Important among these efforts is an extensive Outreach Strategy.[369] Nonetheless, EPA and other agencies need to do more to attend to the myriad groups and subgroups affected by their work. Agencies' efforts, moreover, have been uneven, such that there are some groups and subgroups about which EPA and its counterparts still know relatively little. It should be noted, too, that the composition of the affected groups may be changing rapidly in some areas, such as cities that are ports of entry for immigrant and refugee groups or rural and other areas where particular groups have settled.[370] Thus ongoing and constant efforts are necessary to learn about and attend to the changing contours of affected groups and subgroups. These efforts are most usefully undertaken together with the affected groups themselves, who will often be able to alert non-members to nuances about which they would otherwise not have knowledge. Even laudable agency efforts to identify and address the needs of a non-majority group may be partial to the extent that they fail to appreciate the existence of other affected groups or subgroups. The

---

[366]U.S. Environmental Protection Agency, *Asian American and Pacific Islander Primer* available at www.epa.gov/aapi/primer.htm.

[367]Id.

[368]These efforts place EPA at the forefront of federal agencies in implementing Executive Order13216 (and its predecessor) on Increasing Opportunity and Improving Quality of Life of Asian Americans and Pacific Islanders.

[369]U.S. Environmental Protection Agency, Office of Administration and Resource Management, *Asian American and Pacific Islander Outreach Strategy.* (No. EPA-202-K-01-003) (September 2001) available at www.epa.gov/aapi/outreach.htm.

[370]See, e.g., Kerry Kirk Pflugh, Bureau Chief, Raritan Watershed, Division of Watershed Management, New Jersey Department of Environmental Protection, *National Risk Communication Conference, Proceedings Document,* "Community Outreach to At-Risk Urban Anglers: A Case Study in Risk Communication of Fish Consumption Advisories" II-32 (2001).

Laotian Organizing Project points, for example, to a state fish consumption warning sign at a popular fishing site in Richmond, CA written in English, Spanish, and Vietnamese and notes:

> *The Vietnamese language translation is useless to a predominantly Laotian population.*[371]

These different groups are likely to differ with respect to their concerns and needs relevant to risk communication. This is a crucial point. The risk communication literature, including Volume 4 of EPA's *Guidance for Assessing Chemical Contaminant Data for Use in Fish Advisories*, describes "needs assessment" or determining "what the audiences want and need to know" as an initial step in the risk communication process.[372] The answer to this question is likely to differ in important respects from group to group, and even from subgroup to subgroup. *The best   if not only   way to determine the concerns and needs of a particular group is to secure the involvement of group members in the process.* This involvement is crucial at every point in the risk communication process. It is especially important at the point of needs identification, if the resulting advisories and other communication efforts are to be relevant to the group   and if they are to be perceived by the group as being relevant.

The importance of affected group involvement at the point of identifying needs and defining a research agenda has been echoed by numerous communities and tribes. For example, consider the account of recent efforts by the Alaska Native Science Commission to this end as part of the Traditional Knowledge and Contaminants Project, by Pat Cochran, Executive Director:

> *The project objectives are, first of all, to use our own native ways of knowing, learning, and teaching to gather information. We held our own talking circles in our own communities. We did not send out survey forms. We didn't have people that had focus groups. We went and sat with our people for days at a time   laughing, singing, dancing, and eating a lot of food   because this is a part of what we all do. So, we could really gain the knowledge from our communities. Our communities, we understand, are the first observers of what happens on our land, to the people, in the air, in the water, and in the environment around us. Long before a researcher or scientist or anyone else enters the community, our people are the ones who perceive what happens every day, and also generationally over centuries and beyond from information that has come down from their people. We [are] providing grant opportunities to our communities and we are looking at developing a common research agenda that answers concerns and questions about our communities and not just somebody's Ph.D. dissertation topic. And we are also developing a database. We held regional meetings all across the state of Alaska*[373]

---

[371]Laotian Organizing Project, *Fighting Fire with Fire* 5 (2001).

[372]See, e.g., *National Risk Communication Conference, Proceedings Document* 14 (2001); U.S. Environmental Protection Agency, *Guidance for Assessing Chemical Contaminant Data for Use in Fish Advisories, Volume IV: Risk Communication* 3 (1995).

[373]Patricia Cochran, Executive Director, Alaska Native Science Foundation, *National Risk Communication Conference, Proceedings Document* II-20 (2001).

3. Message Content

What constitutes appropriate and relevant message content is likely to differ from group to group. General, "one-size-fits-all" recommendations, therefore, are likely to be unuseful. Rather, the important point is that content that is appropriate and relevant to a particular affected group cannot be determined apart from the involvement of members of that group. In addition to local knowledge, group members will often have extensive expertise in message development and community outreach for their particular community or tribe. Their involvement in every aspect of content development and advisory design is indispensable.

Several considerations are relevant. Advisory content should be culturally appropriate from the perspective of the particular affected group or subgroup. As documented in Part A., above, it may be culturally inappropriate to include various recommendations to eliminate or reduce fish consumption, or to alter practices including procurement of fish, species and parts consumed, and preparation methods. Here, there are likely to be vast differences among affected groups as to what is and is not acceptable. Advisory content thus needs to be developed in a manner that is respectful of these differences. Involvement by members of the particular affected group is, again, crucial.

Advisory content should address the needs identified by the particular affected community. This should include the needs of any subgroups within the larger group, such as nursing infants; children; pregnant women and women of childbearing age; elders; traditionalists versus modernists in terms of practices that implicate fish consumption; and subgroups defined by geographical region. Other needs, too, may emerge as important to a particular group. For example, according to the summary of the important themes that emerged from the breakout group designated "Cultural Enclaves Native American and Other Cultural and Traditional Communities:"

> *Fish advisories should contain information on the nature and sources of the contamination so that the affected community is empowered to take action to reduce pollution source and clean up existing contaminated sites or obtain financial compensation for the loss of the natural resources.*[374]

To address the needs of some affected groups, advisories should emphasize the health and cultural benefits of eating fish or of participating in particular practices.

Advisories should be provided in the language(s) of the affected communities, groups, or peoples. Many members of affected groups are limited-English proficient; some, especially recent immigrants and refugees, may have no English. For example, EPA reports that "[a]n estimated 40-50% of [Asian American and Pacific Islanders] are limited-English proficient."[375] Many agencies have recently worked to provide language-appropriate warnings (perhaps as a result of

---

[374]*National Risk Communication Conference, Proceedings Document* I-11 (2001).
[375]U.S. Environmental Protection Agency, *Asian American and Pacific Islander Primer* available at www.epa.gov/aapi/primer.htm.

studies showing a particular group's lack of awareness of advisories, as was the case on the Lower Fox River, where Wisconsin recently posted signs in English and Hmong), and there has been considerable progress in this regard. For example, Chee Choy, Project Manager for the Columbia Slough Sediment Project, Bureau of Environmental Services, Portland, Oregon, recounts the challenges and ultimate success   in important part because of the partnership between the City and the various affected groups   of one such effort:

> *A committee comprising people from various community organizations (such as [Environmental Justice Action Group] EJAG, [International Refugee Center of Oregon] IRCO, Urban League, Coalition of Black Men, Lutheran Family Services Center, Russian Oregon Social Services, Confederated Tribes, etc.) helped the City of Portland to rewrite the technical fish advisory brochure originally written by the Oregon Health Division. This process was challenging because of the differences in opinion among the various communities regarding the usage of appropriate words in the advisory. While many committee members did not object to literally translating the word "DANGER," which was stamped across a picture of a carp, into their respective languages, the Russian community representatives strongly insisted on using "CAUTION" rather than "DANGER." After much deliberation, the committee reached a compromise to use the word "CAUTION" [and translate the advisory into six appropriate languages].[376]*

Even where agencies have made progress, however, they may have yet to identify and address the needs of all the relevant communities for language-appropriate advisories. Recall the Laotian Organizing Project's dismay when a state fish consumption warning sign at a popular fishing site in Richmond, CA was written in English, Spanish, and Vietnamese: *"The Vietnamese language translation is useless to a predominantly Laotian population."*[377] Similarly, Hawaii's Thousand Friends recommends that agencies:

> *Partner with local groups in Hawai'i to create information sheets/brochures in the Hawaiian language for distribution in immersion schools.[378]*

Advisories should be designed to account for limited literacy or illiteracy in the affected group. Some groups come from a tradition of orality.[379] They may not have a written language or may not be literate in their language to the extent it has been written down. Or they may be

---

[376]Chee Choy, Project Manager, Columbia Slough Sediment Project, Bureau of Environmental Services, City of Portland, Oregon, *Comments on the NEJAC Draft Fish Consumption Report* 5 (Feb. 1, 2002) (The commenter notes that the comments are "based on my personal experiences and opinions as a first-generation immigrant working as a Project Manager for the Bureau of Environmental Services, City of Portland, on the Columbia Slough Sediment Project in Portland, Oregon. This statement does not necessarily reflect the opinions of the City of Portland.").

[377]Laotian Organizing Project, *Fighting Fire with Fire* 5 (2001).

[378]Hawaii's Thousand Friends (Written Comments, March 11, 2002).

[379]See, e.g., id. ("The Native Hawaiian culture is an oral culture, so written information sheets and/or brochures will not always reach the intended audience, and more culturally sensitive methods should be developed.").

resistant to reducing communication to writing, preferring instead to give and receive information orally. Some groups have had less formal education, such that some of their members may be illiterate. In all of these cases, advisories should not rely on written words, but on devices such as spoken words, demonstration, or graphics.

Advisories should be accessible. They should use words that are understandable to the particular affected group; they should avoid jargon. To the extent possible, they should use short, manageable sentences. They should employ visual aids such as charts, pictures, models, posters, and hands-on demonstrations. Kristine Wong, the former Project Director of the Seafood Consumption Information Project, which focused on "conducting community-based research, education, outreach, and advocacy on the issue of contaminated fish consumption in San Francisco Bay," observes:

> *[M]any terms used frequently in health warnings need to be changed to reflect the common language of those who fish for food. For example, the term "sportfish" is used in the San Francisco Bay health advisory, yet those who catch and eat bay fish do not interpret the term "sportfish" as the fish that they themselves consume on a regular basis. During our regular visits to the fishing piers we conducted an informal survey to see if people actually understood that "sportfish" applied to all the fish that were being caught in the bay. Most interpreted the term "sportfish" to be the jumbo-sized fish caught on fishing boats, confirming our suspicions.[380]*

As Hawaii's Thousand Friends urges:

> *Use the local name of the fish in any outreach.[381]*

Although, in order to be sufficiently informative, advisories will need to convey complex information (e.g., about risk, contaminants' health effects, sources of contamination), there are more and less accessible ways to do this. Daisy Carter, Project AWAKE, Coatopa, Alabama, explains:

> *We believe enough books, pamphlets, policies, and manuals have been written. We have become a paper-filled society to the limit. But the question is, who is reading this material? Most people and especially the impacted communities do not take the time to read these large manuals; yet this is the method EPA and states use to get their information out. This is not the best approach to reach these communities. When asked what is being done, the reply is, "well, we have this book." What is the problem? Document upon document, volume upon volume is available, waiting to be read and complied with."*

---

[380]Kristine Wong, Former Project Director, Seafood Consumption Information Project, *Comments to the National Environmental Justice Advisory Council* Vol III-65-67 (Annual Meeting Transcript) (Dec. 4, 2001).

[381]Hawaii's Thousand Friends (Written Comments, March 11, 2002).

Finally, advisories should be designed to facilitate the two-way exchange that is the hallmark of good risk communication. *Importantly, as many affected groups have noted, advisories need to make available information about the nature, extent, and sources of the contamination that is giving rise to the advisory.* Thus, at a minimum, they should include contact information for the appropriate agencies, tribal government bodies and/or community groups, so that there is a place to lodge comments, ask questions, or obtain further information. Posted signs, for example, often leave those affected with unanswered questions.[382] Advisories should also provide additional relevant information, including information about the nature, extent, and sources of contamination that would enable those affected to participate not only in risk communication efforts but also in risk assessment and risk management decisions. Joanne Bonnar Prado, of the Washington Department of Health, emphasizes just this perspective:

> *[O]ne of the things that I've learned . . . is that we need to incorporate really thoroughly issues of source and where the sources [of contamination] are coming from . . . We understand that, [but] we do not talk about it much within our – or at all within our – health communications about source and source reduction. . . . So supplying information about sources, source reduction that individuals and communities and governments and all the various strategies that can be used on a local, statewide, and worldwide basis to reduce mercury – and this would apply to really all contaminants I would think – is really appropriate for this particular issue.[383]*

4. Medium

What constitutes an effective and appropriate medium for conveying the message will vary from group to group. Sometimes, it will be most effective to try to reach people via multiple media routes. Again, general "one-size-fits-all" recommendations are likely to be unuseful. Again, members of the affected group will possess valuable knowledge about the best medium from their perspective, and should therefore be involved in choices among media.

Several observations can be made. The medium chosen should take into account the habits and customs of the affected groups; it should take into account the access enjoyed by the affected groups. There has been some recent work identifying different media sources as more or less likely to be used or preferred by various affected groups.[384] For example, of those in the Laotian communities in West Contra Costa County who had heard of the health warning in place

---

[382]See, e.g., John M. Cahill, Director, Bureau of Community Relations, New York State Department of Health, *National Risk Communication Conference, Proceedings Document* II-43-44 (2001).

[383]Joanne Bonnar Prado, Washington State Department of Health, *Comments to the National Environmental Justice Advisory Council* Vol III-13 (Annual Meeting Transcript) (Dec. 4, 2001).

[384]See, e.g., John M. Cahill, Director, Bureau of Community Relations, New York State Department of Health, *National Risk Communication Conference, Proceedings Document* II-45-49 (2001) (presenting an extensive assessment of the advantages and disadvantages of twelve different categories of media/formats for various audiences, and cataloging available community channels and potential partners).

for San Francisco Bay fish, nearly 60% had heard of it through television news, 37.8% though word of mouth from friends and family, 18.9% via signs at various piers, and 14.4% through the newspaper; others had heard of the advisory though church, a local community-based organization, school, the doctor's office, and the welfare office.[385] Many members of affected communities of color, low-income communities, tribes, and indigenous peoples do not have access to the Internet as a means of apprising themselves of current advisories posted on agencies' websites. According to John Cahill, Director, Bureau of Community Relations, New York State Department of Health:

> *Last year, 56 percent of Americans used the Internet. However, only 23 percent of African Americans had Internet access, compared to 46 percent of White households. A majority, 82 percent, of Americans earning $75,000 or more had access, compared to only 38 percent of those earning less than $30,000.*[386]

Some of those affected may not have a telephone, and so cannot readily call numbers listed on signs or in pamphlets. To the extent information is distributed by agencies or others who give out fishing licenses, Native Americans and others who are not required to obtain a license to fish will not receive information distributed in this way; neither will those who for any number of reasons simply haven't obtained a license. John Cahill points out, for example, that a recent survey of anglers along New York's Hudson River revealed that only 57.5% of them had licenses; and a series of focus groups among Latino anglers in Buffalo found that only about half of them were licensed.[387]

The medium chosen should make advisory information easy to locate and access. Some current advisories may require several steps to locate and access (e.g., the need to consult a fishery regulations book, as in Maine; the need to write to the Department of Natural Resources or to go to local offices or state parks (or on-line), as in Wisconsin; the need to sort through fairly complex information, as in Michigan), which steps impose greater hurdles for those whose educational background or financial resources do not afford them the tools to navigate governmental bureaucracies.

Here again, agencies are making strides although there is work yet to do, and agencies need to ask those affected what would work for them.

5. Implementation

Members of affected communities and tribes will often be particularly well-positioned to take the lead in implementing the advisory and outreach strategy that has been developed by and for their group. Members of affected groups will be active in or aware of community

---

[385]Audrey Chiang, Asian Pacific Environmental Network, *A Seafood Consumption Survey of the Laotian Community in West Contra Costa County, California* 30 (1998).

[386]John M. Cahill, Director, Bureau of Community Relations, New York State Department of Health, *National Risk Communication Conference, Proceedings Document* II-43 (2001).

[387]Id. at II-42-43.

organizations, churches and other religious organizations, clubs, schools, and other entities that could play a role in getting the message out and facilitating risk communication. Members of affected groups will likely know precisely which community festivals, ceremonies, or events are likely to be well-attended and appropriate venues for outreach. For example, Detroiters Working for Environmental Justice not only prepared a pamphlet, together with the Lake Erie Binational Public Forum, directed at those eating fish from Lake Erie, the Detroit River, and the Rouge River, but they also work to distribute the pamphlet at local health fairs.[388] Members of affected groups will often be able to put together creative ideas for outreach   a product of their knowledge of norms in the community or tribe; their on-the-ground connections; their shared experience   especially, shared practices exposing them to environmental risks; and their involvement in prior organizing efforts.

Implementation by members of affected groups may also facilitate environmental justice along multiple dimensions. In addition to capacity-building, discussed below, looking to affected groups for implementation may enable them to dovetail efforts regarding fish consumption with other health and environmental outreach efforts (e.g., regarding possible contaminants in breast milk, regarding the value of Native foods in countering diabetes, or regarding nutrition in general) and/or other community-building efforts   efforts that may already be well-established, which would in turn enhance the likelihood that data about fish consumption practices would be complete and accurate, and that advisories regarding these practices would be received. For example, the Asian Pacific Organizing Network explains, in the context of its survey of Laotian communities in West Contra Country, California:

> Active participation by community leaders who are recognized and respected in the community brings trust and credibility to a survey that could otherwise be seen as intrusive. In this survey project, community leaders made the initial contact with people in the community, explained the goals of the survey to participants, and answered any questions and allayed any fears that people may have. Such collaborative work helped establish important relationships between community leaders and APEN's Laotian Organizing Project (LOP) as a young, emerging organization within the community.

> Organizationally, APEN is committed to working with youth, in order to foster new leadership within the community. Therefore, 'survey teams' of youth and established community leaders carried out the survey together.[389]

Agencies, together with affected groups, should consider shifting current approaches to outreach so that it is primarily grassroots, community-based organizations and groups that do the outreach in their respective communities. Where this is appropriate, these groups should be funded to take on this responsibility. For example, they could be hired as contractors to the

---

[388]Telephone Interview with Michelle Shewmaker, Detroiters for Environmental Justice (Oct. 26, 2001); Detroiters Working for Environmental Justice and Lake Erie Binational Public Forum, *A Family's Guide to Eating Fish from the Detroit Area* (pamphlet).

[389]Audrey Chiang, Asian Pacific Environmental Network, *A Seafood Consumption Survey of the Laotian Community in West Contra Costa County, California* 8 (1998).

relevant agency. Or, they could receive grants to conduct this work. As Marianne Yamaguchi, Director, Santa Monica Bay Restoration Project, notes, some agencies and others in Southern California are already taking this approach, with benefits not only in terms of effective and appropriate implementation but also in terms of capacity building.[390] Funding and capacity-building are discussed further below, in Section 7.

6. Evaluation

Affected group involvement is critical to evaluating the success of risk communication efforts in general and consumption advisory programs in particular. This involvement is important at every point of evaluation, but is particularly necessary to evaluation in the early stages of risk communication (what *Volume IV* and the risk communication literature term "formative evaluation") and at the point of assessing whether the objectives of risk communication efforts have been met (what *Volume IV* and the risk communication literature term "summative evaluation"). Given the potential for differences in the definitions of "effectiveness" adopted by agencies and various affected groups   and the likelihood that differences in objectives would flow therefrom   it will be important for those affected to be able to ensure that *their* perspectives are being incorporated into any evaluations.

Affected groups will be able to work together with agencies to determine the extent to which it is useful to focus evaluation on particular "products" (e.g., number of radio spots, number of pamphlets distributed, numbers of health fairs visited), on outcomes indicating awareness (e.g., awareness of advisories' content and recommendations), on behavioral outcomes (e.g., extent to which consumption levels are reduced so that they fall within recommendations, extent to which species consumed changes from less safe to safer species, extent to which preparation methods change so that exposure to contaminants is avoided), or on more broadly crafted outcomes (e.g., increased knowledge within effective group of contamination, its sources, and related regulatory efforts, increased involvement by community members in decision making regarding risk from contaminated aquatic ecosystems, improved trust and enhanced relationships among agencies and affected communities and tribes, improved health in the affected group).

Agencies should ensure that "evaluation" includes assessment not only of the particular advisory program or outreach effort, but of its risk communication efforts more generally. Affected groups can usefully aid agencies in evaluating their risk communication efforts, and in evaluating connections between risk communication and risk assessment and management. For example, related to the issue of two-way communication, consider the question: How should agencies *register* the responses of those affected?[391] For example, if an affected group receives and understands the information contained in an advisory but nonetheless rejects its advice that fish consumption be reduced, how should this response be incorporated into agencies' policy choices regarding the role of fish consumption advisories? How, in the first place, should agencies ensure that they are correctly interpreting the responses of affected groups   have the

[390]E-mail Communication, Marianne Yamaguchi, Director, Santa Monica Bay Restoration Project (Oct. 23, 2001).
[391]Catherine A. O'Neill, *Risk Avoidance and Environmental Justice* (forthcoming).

practices remained the same because those affected do not understand the advisories; because they understand but do not believe or agree with the advisories' accounts of the contamination or its health effects; because they understand and in some sense agree with the advisories' accounts of the contamination or its health effects, but nonetheless cannot for economic and/or for traditional, cultural, or religious reasons change their practices? The need for "interpreters" from within the relevant community, group or tribe seems clear. And to the extent that those who decline to "comply" with advisories should be taken to be lodging a kind of protest   that is, to the extent that noncompliance itself should be taken as an expressive act, indicating resistance to agencies' reliance on risk avoidance rather than risk reduction[392]   how will this view be taken into account when agencies decide how much to rely on advisories versus how much to focus on cleanup and prevention?

Finally, agencies should ensure that "evaluation" includes vigilant and careful re-assessment of the health of the resources that are the subject of advisory or closure, so that they are opened again for fishing and advisories are lifted as soon as is appropriate. This may be a particular issue in the case of shellfisheries closed due to the presence of acute contaminants, whose short-term life span means that re-certification may be appropriate in fairly short order.[393] This is especially important given communities' and tribes' reliance on these resources for economic, subsistence, and other reasons. Of course, agencies will need to be sure that fish are safe for consumption before doing so, and this implicates current limitations in agencies' ability to measure the presence of contaminants. For example, current methods are unable to detect below certain levels for some persistent and bioaccumulative contaminants (e.g., dioxins)   yet even very small quantities may have an effect on human and environmental health. Thus, even if it can be said that contaminant levels in a particular river stretch have been reduced to non-detectable levels, this may not mean that they have been reduced to safe levels   only that current measurement methods are at their limit. To remedy this gap in agencies' ability to determine the safety of fish for human consumption, agencies need to conduct research to improve current measurement abilities. In the meantime, agencies need to inform affected groups of the detection limit issue (and other relevant issues) if an agency chooses to alter or lift advisories under such circumstances.

7. Funding and Capacity-Building

As noted above, capacity-building or capacity-augmentation is in and of itself an environmental justice issue, for both communities and tribes. Involvement by those affected at each point in the risk communication process would go far toward enabling those affected to shape the process so that it is not only relevant and appropriate, but also useful and empowering from the perspective of the community or tribe. In addition to the aspects of capacity-building discussed above, affected groups will be able to identify other, current needs in this regard.

---

[392]Id.

[393]Telephone Interview, Jay Zischke, Marine Fish Program Manager, Suquamish Tribe (Oct. 17, 2001).

Among the issues that have been identified is the need to ensure that the fruits of its work are returned to the affected group. The information gathered   e.g., as part of baseline assessment of fish consumption rates and practices, as part of evaluation processes, or otherwise   needs to get back to the affected group for them to use for their own purposes. Hopefully, the involvement of the affected group from the outset of the process means that its needs have been identified and the results meet those needs. Nonetheless, the information may be valuable to the group in the longer term, as a foundation for other projects, as historical documentation of practices at a particular point in time, or for any number of reasons. In some cases, a community or tribe may want to be custodian of the information about their group, to ensure that they have some amount of control over the ends to which it may be put in the future. Whatever the reasons, it may be important to capacity-building and empowerment that the information about a particular group be returned to that group. Daisy Carter, Project AWAKE, Coatopa, Alabama, highlights communities' lack of empowerment when information is gathered *from* them, but not necessarily for and with them:

> *EPA knows all the problems that exist in every community, state and country. EPA is aware of what is wrong. They know who is impacted by the various contaminants and to what degree citizens are unfairly treated. They know what injustices are being done. They also impose fines upon various companies. It is the policy of these companies and EPA to keep citizens who are at risk seeking and searching for answers and assistance to eliminate their problems and suffering. EPA wants to keep citizens, people of color, and impacted communities talking and asking for help so that EPA can stay informed and keep abreast of the status of the burdens and injustices in these communities.*

In addition, as noted in Chapter 1 in the context of research in general, funding is crucial to the ability of affected communities and tribes to be involved in research, including research about risk communication. Although community and tribal members have considerable expertise to offer, they often have minimal or no funding to support their work. *To a person*, community members, tribal members, inter-tribal organization staff, and state and local agency representatives who work with affected groups stressed the importance of adequate funding. Diane Lee, a research scientist with the California Department of Health Services who has worked extensively with communities as part of the Palos Verdes Fish Contamination Outreach and Education Project and other studies in the San Francisco Bay area, is emphatic:

> *I cannot underscore enough the need to provide funding to affected communities so that they can participate fully in every aspect of the research process, from needs assessment to dissemination of the results. Funding, moreover, needs to be provided on an on-going, rather than one-time, basis.*[394]

Again, EPA and other agencies have often provided much-needed support. For example, the EPA's Office of Water, together with Minnesota's Department of Health, recently sponsored the National Risk Communication Conference to bring together representatives of federal, tribal,

---

[394]Telephone Interview, Diana Lee, Research Scientist, California Department of Health Services (Oct. 26, 2001).

state, and local health and environmental agencies, affected communities, tribes and Alaskan Native villages, and other interested in risk communication about contaminated fish. Importantly, EPA secured funding for several community, tribal, and village representatives who otherwise likely would not have been able to attend. This was an impressive undertaking that produced a rich exchange and a source of information and experience that should continue to advance deliberation in this area. EPA also recently gave a small grant to the California Department of Health Services "to explore and develop methods of communicating with diverse communities about fish contamination issues" in San Francisco Bay, which CDHS was able to turn around and share with community organizations working on the issue.[395] As California Department of Health Services explains:

> Our participatory approach aims to build local partnerships through collaboration with community-based organizations (CBOs) and local agencies that serve fishing populations. A limited number of stipends will be provided to selected groups to assist them in developing and pilot testing educational materials or activities.[396]

Affected communities and tribes have commended EPA's efforts to this end.

However, they noted that the need for funding to enable communities and tribes fully to be involved in research and decisions affecting risk assessment, management, and communication far outstrips the funding that has been so far made available. Funding needs to be regularized and allocated as a part of agencies' budgets, so that affected groups can be assured on-going support for their efforts (rather than piecemeal or one-time funding). The participation of community groups is vital to the success of agencies' risk communication efforts; agencies should not count on community groups to donate their time and expertise when others important to risk communication efforts (e.g., agency staff and contractors) are compensated and supported. Among other things, agencies should contract with grassroots community groups to undertake outreach these groups will be uniquely positioned to provide this service to agencies and they should be compensated for doing so. Agencies should also combine financial support with technical and other in-kind support. Here again, agencies and affected groups can be creative, as some have demonstrated. For example, as part of its Palos Verdes Fish Contamination Outreach and Education Project, California Department of Health Services held a free "train the trainer" workshop for community-based organizations, agencies, and others, during which participants were trained in conducting their own educational programs for fishing populations.[397] After the

---

[395]California Department of Health, Environmental Investigations Branch, *San Francisco Bay Fish Consumption Outreach and Education Project* (factsheet available from California Department of Health Services).

[396]Id.

[397]California Department of Health, Environmental Investigations Branch, *Palos Verdes Shelf Outreach and Education Project on Fish Contamination Issues* (factsheet available from California Department of Health Services).

training, community-based organizations received a stipend to develop and implement a pilot educational activity for the community they serve. The type of activity was determined by the community-based organization and included a wide range of activities (e.g., organizing a table at a health fair, conducting a workshop, putting together a media kit).[398]

---

[398]Id.

CHAPTER IV: AMERICAN INDIAN TRIBES AND ALASKAN NATIVE VILLAGES

In determining how EPA should improve the quality, quantity, and integrity of aquatic ecosystems, what special considerations should EPA take into account when protecting the health and safety of federally recognized tribal governments and their members?

American Indian tribes and Alaskan Native villages and their members ("AI/ANs") share many of the concerns explored in the preceding chapters. However, the particular circumstances of AI/ANs also warrant separate discussion. Tribes' political and legal status is unique among affected groups. Tribes are governmental entities, recognized as possessing broad inherent authority over their members, territories and resources. As sovereigns, federally recognized tribes have a government-to-government relationship with the federal government and its agencies, including the EPA. Tribes' unique legal status includes a trust responsibility on the part of the federal government. For many tribes, it also includes treaty rights. Other laws and executive commitments, too, shape the legal obligations owed to AI/AN tribes and villages and their members.

There are some 556 federally recognized tribal governments in the United States, including 223 Alaska Native villages.[399] At the time of the 1990 census, about 1.9 million AI/ANs lived in the United States.[400] In 1993, the Bureau of Indian Affairs estimated that 1.2 million AI/ANs lived within Indian country on lands reserved for their tribes as permanent homelands.[401] "Indian country," which includes reservations, dependent Indian communities, and Indian allotments, comprises approximately 53 million acres of land, much of which is found in remote areas of the nation.[402] The remaining AI/ANs live in urban areas and comprise a growing segment of the Native population.

---

[399]"Federally recognized" means that these tribes and groups have a special legal relationship with the United States. Additionally, a number of tribes and indigenous groups do not have federally recognized status, although some of these tribes are state-recognized or are in the process of seeking federal recognition.

[400]AI/ANs are among the fastest growing ethnic/minority populations in the nation. The 1990 census showed a 37.9% increase over the population of AI/ANs in the 1980 census. For additional facts and general information, see the Bureau of Indian Affairs' homepage at www.doi.gov/bia/aitoday/q and a.html.

[401]For additional facts and general information, see the Bureau of Indian Affairs' homepage at www.doi.gov/bia/aitoday/q and a.html.

[402]The term "Indian country" is defined by federal law as including "(a) all land within the limits of any Indian reservation under the jurisdiction of the United States Government, notwithstanding the issuance of any patent, and, including rights of way running through the reservation, (b) all dependent Indian communities . . . and (c) all Indian allotments, the Indian titles to which have not been extinguished, including rights-of-way running through the same." See 18 U.S.C. § 1151.

Part A of this chapter outlines the legal status of AI/ANs. Part B of this chapter addresses the particular issue of treaty rights. Part C of this chapter outlines issues particular to Alaska Natives. Finally, Part D examines tribes' susceptibilities and co-risk factors; while some of these will also be applicable to other affected groups, the particular combination discussed here is unique to AI/ANs.

A. LEGAL STATUS

Federally recognized Indian tribes possess a unique political and legal status that distinguishes them from all other ethnic and minority groups in the United States. Although subject to applicable federal law, tribes have long been recognized as separate sovereigns possessing broad inherent authority over their members and territories. As governments, the relationship between federally recognized tribes and the federal government is described as "government-to-government" and, in 1994 and 2000, President Clinton explicitly directed each federal agency to operate within this relationship[403] and to maintain it through meaningful consultation and coordination with tribes.[404] Among other things, the government-to-government relationship means that federal agencies may not treat Indian tribes as "interest groups" or simply as part of the general public.

The cornerstone of the government-to-government relationship is the federal government's trust responsibility to federally recognized Indian tribes to protect their status as self-governing entities and their property rights. The trust responsibility is based on treaties, statutes, executive orders, and the historical relations between the federal government and tribes. In practice, the trust responsibility gives rise to distinctive fiduciary obligations on the part of federal agencies that must be "exercised according to the strictest fiduciary standards."[405] The United States Supreme Court has stated that federal officials are "bound by every moral and equitable consideration to discharge the federal government's trust with good faith and fairness" when dealing with tribes.[406]

Also related to the trust doctrine is Congress' plenary power over Indian affairs. Under the plenary power doctrine, the federal government is vested by the Constitution with exclusive authority over relations with Indian tribes.[407] Because the power of Congress is exclusive, states

---

[403]See Executive Memorandum on Government-to-Government Relations with Native American Tribal Governments (Apr. 29, 1994).

[404]See Executive Order No. 13084 (May 14, 1998). On November 6, 2000, President Clinton issued a new order strengthening the policy on tribal consultation. See Executive Order No. 13175 (Nov. 6, 2000).

[405]Nance v. Environmental Protection Agency, 645 F.2d 701, 710 (9th Cir. 1981).
[406]United States v. Payne, 264 U.S. 446, 448 (1924).
[407]See Morton v. Mancari, 417 U.S. 535 (1974).

generally lack authority over Indian tribes and tribal members within Indian country, unless Congress has expressly delegated that authority to states.

Due to the special legal status of tribes, and because the jurisdictional rules applicable to Indian country left EPA unable to pursue its usual practice of delegating primary enforcement responsibility to states that so request, EPA developed special regulations and policies concerning environmental regulation on Indian reservations and the role to be played by tribal governments. On November 8, 1984, EPA adopted a formal policy, the "EPA Indian Policy for the Administration of Environmental Programs on Indian Reservations" ("Indian Policy"). The Indian Policy sets forth nine principles by which the EPA will pursue its objectives including, but not limited to EPA's commitment to work with tribes on a government-to-government basis, to recognize tribes as the primary decision-makers for environmental matters on reservation lands, to help tribes assume program responsibility for reservations, to remove existing legal and procedural impediments to tribal environmental programs, and to encourage tribal, state, and local government cooperation in areas of mutual concern. Following the adoption of the Indian Policy, every EPA Administrator since has reaffirmed the principles set forth therein. Most recently, on July 11, 2001, EPA Administrator Christine Todd Whitman again reaffirmed the Agency's commitment to the Indian Policy.

A major goal of the Indian Policy is to eliminate statutory and regulatory barriers to the assumption of federal environmental programs by Indian tribes. As originally enacted, most of the federal environmental laws mentioned tribes or Indian reservations and none provided for direct participation by tribal governments. To date, however, tribal amendments to four major federal environmental laws--the Safe Drinking Water Act, Clean Water Act, Clean Air Act, and Comprehensive Environmental Response, Compensation, and Liability Act--have been enacted.[408] Despite these amendments and the Indian Policy, federal funding for tribal environmental programs and environmental enforcement within Indian country has been inadequate and inequitable, particularly in light of the billions of federal dollars spent on state environmental efforts over the last three decades. While funding for tribal programs has increased substantially in recent years, inadequate funding for tribal programs is considered by many to be an environmental justice issue and also is one of the key factors impeding effective consultation with tribes due to the limited capacity of tribal environmental programs. As discussed further in Chapter 2, while some tribal governments are moving forward in participating under federal environmental programs, few tribes have actually been authorized by EPA to assume primary regulatory and enforcement responsibilities for these program on their reservations. Where tribes have not yet assumed these responsibilities, EPA remains responsible for implementing and enforcing the federal environmental laws within Indian country pursuant to these laws and the federal trust responsibility owed to tribes.

---

[408]See, generally, Jane Marx, Jana L. Walker, and Susan M.. Williams, *Tribal Jurisdiction Over Reservation Water Quality and Quantity*, 43 South Dakota Law Review 315 (1998).

As noted in Chapter 2, tribes may be involved as co-managers of cleanup and restoration efforts. For example, the Lower Elwha Klallam Tribe recently signed an agreement with federal and state agencies recognizing its role in overseeing cleanup of a contaminated (with dioxins and PCBs) area affecting important off-reservation resources.[409] The Menominee Indian Tribe of Wisconsin and the Oneida Tribe of Indians of Wisconsin are among the Natural Resource Trustees addressing cleanup and restoration of the Fox River and Green Bay.[410] In these roles, tribes will have environmental justice concerns of a different and often complex nature.

B. TREATY RIGHTS

Treaties preserve important tribal rights. "A treaty, including one between the United States and an Indian tribe, is essentially a contract between two sovereign nations."[411] The United States entered into more than 400 treaties with Indian tribes under which tribes typically gave up large parts of their aboriginal territories in exchange for explicit promises from the federal government. Because the United States received rights to land from the tribes, the United States Supreme Court has described a treaty as a grant of rights from the Indians with a reservation of all those rights not granted.[412] Thus, a treaty does not have to reserve expressly hunting and fishing rights within an Indian reservation for such rights to exist; rather, such on-reservation rights exist unless expressly given up by the tribe.[413] In many treaties, tribes expressly reserved certain rights in lands and waters outside their reservations. For example, today, many tribes possess treaty rights to fish, hunt, and gather at all "usual and accustomed" places. In 1871, Congress ended the practice of entering into treaties with Indian tribes, but subsequently engaged in the practice of ratifying agreements with tribes negotiated by the Executive Branch. While the United States Supreme Court has ruled that Congress has the power to break treaties with tribes, unless clear congressional intent exists to abrogate a treaty, a treaty continues in effect.[414]

C. ALASKA NATIVES

The term "tribe," and the recognition of a particular political and legal status that this term entails, applies to Alaska Native villages as well as to American Indian tribes in the forty-eight

---

[409]L. Harris, *Tribe Will Oversee Pulp Mill Cleanup*, Northwest Indian Fisheries Commission News 8 (Spring, 2000).
[410]U.S. Environmental Protection Agency, *Intergovernmental Partners Negotiate Fox River Interim Agreement* (factsheet, 2001).
[411]See Washington v. Washington State Commercial Passenger Fishing Vessel Assoc., 443 U.S. 658, 675 (1979).
[412]See United States v. Winans, 198 U.S. 371 (1905) ("In other words, the treaty was not a grant of rights to the Indians, but a grant of rights from them—a reservation of those not granted.")
[413]See Menominee Tribe of Indians v. United States, 391 U.S. 404 (1968).
[414]See United States v. Dion, 476 U.S. 734 (1986).

contiguous states.[415] Indeed, as noted above, of the 556 federally recognized tribal governments within the United States, 223 of these are Alaska Native villages. While several aspects of tribes' particular political and legal status are common to American Indian tribes and Alaska Native villages, there are also important differences. This section, therefore, briefly outlines the unique circumstances of Alaska Native villages in this regard.

Consistent with their status as federally recognized tribes, Alaska Native villages have a government-to-government relationship with the federal government and its agencies, including the EPA. The rights and responsibilities that flow from this relationship are described above, in Section A, and apply equally to Alaska Native villages. Among other things, under current federal law and policy, federal agencies are directed to operate within the government-to-government framework, and to consult with tribes, including Alaska Native villages, as sovereign entities.

The federal trust responsibility is similarly applicable to Alaska Native villages.[416] The trust responsibility requires the federal government and its agencies to uphold the highest fiduciary standards when its actions affect the well-being of Alaska Native villages, their property (including subsistence rights),[417] resources, and culture. The object of the trust responsibility is the furtherance of the self-determination and cultural integrity of tribes and Alaska Native villages.

However, there are also important differences between the legal, political, historical and other circumstances of Alaska Native villages and their members and those of tribes and their members in the lower forty-eight states. For example, Alaska Native villages and the United States government did not enter into any treaties. And, while Alaska Natives have been included by Congress in legislation generally applicable to American Indians,[418] Congress has also legislated separately with respect to Alaska Native villages and their members. Alaska Native land and subsistence rights, for example, are importantly affected by the Alaska Native Claims Settlement Act (ANSCA)[419] and by the Alaska National Interest Lands Conservation Act (ANILCA).[420] In addition, special recognition of and exceptions for Alaska Native subsistence rights have been

---

[415]See, e.g., *Noatak v. Hoffman*, 896 F.2d 1157 (9th Cir. 1990); *Native Village of Tyonek v. Puckett*, 890 F.2d 1054 (9th Cir. 1989); see generally, Eric Smith and Mary Kancewick, *The Tribal Status of Alaska Natives* 61 University of Colorado Law Review 455 (1990).

[416]*People of Togiak v. United States*, 470 F. Supp. 423 (D.D.C. 1979).

[417]Id.

[418]See, e.g., Indian Self-Determination Act, Public Law No. 93-638, 88 Stat. 2206 (codified in scattered sections of the United States Code; see especially 43 U.S.C. §§ 1601-1624; Indian Financing Act of 1974, 25 U.S.C. § 1452(c).

[419]43 U.S.C. §§ 1601-1628.

[420]16 U.S.C. §§ 3101-3133.

included in federal statutes and treaties concerned with protection of animals, birds, and their habitat, such as the Marine Mammal Protection Act[421] and the Endangered Species Act.[422]

The special circumstances of Alaska Native villages are also relevant to their ability to choose to accept responsibility for administering federal environmental statutes. For example, because the United States Supreme Court held in *Alaska v. Native Village of Venetie*,[423] that only one Indian "reservation" -- the Annette Island Reserve -- exists in Alaska and that land conveyed by the federal government to Alaska Native villages under ANCSA was not "Indian country," and because the language of the Clean Water Act recognizes the power of tribes to establish water quality standards throughout their "reservations," Alaska Native villages are unable to assume regulatory authority or to participate in the same manner or to the same extent under the Act as tribes located in the lower forty-eight states. Alaska Native villages and their members have also identified other hurdles particular to their efforts to manage (or co-manage) and to access resources that are important for subsistence uses. Important among these has been a historical lack of attention to, funding for, and technical assistance supporting the environmental management efforts of Alaska Native villages.

Finally, it is important to recognize that the particular historical, economic, ecological, and cultural circumstances of Alaska Native villages and their members give rise to several issues that are less likely to be of concern elsewhere. These circumstances range from Alaska's unique climates, including its Arctic climate;[424] to its historical military use by the U.S. Department of Defense and the continuing legacy of contamination at the hundreds of formerly- and currently-used defense sites;[425] to the exploitation of its wealth of mineral and petroleum resources and the

---

[421] 16 U.S.C. § 1371(b).

[422] 16 U.S.C. § 1539(e).

[423] 118 S. Ct. 948 (1998).

[424] See, e.g., Interagency Collaborative Paper, *Contaminants in Alaska: Is America's Arctic at Risk?* (issued by the U.S. Department of the Interior, U.S. Environmental Protection Agency, Alaska Department of Environmental Conservation, Alaska Department of Health and Social Services, University of Alaska Institute for Circumpolar Health Studies, Alaska Federation of Natives, Alaska Native Science Commission, Alaska Inter-Tribal Council, Native American Fish and Wildlife Society, Alaska Native Tribal Health Consortium, Alaska Community Action on Toxics, and North Slope Borough, September 2000). This paper describes the cold, northern Arctic as a sink for numerous environmental contaminants transported from elsewhere; notes the particular persistence of these contaminants in this environment, given the slower rate of breakdown in the colder climate; and citing POPs, as well as metals as among the contaminants of concern for Arctic fish, wildlife, and people. Id.

[425] Alaska hosts approximately 700 formerly-used defense sites, five military Superfund sites, and weapons testing ranges encompassing an area equal in size to the state of Kansas. These sites are contaminated with PCBs, dioxins, radioactive waste, and a variety of other pollutants resulting from the use of solvents, fuels, and chemical munitions. See, e.g., Pamela K. Miller, Director, Alaska Community Action on Toxics, Testimony to the National Environmental Justice Advisory Council, Dec. 4, 2001 (Written Testimony).

resulting environmental harms; to the remoteness and relative poverty of many of its rural villages, resulting, among other things, in the fact that only 40% of Alaska Native families have basic sanitation services such as piped drinking water and flush toilets, and more than half of these systems are rudimentary at best.[426] For example, Pamela K. Miller, Director, Alaska Community Action on Toxics, relates:

> *The north has become a hemispheric sink for persistent organic (POPs) . . . Many persistent pollutants originate from thousands of miles away, traveling northward via wind and ocean currents and in the bodies of migratory animals. . . . Northern ecosystems, wildlife, and people are the ultimate repositories for persistent pollutants. . . . Cold-water bodies of the Arctic are important sinks [for example] for lindane. Levels of [lindane] in seawater are an order of magnitude higher in the Arctic than in tropical and subtropical regions. . . . Lindane was among the organochlorine contaminants detected in blood samples from Alaska Native women participating in a pilot study conducted [in 1996].*[427]

June Gologergen Martin, Coordinator, National Environmental Health & Justice, St. Lawrence Island Project, explains:

> *Whanga aatqa yupiigestun Yatgawen, Sevungami allgeqawunga. Hello, my name is June Gologergen Martin. My Siberian Yupik name is Yatgawen. I was born on St. Lawrence Island in the village of Savoonga, Alaska. As a Siberian Yupik native, I grew up going to North East Cape during the summer months in the mid-1960s. . . .*

> *We live a subsistence lifestyle. We are rich in our culture; our Siberian Yupik language is very strong. Our families still hunt walrus, seals, bowhead whales, halibut, crabs, different species of seabirds and fish in the Bering sea, lakes, and rivers, like the Suqi River in North East Cape . . . We also gather edible plants, roots, seabird eggs, marine plants and seaweed.*

> *During the earlier years of my life, there were talks of not consuming fish and wildlife and edible plants around the North East Cape military site. These warnings came from our elders and leaders. We were told not to subsistence fish in the Suqi River at North East Cape. We were confused and alarmed about this warning from our elders and leaders. If we cannot consume our subsistence fish, marine mammals and other plants due to contamination by military debris left behind, our spirit slowly dies within us!*

---

[426]See, e.g., Videotape: *The Forgotten America -- Alaska's Rural Sanitation Problem* (The Media Support Center for the Alaska Department of Environmental Conservation).

[427]Pamela K. Miller, Director, Alaska Community Action on Toxics, Testimony to the National Environmental Justice Advisory Council, Dec. 4, 2001 (Written Testimony).

Our uncles and possibly our fathers and others who have spent time at North East Cape military site began dying of cancer-related illnesses. Our elders knew why this was happening. They knew that whatever contaminants the military left behind might have been the cause of these deaths. . . .

[We] urge NEJAC to review information on St. Lawrence Island regarding North East Cape and the Native Village of Gambell military clean-up project and recommend that St. Lawrence Island be considered a Superfund site so that there is complete restoration . . . [428]

Rosemary Ahtuangaruak, Native Village of Nuiqsut, explains:

I am from the Native Village of Nuiqsut on the north slope of Alaska, 60 miles west of Prudhoe bay and 130 miles southeast of barrow. We are an Inupiat village, which relies upon the subsistence resources for our survival. The land, sea, and air provide for us and we, in turn, protect them . . .

The long dark months of winter can have many starvation moons until the natural resources of subsistence return. The concerns now are not only can we put enough away but if the supply is safe to consume. . . . [O]ur attempts to harvest are coming back empty and our nets are getting few fish. . . .

The national need for energy is ignoring the need we have for subsisting. We are going without multiple subsistence resources for the benefit of our nation's energy need. There are not means for us to address the assault on our resources, which our elders have taught us to use. The recognition of our loss is belittled in the many public meetings, which come to our village as a public process without the incorporation of our concerns into the proper framework to address them. . . .

The people of Nuiqsut rely upon the fish harvesting and the last six years have seen the devastation of our fish stocks. . . . I feed three families with the harvesting I do and they go without as well as me. I eat fish or whale two times a day and 5-7 days out of the

---

[428] June Gologergen Martin, Coordinator, National Environmental Health & Justice, St. Lawrence Island Project, Testimony to National Environmental Justice Advisory Council, Dec. 4, 2001 (Written Testimony); accord, Kendra Zamzow, National Institute of Environmental Health Sciences Grant Researcher, Testimony to National Environmental Justice Advisory Council, Dec. 4, 2001 (Written Testimony)(noting that the U.S. Department of Health and Human Services disseminated a fish consumption advisory urging that no fish from the Suqi River be eaten, given PCB contamination in even very small (4" long) fish, and pointing out that the Suqi and its fish and wildlife are also contaminated with five PAHs (polycyclic aromatic hydrocarbons), dissolved arsenic, lead, and zinc).

week. I have to dig through the ice and in three days, I got only 1-2 fish. This cannot feed my family as well as the extended family members. We are concerned about the quality of the fish, as the meat has changed, they are yellow and not as fat as usual, and they have a bitter taste. Every fisherman in our village has faced the same hardships. We depend on the healing qualities of this resource and now it is being considered a bad thing. The social, economical, cultural, and medicinal [aspects] of our resources are needed to sustain our health . . .[429]

Dr. Delores Garza, Alaska Native Science Commission, explains:

In rural Alaska we have many communities that are still relegated to the "honey bucket." That means that there is no sewer system. The sewage goes into a five-gallon white-lined bucket that's lined with a garbage bag. It goes out to the dump and it's thrown out on the surface. In Southwestern Alaska, primarily in the Yupik area where you have communities built in areas that you might consider bogs, they have high water tables. The sewage is leaching and is contaminating the fresh water source. . . . So you have communities that now may have 70, 80 percent unemployment trying to find the gas money to take their boat upriver or to take their four-wheeler farther out to get fresh water, and while Alaska has worked to reduce the number of communities that have to rely on this honey bucket system, that is still a big issue in many communities in Southwestern Alaska.[430]

Thus, while Alaska Native villages and their members may share many of the concerns articulated by various affected groups throughout this Report, it is critical that EPA and other agencies listen and attend to the particular issues articulated by Alaska Native villages and their members. And, here as elsewhere, this will mean recognizing that there will often be differences *among* the concerns of various Alaska Native villages.

D. TRIBES' UNIQUE SUSCEPTIBILITIES AND CO-RISK FACTORS

Commonly cited statistics all seem to agree that AI/AN's economic wealth, public health, and education are the worst of any group in the nation. Poverty and unemployment rates among AI/ANs are the highest for any ethnic group in the country, and education, per capita income, and home ownership are among the lowest.[431] One out of every three AI/ANs lives

---

[429]Rosemary Ahtuagaruak, Native Village of Nuiqsut, Testimony to the National Environmental Justice Advisory Council, Dec. 4, 2001 (Written Testimony).

[430]Delores Garza, Alaska Native Science Commission, Testimony to the National Environmental Justice Advisory Council, Dec. 4, 2001 (Annual Meeting Transcript, Vol III-89).

[431]See, e.g., *National Gambling Impact Study Commission Report*, "Native American Tribal Gambling" 6-5 (Jun. 18, 1999).

below the poverty line; approximately 90,000 AI/AN families are homeless or underhoused; and one out of every five AI/AN households lacks adequate plumbing.[432] The statistics are even more disheartening for Alaska Native villages. Only 40% of Alaska Native families have basic sanitation services such as piped drinking water and flush toilets, and more than half of these systems are rudimentary at best.[433] Climate poses a significant challenge to the use of conventional sanitation systems in these communities, which are typically far removed from urban areas. And, the lack of economic development in most Alaska Native villages makes it impossible for these subsistence-based families to pay the cost of bringing in appropriate and sustainable sanitation services.[434]

Health care data on AI/ANs is scarce and unreliable. Significantly, the health status of AI/ANs is far below the health status of the general population in this country, and unmet AI/AN health needs are alarmingly high. This disparity in health status is reflected clearly in the death rates for AI/ANs. For example, AI/ANs have the highest suicide rate (70% higher than the rate for the general population) and the lowest life expectancy of any population in this hemisphere except Haitians.[435] Compared to death rates for all other races in the United States, AI/ANs have a death rate for diabetes mellitus that is 249% higher; a death rate for pneumonia and influenza that is 71% higher; a death rate for tuberculosis that is 533% higher; and a death rate from alcoholism that is 627% higher.[436]

AI/ANs also have a unique set of cancer problems ranging from inadequate screening to under-diagnosis and -reporting of cancer to lack of access to quality health care and new cancer treatments. For example, the leading cause of death for AIs is lung cancer, and AN women have the highest cancer and lung cancer mortality rates of any major racial female group.[437] Recently, the Association of American Indian Physicians reported that cancer is the third leading cause of death for all AI/ANs of all ages; the second leading cause of death for all AI/ANs over age 45; and the leading cause of death for AN women. The Association also reported that, in most parts

---

[432]Id.

[433]See, e.g., Videotape: *The Forgotten America -- Alaska's Rural Sanitation Problem* (The Media Support Center for the Alaska Department of Environmental Conservation).

[434]Id.

[435]See, e.g., Wallwork Winik, Lyric, "There's A New Generation with a Different Attitude," Parade Magazine 6-7 (July 18, 1999).

[436]Proposed IHCA Amendments of 2000, Section 2(h), prepared by the National Steering Committee for the Reauthorization of the Indian Health Care Improvement Act, P.L. 94-437 (Oct. 6, 1999), and based on data used by the Indian Health Service for the FY 2001 budget development.

[437]See National Cancer Institute, National Institute of Health, HHS, Office of Special Populations Research Web Site, *The Cancer Burden* available at www.ospr.nci.nih.gov.burden.htm.

of the country, AI/ANs have poorer survival rates from cancer than do whites, African Americans, Hispanics, and Asians.[438]

AI/ANs are particularly susceptible to health impacts from pollution due to their traditional and cultural uses of natural resources and, in fact, AI/ANs "have greater exposure risks than the general population as a result of their dietary practices and unique cultures that embrace the environment."[439] Fishing, hunting, and gathering often are part of a spiritual, cultural, social, and economic lifestyle, and the survival of many AI/ANs depends on subsistence hunting, fishing, and gathering. In some instances, the right to engage in these activities is legally protected by treaty. Additionally, many AI/ANs also use water, plants, and animals in their traditional and religious practices and ceremonies. As a result, contamination of the water, soil, plants, and animals and the subsequent accumulation of these contaminants in the people through ingestion, inhalation, and contact not only endangers the health of AI/ANs, but also threatens the well-being of their future generations[440] and undermines the cultural survival of tribes and Alaska Native villages. For example, tribes near the Hanford Nuclear Reservation have been working with the Agency for Toxic Substances and Disease Registry to design health assessments focusing on exposure effects from food consumption and other activities. These tribes want to learn if the Hanford releases affect native food items and local materials used in tribal products like storage and cooking baskets, mats, and clothing.[441] Similarly, tribes located in coastal northern California are concerned about the pesticide exposure of some 300 traditional basketmakers who gather their own materials from the forests and roadsides. Basketweavers are exposed to pesticides as they tend and gather basketry materials; as they weave (weavers often hold one end of the grasses

---

[438]K. Marie Porterfield, *American Indian Cancer Statistics Under Reported*, Indian Country Today C-1 (Jul. 26, 2000).

[439]See Agency for Toxic Substances and Disease Registry, *Focus on American Indian and Alaska Native Populations* 1-2.

[440]A number of studies have shown that children are uniquely susceptible to pollution and contaminants. For example, since 1992, the Agency for Toxic Substances and Disease Registry has funded research in the Great Lakes states focusing on the health effects of high risk populations, including American Indians, from persistent toxic substances found in fish. One study found that newborns born to mothers who consumed only 2.3 PCB-contaminated Great Lakes fish meals per month scored lower on the Neonatal Behavioral Assessment Scale. See Agency for Toxic Substances and Disease Registry, *Focus on American Indian and Alaska Native Populations* 2-3. Additionally, in Oklahoma, Indian children also suffer harm from their environment. The Tar Creek Superfund Site, a former lead and zinc mine, occupies 40 square miles within the boundaries of the former Quapaw Indian Reservation. Both the Quapaw Tribe's powwow grounds and campgrounds are contaminated from mine tailings, and the EPA Region 6 reports that approximately 25% of the Quapaw children have elevated blood lead levels compared with a statewide average of 2%. See U.S. Environmental Protection Agency, *Region 6 Environmental Justice Update* 7 (May 2000).

[441] See Agency for Toxic Substances and Disease Registry, *Focus on American Indian and Alaska Native Populations* 5.

or other materials in their mouths as they weave); and as they wear, cook with, and use the finished baskets. Because a disproportionate number of American Indian residents in Humboldt County, California have been diagnosed with cancer, tribes believe studies are needed to determine the exact cause of such cases.[442]

Significantly, where such traditional, cultural, and subsistence activities are involved, federal and state environmental standards used to protect the general non-Indian/non-Native population may not afford tribes and Alaska Native villages adequate protection from environmental harm.[443] Again, although several of the major federal environmental laws have been amended to allow federally recognized tribes to assume primacy for certain programs,[444] to date, only a few tribes have EPA- approved or -promulgated environmental programs.[445] Based on all of the foregoing, federally recognized tribes and AI/ANs suffer a disproportionate burden of health consequences due to their exposure to pollutants and hazardous substances in the environment. This is particularly so for AI/AN infants and children.[446]

---

[442] See Chuck Striplen, Mutzun Oholone Tribe, *Native Subsistence in a Toxic Environment: A Tribal Viewpoint* 14, (EPA's OPPTS Tribal News) (Fall/Winter 1999-2000).

[443]See, e.g., City of Albuquerque v. Browner, 97 F.3d 415 (10th Cir. 1996), *cert. denied*, 118 S. Ct. 410 (1997) (upholding the EPA's approval of the Pueblo of Isleta's water quality standards that were more stringent than the state water quality standards, and which included a ceremonial use standard).

[444]Since 1986, the Safe Drinking Water Act, Clean Water Act, and Clean Air Act have been amended to afford tribes substantially the same opportunities as states to assume responsibility for certain programs or purposes.

[445]For example, as of July 13, 2000, the EPA reported that only 15 tribes have EPA-approved or -promulgated water quality standards and no tribes are authorized to administer the National Pollutant Discharge Elimination System or to establish Total Maximum Daily Loads. See 65 Fed. Reg. 43,585 (Jul. 13, 2000).

[446]For example, a New York State Department of Health study of lactating women and their infants linked breast feeding and infant exposure to hazardous substances. This study compared PCB levels in the breast milk of Mohawk women who gave birth between 1986 and 1992 with a control group. The study found that although the PCB concentrations in the breast milk of Mohawk mothers decreased over time, their infants had urine PCB levels ten times higher than that of their mothers. See Agency for Toxic Substances and Disease Registry, *Focus on American Indian and Alaska Native Populations* 3-4. See also Winona Laduke, *All Our Relations, Native Struggles for Land and Life* 11-23 (1999).

APPENDIX A: NEJAC EXECUTIVE COUNCIL MEMBERS

List of Members by Stakeholder Category

ACADEMIA - 5

Veronica Eady - 1 year
Tufts University
Department of Urban and
Environmental Policy
Tufts University
97 Talbot Avenue
Medford, MA 02155
Phone: (617) 627-2220
Fax: (617) 627-3377
E-mail:
Veronica.Eady@tufts.edu

Tseming Yang - 2 years
Professor
Vermont Law School
Chelsea Street, Whitcomb House
South Royalton, VT 05068
Phone: 802/763-8303 ext 2344
Fax: 802/763-2663
E-mail: tyang@vermontlaw.edu

Eileen Gauna - 1 year
Professor
Southwestern Univ. School of
Law
675 South Westmoreland Avenue
Los Angeles, CA 90005
Phone: (213)738-6752
Fax: (213)383-1688
E-mail: egauna@swlaw.edu

Graciela I. Ramirez-Toro-1 year
Director for the Center for
Environmental Education,
Conservation and Interpretation
Inter American University of PR
P. O. Box 5100
San Germán, PR 00683
Ph: (787) 264 1912 ext. 7630
Fax: (787) 892 2089
E mail: cecia@prtc.net

Richard Gragg, III - 2 years
Assistant Professor/Associate
Director
Environmental Science Institute
Florida A&M University
Tallahassee, FL 32307-6600
Phone: (850) 599-8549
Fax: (850) 561-2248
E-mail:
richard.graggiii@famu.edu

INDUSTRY/BUSINESS - 4

Robert L. Harris - 2 years
Vice President
Environmental Affairs
Pacific Gas and Electric Company
P. O. Box 770000
San Francisco, CA 94177-0001
Ph: (415) 973-3833
Fax: (415) 973-1359
E-mail: rlh6@pge.com

Jana L. Walker- 1 year
Law Office of Jana L. Walker
141 Placitas Trails Road
Placitas, NM 87043
Phone: (505) 867-0579
Fax: (505) 867-0579
E-mail: ndnlaw@sprintmail.com

Kenneth J. Warren, Esq. - 2 years
Chair of Environmental Department
Wolf, Block, Schorr and Solis-
Cohen
1650 Arch Street, 22nd Floor
Philadelphia, PA 19103
Phone: (215) 977-2276
Fax: (215) 977-2334
E-mail: kwarren@wolfblock.com

COMMUNITY-5 (1 vacancy)

Larry Charles - 2 years
Executive Director
ONE/CHANE, Inc.
2065 Main Street
Hartford, CT 06102
Phone: (860) 525-0190
Fax: (860) 522-8266
E-mail: lcharles@snet.net

Harold Mitchell - 1 year
Director
Regenesis, Inc.
101 Anita Drive
Spartanburg, SC 29302
Phone: (864) 542-8420
Fax:: (864) 582-0001
E-mail regenesisinc@aol.com

Mary Nelson - 1 year
President
Bethel New Life, Incorporated
4950 West Thomas
Chicago, IL 60651
Phone: 773-473-7870
Fax: 773-473-7871
E-mail: mnelson367@aol.com

Peggy Shepard – 1 year
Executive Director
West Harlem Environmental Action
271 West 125th Street, Suite 211
New York, NY 10027
Phone: (212) 961-1000
Fax: (212) 961-1015
E-mail: peggy@weact.org

NON GOVERN/ENVIRONMENTAL
GROUP 5 (1 vacancy)

Wilma Subra - 2 years
LEAN Representative
Subra Company, Inc.
P. O. Box 9813
3814 Old Jeanerette Rd.
New Iberia, LA 70562
Phone: (337) 367-2216
Fax: (337) 367-2217
E-mail: SubraCom@aol.com

Jason S. Grumet – 3 years
Executive Director
National Commission on
 Energy Policy
1616 H St., NW 6th Floor
Washington, DC 20006
Phone: 202-637-0400 x12
Fax: 202-637-9220
E-mail: hreese@energycommission.org

Judith Espinosa - 3 years
Director, ATR Institute
University of New Mexico
1001 University Blvd.,
SE, Suite 103
Albuquerque, NM 87106-4342
Phone: 505-246-6410
Fax: 505-246-6001
E-mail: jmespino@unm.edu

Rev. Adora Iris Lee - 3 years
Director of EJ Programs
United Church of Christ
Justice and Witness Ministries
110 Maryland Ave., NE, Suite 207
Washington, DC 2002
Phone: 202-543-1517
Fax: 202-543-5994
E mail: adoracrj@aol.com

STATE/LOCAL   4 (1 vacancy)

Jane Stahl - 1 year
Deputy Commissioner
Department of Environmental Protection
State of Connecticut
79 Elm Street, 3rd Floor
Hartford, CT 06106
Phone: (860)424-3009
Fax: (860)424-4054
E-mail: jane.stahl@po.state.ct.us

Walter S. Handy, Jr. – 3 years
Assistant Commissioner of Health
3101 Burnet Avenue
Cincinnati, OH 45229
Phone: (513) 357-7271
Fax: (513) 357-7290
E-mail:
walter.handy@chdburn.rcc.org

Lori F. Kaplan – 3 years
Commissioner
Indiana Department of Environmental Management
100 North Senate Avenue, P.O. Box 6015
Indianapolis, IN 46206-6015
Phone: (317) 232-8611
Fax: (317) 233-6647
E-mail: lkaplan@dem.state.in.us

TRIBAL/INDIGENOUS - 3

Anna Frazier - 2 years
Coordinator
DINE' C.A.R.E.
HCR-63, Box 263
Winslow, AZ 86047
Phone: (928) 657-3291
Fax: (928) 657-3319
E-mail: dinecare@cnetco.com

Pamela Kingfisher - 2 years
Indigenous Women's Network
13621 FM 2769
Austin, TX 78726
Phone: 512-288-6003
Fax: (512) 258-1858
E-mail pame@indigenouswomen.org

Terry Williams - 3 years
Fisheries and Natural Resources Commissioner
The Tulalip Tribes
6700 Totem Beach Road
Tulalip, WA 98271-9694
Phone: (360) 651-4000
Fax: (360) 651-3701
E-mail: dwilliams@tulalip.nsn.us

Terms of Expiration:
1 year = 12/31/2002
2 years = 12/31/2003
3 years = 12/31/2004

APPENDIX B: NEJAC FISH CONSUMPTION WORK GROUP MEMBERS

Coleen Poler (Work Group Co-Chair)
NEJAC Indigenous Peoples Subcommittee
Sokaogon Defense Committee
2915 Ackley Circle Road
Crandon, WI 54520
Ph: 715-365-8995
Fax: 715-365-8977
polersdc@newnorth.net

Leonard E. Robinson (Work Group Co-Chair)
NEJAC Air & Water Subcommittee
TAMCO Steel
12459 Arrow Highway
Rancho Cucamonga, CA 91739
Ph: 909-899-0631 x.203
Fax: 909-899-1910
RobinsonL@tamcosteel.com

Daisy Carter
NEJAC Air & Water Subcommittee
PROJECT AWAKE
Route 2, Box 282
Coatopa. AL 35470
Ph: 205-652-6823
fax: 205-652-6823 or 205-652-9343
pawake@sumternet.com

Patricia Cochran
Alaska Native Science Commission
University of Alaska Anchorage
3211 Provident Drive
Anchorage, Alaska 99508
Ph: 907-786-7704
Fax: 907-786-7731
anpac1@uaa.alaska.edu

Josee Cung
Minnesota Department of Natural Resources
Southeast Asian Program- Commissioner's Office
500 Lafayette Road, Box 10
St. Paul, MN 55155-4010
Ph: 651-297-4745
Fax: 651-296-6047
josee.cung@dnr.state.mn.us

Ticiang Diangson
Supervising Planning and Development Specialist
Seattle Public Utilities
710 Second Ave. #505
Seattle, WA 98104
Ph: 206-684-7643
Fax: 206-684-8529
ticiang.diangson@ci.seattle.wa.us

Pamela Kingfisher
NEJAC Health & Research Subcommittee
Indigenous Women's Network
13621 FM 2769
Austin, TX 78726
Ph: 512-401-0090
Fax: 512-258-1858
pjkingfisher@yahoo.com

Brian Merkel
University of Wisconsin- Green Bay
College of Human Biology
Green Bay, WI 54311-7001
Ph: 920-465-2262
Fax: 920-465-2769
MerkelB@uwgb.edu

Bark Merrick
Earth Conservation Corps
1st and Potomac Ave.
Washington, D.C.
Ph: 202-554-1960

Lawrence Skinner
New York State Dept. of Environmental Conservation
Bureau of Habitat
50 Wolf Rd. R. 576
Albany, N.Y. 12233-4750
Ph: 518-457-0751
Fax: 518-485-8424

Moses D. Squeochs
NEJAC Indigenous Peoples Subcommittee
14 Confederation Bands of Yakama Nation
P.O. Box 151
Toppenish, WA 98948
Ph: 509-865-5121
Fax: 509-865-6850
mose@yakama.com

Velma Veloria
1265 South Main Street, Suite 203
Seattle, WA 98144 or
P.O. Box 40600
Olympia, WA 98504-0600
Ph: 360-786-7862
Fax: 360-786-7317
veloria_ve@leg.wa.gov

Jana L. Walker
Attorney
NEJAC Indigenous Peoples Subcommittee
Law Office of Jana L. Walker
141 Placitas Trails Road
Placitas, New Mexico 87043
Ph: 505-867-0579
ndnlaw@sprintmail.com

Patrick West
Professor Emeritus, University of Michigan
29377 Sunny Beach Additive Road
Grand Rapids, MN 55744
Ph: 218-326-2170
pswest@paulbunyan.net

Damon Whitehead
NEJAC Air & Water Subcommittee
Earth Conservation Corps
1st Street and Potomac Avenue, SW
Washington, DC 20003
damon@anacostiariverkeeper.org

Terry Williams, Commissioner
Fisheries & Natural Resources
Tulalip Tribes
7615 Totem Beach Road
Marysville, WA 98271
Ph: 360-651-4471
Fax: 360-651-4490
twilliams@tulalip.nsn.us

Marianne Yamaguchi
NEJAC Air & Water Subcommittee
Santa Monica Bay Restoration Project
320 West 4th Street, Suite 200
Los Angeles, CA 90013
Ph: 213-576-6614
Fax: 213-576-6646
myamaguc@rb4.swrcb.ca.gov

Alice Walker (WorkGroup DFO)
Co-Designated Federal Official
Office of Water
NEJAC, Air and Water Subcommittee
OW Environmental Justice Coordinator
Ph: 202-564-0498
Fax: 202-529-7534
Walker.Alice@epa.gov

Danny Gogal (WorkGroup DFO)
DFO, NEJAC Indigenous Peoples Subcommittee
USEPA Headquarters
Office of Environmental Justice- 2201A
1200 Pennsylvania Avenue, N.W.
Washington, DC 20460
Ph: 202-564-2576
Gogal.Danny@epa.gov

Charles Lee (NEJAC DFO)
Associate Director for Policy and Interagency Liaison
Office of Environmental Justice- 2201A
USEPA Headquarters
1200 Pennsylvania Avenue, N.W.
Washington, DC 20460
Ph: 202-564-2597
Lee.Charles@epa.gov

Catherine O'Neill (Meeting Report Consultant)
Associate Professor
Seattle University School of Law
900 Broadway
Seattle, Washington 98122
Ph: 206-398-4030
Fax: 206-398-4077
oneillc@seattleu.edu

APPENDIX C: FISH CONSUMPTION WORK GROUP PROPOSALS

The following proposals were developed by the National Environmental Justice Advisory Council (NEJAC) Fish Consumption Work Group (FCWG) for deliberation and action by the NEJAC Executive Council. While elements of these proposals were incorporated into the six Consensus Recommendations adopted by the NEJAC Executive Council, these proposals were not adopted by the NEJAC Executive Council.

The following proposals of the FCWG are set forth as "Overarching Proposals" and "Focused Proposals." Overarching proposals are intended to set forth the FCWG's proposals in broad terms. Each group of overarching proposals is in turn elaborated by one or more focused proposals. In every case, the proposals should be understood to refer to the contamination and depletion of aquatic ecosystems and all of their components, including fish, shellfish, marine invertebrates, aquatic plants, and wildlife. They should be understood to apply to efforts to address contamination wherever it may affect aquatic ecosystems, including contamination in surface waters, sediments, groundwater, soils, and air. Finally, they are meant not only to cleanup current contamination and prevent future contamination, but to do so in a manner that rectifies disproportionate impacts, so that all affected people or groups   including people of color, low-income people, American Indians, Alaska Natives, Native Hawaiians and other Pacific Islanders, and other indigenous people located within the jurisdictional boundaries of the United States   are able to live in a healthful environment, in this generation and all generations to come.

Chapter One

The contamination of fish, aquatic plants, and wildlife is an especially pressing concern for many communities of color, low-income communities, tribes, and other indigenous peoples, whose consumption and use practices differ   often profoundly so   from those of the general population. Members of these groups often consume far greater quantities of fish, aquatic plants, and wildlife; they consume fish, plants, and wildlife at different frequencies, in accordance with seasonal availability and other cultural considerations; they consume and use different species and parts; and they employ different methods in procuring and preparing the fish, aquatic plants, and wildlife that they use. Thus, communities of color, low-income communities, tribes, and other indigenous peoples are among the most highly exposed to contaminants in the fish, plants, wildlife, and aquatic environment. For example, empirical studies document 90th percentile fish consumption rates for various affected communities and tribes at 225 g/day, 242 g/day, and 489 g/day (respectively, urban fishers on Los Angeles Harbor; ten Asian and Pacific Islander communities in King County, WA; and the Suquamish Tribe). Although EPA's revised default assumptions of 17.5 g/day, representing the 90th percentile of the general population, and 142.4 g/day, representing the 99th percentile of the general population are a marked improvement over its previous assumption of 6.5 g/day, the revised defaults still considerably underestimate exposure for many affected communities and tribes.

Overarching Proposals

I-1. The FCWG proposes that EPA work with affected groups to develop and use fish consumption rates that are appropriate for various higher-consuming communities and tribes whenever EPA conducts activities that affect these higher-consuming groups, for example, when it develops water quality criteria; when it sets and approves state and tribal water quality standards; when it sets and approves cleanup levels for water and sediments; when it addresses cross-media contamination (e.g., mercury emissions to air); and when it provides other relevant guidance.

FCWG proposes that EPA work in particular with those affected groups for which few or no empirical data exist, ensuring that studies are undertaken systematically to provide a full account of all affected groups' consumption practices. FCWG notes that, among other things, an appropriate fish consumption rate must account for affected groups' different consumption frequencies or patterns due to seasonal availability and other cultural considerations, particularly those that result in acute or peak exposures.

I-2. The FCWG similarly proposes that EPA account for other aspects of communities' and tribes' different exposure circumstances when it conducts these various activities, including practices that mean different species are consumed, different parts are used (e.g., the highly contaminated hepatopancreas of crabs, often consumed by Asian and Pacific Islanders and by other island people), and/or different preparation methods are employed than those typically assumed by agencies.

I-3. The FCWG proposes that EPA remedy, in measurable and reportable ways, the disparities in the level of protection provided by water quality criteria and standards, cleanup standards, air emissions standards, and other relevant environmental standards as between the general population and "subpopulations" comprised of communities of color, low-income communities, tribes, or other indigenous peoples.

Focused Proposals

I-1 through I-3

1. FCWG proposes that EPA work with affected groups to facilitate research documenting these groups' different fish consumption and use practices, focusing on communities of color, low-income communities and tribes:

   a. FCWG proposes that EPA work with affected groups from the outset, so that research questions are framed and studies are designed to reflect accurately the needs and practices of the affected groups;

   b. FCWG proposes that, among other issues to be identified together with affected groups, studies document not only the different quantities of fish consumed by these groups, but also other aspects of these groups' different practices, including the extent to which they consume fish, plants, and wildlife at different frequencies; the extent to which they (or particular members of the relevant group, such as children or elders) consume and use different species or parts; and the extent to which they employ different methods in procuring and preparing the fish, aquatic plants, and wildlife;

   c. FCWG proposes that EPA prioritize research documenting those consumption and use practices about which relatively little is known and/or for which there are not reasonable proxies among current data, including research documenting the consumption and use of subsistence foods other than fish; research documenting consumption and use frequencies that result in acute or peak exposures (e.g., in the case of various Alaska Natives or others for whom seasonal availability or cultural considerations determine practices); and research documenting consumption and use among groups or in regions of the country for which few data exist (e.g., Native Hawaiians, among others).

2. FCWG proposes that EPA work with affected groups to ensure that EPA accurately and appropriately accounts for these groups' different fish consumption and use practices in all of its activities, including instances in which:

   a. EPA develops water quality criteria;

   b. EPA approves state or tribal water quality standards;

   c. EPA sets state or tribal water quality standards;

   d. EPA approves or sets cleanup levels for surface water and sediments;

e. EPA addresses relevant cross-media contamination (e.g., mercury emissions to air);

f. EPA undertakes relevant programs and initiatives (e.g., the Persistent Bioaccumulative and Toxic (PBT) Control Program); and

g. EPA provides other relevant guidance (e.g., its Guidance for Assessing Chemical Contaminant Data for Use in Fish Advisories).

3. FCWG also proposes that EPA act expeditiously to issue CWA § 304(a) water quality criteria that reflect affected groups' consumption and use practices; FCWG notes that EPA has sufficient data documenting the exposure circumstances of communities of color, low-income communities, tribes, and other indigenous peoples to warrant the issuance of revised criteria and emphasizes that it is unacceptable that criteria are still in effect that employ the outdated 6.5 grams/day fish consumption rate.

4. Specifically, FCWG proposes that EPA take a more active role in ensuring that state and tribal water quality standards are protective of affected groups' consumption and use practices, by assisting states, tribes, and affected groups in their data-gathering efforts; by encouraging states and tribes to employ protective assumptions (e.g., in reliance on EPA's Ambient Water Quality Criteria Methodology), even in advance of federally-mandated deadlines; and, crucially, by disapproving state and tribal standards that do not adequately account for these groups' different practices.

5. FCWG proposes that EPA work together with affected groups to revise its research methods and protocols to ensure that they result in the accurate depiction of these groups' exposure circumstances.

6. FCWG proposes that EPA should then produce and distribute a manual of methods and protocols for determining health risks for persistent and bioaccumulative toxics, for use by tribes and other affected groups who wish to employ local data in investigating and documenting human health risks in their own communities from the consumption and use of fish, shellfish, and other aquatic resources. This manual should include methods that permit analyses of both acute and chronic effects, and incorporation of multiple exposures and cumulative risks.

The contamination of fish, aquatic plants, and wildlife is also troubling to many communities of color, low-income communities, tribes, and other indigenous peoples, because these groups consume and use fish, aquatic plants, and wildlife in different cultural, traditional, religious, historical, economic, and legal contexts than the "average American." For example, many tribes have treaty-guaranteed rights to take fish; the unique legal obligations entailed by these treaties are relevant to EPA's decisions affecting the health of the fish and the fisheries resource. The presence of these different contexts is abundantly demonstrated by both testimonial and social scientific evidence. For some or all of these reasons, particular fish consumption practices are in an important sense indispensable for many of these affected groups.

Overarching Proposals

I-4. FCWG strongly proposes EPA to work with affected groups to enhance its understanding of the ways in which these groups consume and use fish, aquatic plants, and wildlife in different cultural, traditional, religious, historical, economic, and legal contexts than the "average American" fish consumer and to incorporate this evidence into its risk assessment, risk management, and risk communication policies in measurable ways. FCWG proposes EPA, in collaboration with other appropriate federal agencies, to provide funding to affected groups so that they may document their particular cultural, traditional, religious, historical, economic, and legal circumstances, in a manner and for purposes they deem appropriate.

Focused Proposals

I-4

1. In each instance in which these issues are implicated, FCWG proposes that EPA work with the affected group(s) to develop a process for enhancing EPA's understanding of the particular cultural, traditional, religious, historical, economic, and legal context relevant to EPA's decisions in that case. These efforts should be among the first of EPA's fact-finding undertakings, e.g., for each cleanup of contaminated water and sediments under CERCLA. Among other things, such efforts should attend to:

a. The existence of applicable treaties, e.g., many tribes' treaty-guaranteed rights to hunt, fish, and gather;

b. The effects of the decision on resources, places, or sites that are culturally important to Native peoples or other affected groups, including sites protected by the National Historic Preservation Act, other sacred places, and culturally-important resources (whether located on- or off- reservation).

2. FCWG proposes that EPA and each office within EPA develop a strategy for recruitment, retention, and upward mobility for members of affected groups in order to enhance the extent to which EPA staff are familiar with and equipped to understand the particular relevant cultural, traditional, religious, historical, economic, and legal contexts in which they set priorities, undertake research and develop policies.

3. FCWG proposes that EPA increase its efforts to fund and publicize opportunities for community-based and tribally-conducted research documenting the particular cultural, traditional, religious, historical, economic, and legal contexts in which these groups consume and use aquatic resources. FCWG welcomes EPA's recent efforts to this end; however, as noted below in Proposals I-10 through I-11(1), even greater efforts are necessary.

A "suppression effect" occurs when a fish consumption rate for a given group reflects a current level of consumption that is artificially diminished from an appropriate baseline level for that group. The more robust baseline level is suppressed, inasmuch as it does not get captured by the fish consumption rate. Suppression effects may occur because of contamination (people would consume more fish but refrain because the fish are contaminated) and/or depletion (people would consume more fish but cannot because there are fewer fish to be consumed, for a variety of reasons). Such effects have been noted, for example, at Akwesasne, home to the St. Regis Mohawk, where large-scale PCB contamination of the Grasse and St. Lawrence rivers by General Motors, ALCOA, and Reynolds has left tribal members with little choice but to reduce their consumption of fish from these waters. Similarly, the depletion and contamination of salmon and other fish in the usual and accustomed fishing areas of the Tulalip Tribes has left tribal members with fewer fish to catch and consume. When standards are set based on fish consumption rates that do not capture fully this suppressed consumption, they set in motion a sort of downward spiral whereby the further contamination or depletion is permitted, fish consumption rates are further suppressed, and so on.

Overarching Proposals

I-5. FCWG proposes EPA to work with communities of color, low-income communities, tribes, and other indigenous peoples to identify instances in which these groups believe consumption to be suppressed due to contamination and/or depletion, and to conduct research, together with the affected group, to ascertain whether a suppression effect is at work; if so, cleanup and restoration there should be a high priority.

I-6. FCWG further proposes that, wherever suppression effects are at work, EPA employ appropriate baseline levels in providing guidance for states and tribes, and in setting and approving water quality standards, cleanup standards, and other environmental standards in order to avoid the downward spiral due to suppression effects.

Focused Proposals

I-5 through I-6

>   1. FCWG notes that suppression effects need to be accounted for in gathering and interpreting data, and proposes that EPA work with communities of color, low-income communities, tribes and other indigenous peoples to document the existence and extent of suppression effects due to contamination and/or completion. In many cases, increased research documenting the particular cultural, traditional, religious, historical, economic, and legal contexts in which these groups consume and use aquatic resources, proposed above in Proposal I-4(3), will go hand in hand with research documenting suppression effects.

>   2. FCWG proposes that wherever suppression effects are believed to be at work, EPA work together with the affected group to develop appropriate baseline levels for use when EPA provides guidance for states and tribes, and when EPA sets and approves water quality standards, cleanup standards, and other relevant environmental standards. This proposal might be applicable, for example, to EPA's current cleanup work at the Superfund Site on the Duwamish Waterway.

Current risk assessment methods do not adequately account for susceptibilities and co-risk factors that affect individuals' responses to environmental contaminants. These factors include underlying health status (including existing body burdens), baseline diet quality, genetics, socioeconomic status, access to health care, limited English proficiency, age, gender, pregnancy, lactation, and other factors.

Overarching Proposal

I-7. FCWG proposes further research into the extent to which susceptibilities and co-risk factors are clustered in certain subpopulations, including the extent to which there are disparities in current health status and body burden. To the extent that clusters emerge relevant to communities of color, low-income communities, tribes, or other indigenous peoples, FCWG proposes that EPA incorporate these factors into its risk assessment, risk management and risk communication efforts.

Focused Proposal

I-7

>   1. FCWG proposes that EPA undertake research to permit a more thorough understanding of these susceptibilities and co-risk factors and how they are distributed between communities.

>   2. FCWG proposes that, to the extent that clusters emerge relevant to affected groups, EPA develop methods to incorporate this information into its risk assessment, risk management, and risk communication efforts.

Current risk assessment methods evaluate risks as if humans were exposed to only a single contaminant at time, by a single route of exposure (e.g., consuming fish). Members of communities of color, low-income communities, tribes, and other indigenous peoples, however, are often exposed to multiple contaminants at a time or in succession, and often via more than route of exposure. For example, the Fourteen Confederated Tribes and Bands of the Yakama Nation fish in the Columbia River system, where it is the norm for over 100 contaminants to be identified in fish tissues; the northern Ojibwa Tribes are exposed to mercury via multiple natural resource pathways, given its uptake in fish and its presence in and on wild rice; and African-American and low-income communities living along the Mississippi are subject to multiple exposures, including from sources other than surface waters (e.g. consumption of contaminated fish; ingestion of polluted well water; inhalation of toxic air pollutants from surrounding incinerators, refineries, chemical manufacturers, and other industrial sources; and contact with and ingestion of particles from contaminated soils). Some of these multiple exposures and cumulative effects (and their interactions) are known; the vast majority are not well understood.

Overarching Proposals

I-8. Where the nature of cumulative effects are known, FCWG proposes their incorporation into EPA's environmental policy and specific standard setting practices. Where they are not well known, FCWG proposes this as a high priority area for research, given that the potential for cumulative effects are perhaps where the greatest danger to human health lurks.

I-9. Although EPA has made some inroads in accounting for multiple exposures and cumulative risks, it is FCWG's view that EPA simply must take a more aggressive, holistic, and integrative approach, especially where fish consumption levels are very high for communities of color, low-income communities, tribes, and other indigenous peoples and where the mix of contaminants to which these people are exposed may be highly toxic.

Focused Proposals

I-8 through I-9

1. FCWG proposes that EPA study the health impacts of chemical mixtures present in fish tissues, given that consumption and use of fish tissues represent one of the most significant and widespread instances of real life (as opposed to hypothetical) environmental exposures to chemical mixtures. FCWG further proposes that EPA incorporate the results of such studies in its risk assessment, risk management, and risk communication efforts.

2. At the same time, FCWG proposes that EPA avail itself of existing data characterizing the health risks of PCB-mercury mixtures present in fish tissues (e.g., data from the Seychelles and Faroe Islands). Given the availability of this data, and the large number of instances in which fish and wildlife consumption advisories are issued because of contamination from both PCBs and mercury, FCWG proposes that EPA not delay use of this data on the basis of the need for "further study."

Affected communities and tribes are integral to producing relevant, accurate, scientifically defensible data. Affected communities and tribes need, therefore, to be involved at every stage of the research on the issues identified above   from identifying research needs, to designing research methods, to interpreting the resulting data, to determining its importance to agencies' risk assessment, management, and communication efforts. Research should thus be a joint project reflecting and augmenting both affected communities' expertise and EPA and other agencies' expertise.

Overarching Proposals

I-10. FCWG proposes EPA to recognize the expertise of members of affected communities and tribes (including but not limited to tribal and non-governmental reservation-based organizations and organizations serving Alaska Natives), and to involve them or consult with them throughout the process of researching the various issues outlined above. FCWG proposes EPA to expand and publicize effectively the availability of financial and technical assistance for community-based organizations and tribes so that they may be directly involved in conducting research on these issues.

I-11. Importantly, FCWG proposes EPA to make available additional financial and technical resources to communities and tribes to conduct their own research (as was done for the Asian and Pacific Islander fish consumption study in King County, WA (EPA) and for the Suquamish Tribe fish consumption study (ATSDR)), and thereby to augment their expertise.

Focused Proposals

I-10 through I-11

1. FCWG proposes that EPA recognize the need for studies to be designed and administered *by and for* particular communities, groups, or peoples, and that it facilitate this process by, among other things:

   a. Expanding financial and technical assistance to community-based organizations and tribes to conduct appropriate studies;

   b. Taking the lead in identifying and coordinating financial and technical resources that are available through other federal agencies; and

   c. Publicizing these expanded and coordinated resources to affected groups in a regular and timely fashion;

FCWG commends EPA's recent grant initiatives to this end (established together with the ATSDR), including two programs: *Lifestyle and Cultural Practices of Tribal Populations and Risks from Toxic Substances in the Environment* and *Superfund Minority Institutions Program: Hazardous Substance Research.* However the need for funding to enable communities and tribes fully to be involved in research and decisions affecting risk assessment, management, and communication far outstrips the funding that has been so far made available.

2. FCWG proposes that EPA take an active role in establishing and maintaining a system enabling affected groups to share and access results from community-based and tribally conducted research, as well as other research relevant to affected groups' efforts to document and address the nature, extent, and health impacts of contamination in their own communities. Such a system would assist tribes' and communities' efforts to conduct more efficiently their own research, and to participate in or consult with EPA in a timely and informed manner.

3. FCWG emphasizes that, while further research regarding various affected groups' exposure is important, it should not be undertaken at the expense of research that aims to identify the sources of the contamination that burdens these groups and to understand the mechanisms by which substances that have been or are being emitted or discharged from these sources make their way through the environment. Thus, FCWG proposes that further research be conducted to connect the contaminants found in fish, shellfish, and other aquatic resources to the sources of those contaminants.

Current risk-based methods remain controversial as a matter of science, policy and justice.

Overarching Proposals

1-12. To the extent that EPA continues to rely on risk-based and other quantitative methods (e.g., cost-benefit analysis), FCWG proposes EPA to revisit, together with affected communities and tribes, the fundamental assumptions of these methods and to revise these methods to incorporate eco-cultural and spiritual components of risk.

I-13. FCWG strongly proposes that EPA employ the Precautionary Principle at every opportunity as an alternative to risk-based methods.

Focused Proposals

I-12 through I-13

1. FCWG proposes that EPA consider seriously alternative decision making models that permit the multiple and interrelated dimensions of the harms to be acknowledged and addressed. Among these, EPA should consider the model for enlarging current risk assessment methods suggested by Stuart G. Harris and Barbara L. Harper, *Using Eco Cultural Dependency Webs in Risk Assessment and Characterization of Risks to Tribal Health and Cultures.*

2. FCWG proposes that EPA, together with communities of color, low-income communities, tribes, and other indigenous peoples, work to explore and specify the contours of the precautionary principle. FCWG notes that there is a considerable and growing body of work to this end, and proposes that EPA draw on this body of work and support efforts further to develop it.

3. FCWG proposes that EPA actively identify and make use of opportunity for precautionary approaches within existing legislative and other authority, and that EPA consider and advocate appropriate changes to existing laws in order to facilitate precautionary approaches.

4. FCWG notes that preventive and precautionary measures will often at the same time reduce costs to regulated entities (e.g., savings through reduced use of toxic inputs, savings through reduced need to treat and dispose of toxic outputs); these cost savings will be particularly important where the particular regulated entities are an important source of jobs for communities of color, low-income communities, tribes and other indigenous peoples. FCWG proposes, therefore, that EPA make it a priority to identify and undertake prevention opportunities where this is the case.

Chapter Two

Aquatic environments remain contaminated, despite the existence of considerable environmental legal authorities designed to address contamination. About 40% of the waters assessed in the United States still do not support "fishable-swimable" uses; about 10% by volume of all sediments under U.S. waters are seriously contaminated; the list of contaminated soils, sediments, and surface waters yet to be cleaned up is long; and the number of fish consumption advisories in effect has increased steadily over the last several years. Contaminated aquatic environments are the result of releases to various environmental "receiving media"   to surface waters, groundwater, sediment, soils, and air   and movement among these interconnected media. Because people of color, low-income people, American Indians/Alaska Natives, and other indigenous people are disproportionately among the most exposed to this contamination, any lapses in agencies' efforts to prevent, reduce, clean up, and restore contaminated aquatic environments will disproportionately burden these affected groups.

Overarching Proposals

II-1. Given that five contaminants--mercury, PCBs, dioxins, DDT, and chlordane--are responsible for the majority of fish and wildlife consumption advisories, FCWG proposes that the prevention and cleanup of these pollutants in the Nation's waters and restoration of aquatic ecosystems following such contamination be a priority. FCWG further proposes that prevention, cleanup, and restoration efforts focus on all contaminants that are highly toxic, bioaccumulative, and persistent, especially those identified by the Convention on Persistent Organic Pollutants (POPs); and on other contaminants of concern, including lead and other metals, radioactive materials, pesticides, fecal coliform and other bacterial and viral contaminants, sediment and silt loading, water quantity, water temperature changes and other alterations to aquatic ecosystems, and climate change.

II-2. FCWG cannot emphasize strongly enough the need for redoubled, aggressive prevention, cleanup, and restoration efforts to address these contaminants of concern in the surface water, groundwater, sediments, soils and air. FCWG proposes EPA to ensure that efforts to cleanup and restore contaminated aquatic ecosystems are coupled with measures to prevent future contamination.

II-3. Specifically, because mercury is responsible for nearly 79% of all fish and shellfish advisories and because air emissions account for 80% of mercury depositions in water, FCWG proposes that the prevention and cleanup of mercury in the Nation's waters be a top priority for EPA, and that regulations and other efforts here address all significant sources of mercury, regardless of the initial "receiving medium" (e.g., air, soils, water, sediments). Moreover, FCWG proposes EPA to ensure that reductions in mercury accrue equitably to all, and that mercury reduction efforts do not have the effect of creating "hot spots" or other disparate impacts.

II-4. Further, FCWG proposes that prevention and cleanup of dioxin address all significant sources, and that cleanup of PCBs, DDT, and chlordane (production of which are banned), address all significant sources. Similarly, FCWG proposes that prevention and cleanup of all Persistent Bioaccumulative Toxins(PBTs)/Persistent Organic Pollutants (POPs) address all significant sources.

II-5. Finally, because the concentrations in aquatic organisms of mercury and some other contaminants of concern, such as lead, cannot be reduced by cleaning, trimming, and or cooking, FCWG proposes that regulatory authorities should not rely on advisories suggesting these methods as a way to protect public health.

Focused Proposals

II-1 through II-5

1. FCWG proposes that EPA work expeditiously to *prevent* and *reduce* the release of contaminants of concern and to *clean up* and *restore* aquatic ecosystems contaminated by these pollutants. FCWG emphasizes that, in every instance, EPA must set the relevant environmental standards at levels that protect highly-exposed populations, including communities of color, low-income communities, tribes, and other indigenous peoples. FCWG also emphasizes that, in every instance, EPA account for the particular cultural, traditional, religious, historical, economic, and legal contexts in which these affected groups consume and use aquatic resources.

Specifically, FCWG proposes:

a. With respect to mercury:

(i) EPA address these concerns and expedite the issuance of a Maximum Achievable Control Technology (MACT) standard for emissions from utilities, including coal-fired power plants (a MACT standard for utilities is not scheduled to be proposed until December, 2003; meanwhile, coal-fired power plants are the largest single source of mercury air emissions);

(ii) EPA address these concerns in issuing a Maximum Achievable Control Technology (MACT) standard for emissions from institutional, industrial, and commercial boilers;

(iii) EPA address these concerns in issuing a Maximum Achievable Control Technology (MACT) standard for emissions from chlor-alkali plants (although there are only about a dozen chlor-alkali plants in the United States, each plant is the source of large quantities of mercury. Further, chlor-alkali plants may in some cases constitute the most significant sources locally, as in Louisiana, where the two chlor-alkali plants statewide contribute more mercury than all of the coal-fired power plants statewide combined.[447]);

(iv) EPA address these concerns and expedite the (re)-issuance of its Hazardous Waste Combustor rule, and that, in the meantime, EPA not rely on an interim rule that is less protective than the original final rule – which was struck down by a court because it was insufficiently protective;

(v) EPA address these concerns in ensuring compliance with its recently-issued Maximum Achievable Control Technology (MACT) standard for emissions from medical waste incinerators, and in identifying and facilitating further efforts to reduce and eliminate the use of mercury in the first place (including, e.g., efforts similar to OPPTS' voluntary agreements with hospitals and other medical facilities to reduce mercury use; state and local governments' bans on the use of mercury-containing

---

[447]Telephone Interview with Barry Kohl, Department of Geology, Tulane University (October 17, 2001).

medical products;[448] and potential partnerships with private industries to develop and produce alternative, mercury-free products);

(vi) EPA's Office of Air and Radiation and its Office of Water address these concerns and redouble their efforts to address cross-media mercury contamination through various initiatives, including through the TMDL program;

(vii) EPA address these concerns in supporting the United Nations Environment Program's (UNEP) global mercury study and facilitating and participating in the resulting UNEP efforts toward negotiations on global reductions in mercury emissions;

b. With respect to PCBs:

(i) EPA give priority to these concerns in setting or approving cleanup standards under CERCLA; that EPA conduct robust cleanups and decline to employ "use-restricted" or "risk-based" methods for sites affecting communities of color, low-income communities, tribes, and other indigenous peoples; and that, in any event, EPA refuse to rely on projected or current reductions in fish, shellfish, and aquatic resource consumption and use as a justification for less protective cleanup standards or assumptions;

c. With respect to dioxin:

(i) EPA move expeditiously to release the final Dioxin Reassessment and that EPA ensure that the "need for further study and peer review" not be used as a reason to delay further its publication and use, given that dioxin has already been the subject of over a decade of study and sound scientific evidence supports the findings of the draft Dioxin Reassessment;

(ii) EPA address these concerns in ensuring compliance with its recently-issued Maximum Achievable Control Technology (MACT) standard for emissions from medical waste incinerators, and in identifying and facilitating further efforts to reduce and eliminate the use of products that, ultimately, result in releases of dioxin;

(iii) EPA address these concerns in issuing rules and undertaking initiatives to reduce further dioxin emissions to air, particularly from those sources that remain un- or under-controlled, including backyard burning;

(iv) EPA address these concerns in undertaking cleanup of sediments and soils contaminated from historical emissions and discharges of dioxin, given the increasing relative contribution of sediments and soils to dioxin contamination (as other sources are controlled);

(v) EPA work expeditiously to conduct surveys of sediments and soils likely to be contaminated with dioxin, in order to facilitate effective cleanup;

(vi) EPA, as part of its Dioxin Exposure Initiative, work systematically to characterize the exposures of communities of color, low-income communities, tribes, and their members and to link these exposures to their sources;

(vii) EPA ensure the efficacy of standards regulating dioxin, by working expeditiously to improve its ability to measure dioxin levels – because dioxin is highly toxic in even very small quantities and because current methods are not sensitive enough to detect dioxin in very small quantities, EPA cannot ensure that releases at "non-detect" levels are in fact protective of the health of communities of color, low-income communities, tribes, and other indigenous peoples;

---

[448]These bans have the effect not only of requiring the use of alternative, mercury-free health care products and but also of providing incentives for the development and production of improved mercury-free technology and products. Indeed, such alternative, mercury-free health care products are already becoming available. See, e.g., Sustainable Health Care Project website at: www.uml.edu/centers/LCSP/hospitals.

d. With respect to these and other contaminants of concern:

    (i) EPA begin expeditiously to include additional contaminants of concern on its list of Persistent and Bioaccumulative Toxics (PBTs), including lindane, endosulfan, lead and a host of other highly toxic, persistent, and bioaccumulative substances, especially those affecting the aquatic resources on which communities of color, low-income communities, tribes, and indigenous peoples depend;

    (ii) EPA, under the auspices of its PBT Initiative and otherwise, place a priority on efforts to reduce and eliminate the use of PBTs, and to clean up and restore those ecosystems already contaminated with PBTs.

2. FCWG proposes that, similarly, with respect to its efforts under the Clean Water Act and other statutes addressing water quality and quantity, EPA protect highly-exposed populations, including communities of color, low-income communities, tribes, and other indigenous peoples and account for the particular cultural, traditional, religious, historical, economic, and legal contexts in which these affected groups consume and use aquatic resources.

Specifically, FCWG proposes that:

a. EPA issue guidance clarifying that water quality standards (WQS), whether issued by states, tribes or the EPA, account to the greatest extent possible under law for these affected groups' different consumption and use of aquatic resources by, among other things:

    (i) requiring "designated uses" to reflect appropriate rates of consumption and use of fish, shellfish, plants and wildlife by subsistence fishers and other higher-consuming groups;

    (ii) requiring that such "designated uses" be recognized not only for those water bodies where subsistence and other fishing currently occurs, but also for those water bodies where subsistence and other fishing *would* occur, but for the contamination and depletion that give rise to suppressed consumption (described in Chapter One of the Report);

    (iii) requiring that designated uses support cultural, traditional, and ceremonial uses of aquatic resources, particularly where the quality of the relevant water bodies affects tribal and other culturally important resources (whether located on- or off-reservation);

    (iv) requiring triennial reviews of water quality standards under CWA § 303(c)(1) to consider whether state or tribal criteria protect subsistence fishers and other higher-consuming groups where subsistence and other fishing exists, and stipulating that EPA disapprove any criteria that do not protect these groups;

b. EPA issue a Total Maximum Daily Load (TMDL) rule that protects highly-exposed populations, including communities of color, low-income communities, tribes, and other indigenous peoples and accounts for the particular cultural, traditional, religious, historical, economic, and legal contexts in which these affected groups consume and use aquatic resources – especially given that the impaired waters affected by the TMDL rule occur primarily and disproportionately in locations that impact these affected groups;

c. EPA issue a rule for Large Feedlots (also called Concentrated Animal Feeding Operations (CAFOs)) that protects the health and resources of communities of color, low-income communities, tribes, and other indigenous peoples in the process of addressing the siting and regulation of new facilities and the clean up of contamination from existing and former facilities; and that incorporates the NEJAC Resolution on CAFOs;

d. EPA issue a rule for Metal Products and Machinery that protects the health and resources of communities of color, low-income communities, tribes, and other indigenous peoples while attending to issues of economic justice, particularly to the extent those small businesses affected by the rule are an important source of jobs and economic health for members of affected groups (e.g., by focusing on measures that both prevent contamination and reduce costs to regulated sources);

e. EPA make every use of its authority under the National Pollutant Discharge Elimination System (NPDES) program to protect highly-exposed populations, including communities of color, low-income communities, tribes, and other indigenous peoples and account for the particular cultural, traditional, religious, historical, economic, and legal contexts in which these affected groups consume and use aquatic resources, by among other things:

(i) imposing appropriate permit conditions, when EPA possesses the permitting authority;

(ii) disapproving permits that do not impose appropriate conditions, when states or tribes possess the permitting authority; and

(iii) incorporating the NEJAC proposals regarding permitting: *Environmental Justice in the Permitting Process: A Report from the Public Meeting on Environmental Permitting, Convened by the National Environmental Justice Advisory Council in Arlington, Virginia, Nov. 30 Dec. 2, 1999;*

f. EPA explore and implement additional strategies to address non-point source discharges and runoffs to waters that threaten aquatic ecosystems and human health, including but not limited to discharges from agricultural, construction, forestry, and land disposal operations; stormwater runoff; and applications of FIFRA-approved herbicides along irrigation canals and other waterways;

g. EPA make full use of its authority to ensure non-degradation of clean or "pristine" waters;

h. EPA work to protect and restore wetlands, and to oppose efforts by the Army Corps of Engineers that would relax rules designed to restrict development and degradation of streams and wetlands and to limit cumulative adverse effects on the aquatic environment and ecosystem;[449] EPA should take seriously and literally the commitment to "no net loss;"

i. EPA, in writing regulations under the CWA and in acting other authorities, consider the effect of human-controlled timing and quantity of water flows on water temperature, pollutant concentrations, the health and propagation of fish and wildlife, and the overall health of aquatic ecosystems;

j. EPA attend to urban (e.g., Oakland) and rural (e.g., towns along the U.S.-Mexico border; Alaska Native villages; elsewhere in Indian country; Hawai'i) sanitation issues and their impact on the health of humans and aquatic ecosystems.

3. FCWG also proposes that, with respect to its efforts under the Clean Air Act and other statutes addressing air emissions that affect the health of aquatic ecosystems, EPA protect highly-exposed populations, including communities of color, low-income communities, tribes, and other indigenous peoples and account for the particular cultural, traditional, religious, historical, economic, and legal contexts in which these affected groups consume and use aquatic resources.

Specifically, FCWG proposes that:

a. EPA work with Congressional staff, testify before Congress, and otherwise seek to ensure that the National Energy Plan currently being debated:

(i) places stringent limits on releases of NOx, SO2, and mercury from power plants in order to protect communities of color, low income communities, tribes, and other indigenous peoples and the aquatic ecosystems on which they depend; and

(ii) in the event that it includes an emissions trading program for mercury, employs a "cap" that requires significant aggregate reductions in mercury and includes mechanisms to guarantee that disproportionate burdens from these sources on communities of color, low income communities, tribes, and other indigenous peoples are not exacerbated or newly created by trading;

b. EPA evaluate more thoroughly the impacts of air deposition on the health of fish, aquatic plants, and wildlife, and, in turn, on communities of color, low income communities, tribes, and other indigenous peoples that depend on these resources, and that EPA address these impacts, including:

---

[449]The Washington Post Online, "Army Corps Seeks to Relax Wetlands Rules," by Michael Grunwald, p. A01 (June 4, 2001). See also http://washingtonpost.com:80/wp-dyn/articles/A16798-2001June3.html.

(i) through expanded cross-program initiatives; and

(ii) when it considers the residual risks after the application of MACT, as part of the 10-year reviews required under CAA § 112(f);

c. EPA better control NOx to prevent acidification and eutrophication;

d. EPA make every use of its authority under the Title V Air Operating Permit program to protect highly-exposed populations, including communities of color, low-income communities, tribes, and other indigenous peoples and account for the particular cultural, traditional, religious, historical, economic, and legal contexts in which these affected groups consume and use aquatic resources, by among other things:

(i) imposing appropriate permit conditions, when EPA possesses the permitting authority;

(ii) disapproving permits that do not impose appropriate conditions, when states or tribes possess the permitting authority; and

(iii) incorporating the NEJAC proposals regarding permitting: *Environmental Justice in the Permitting Process: A Report from the Public Meeting on Environmental Permitting, Convened by the National Environmental Justice Advisory Council in Arlington, Virginia, Nov. 30 Dec. 2, 1999.*

4. FCWG also proposes that, with respect to its efforts under the Comprehensive Environmental Response, Compensation, and Liability Act (CERCLA), and other statutes addressing cleanup and restoration of contaminated environments, EPA protect highly-exposed populations, including communities of color, low-income communities, tribes, and other indigenous peoples and account for the particular cultural, traditional, religious, historical, economic, and legal contexts in which these affected groups consume and use aquatic resources.

Specifically, FCWG proposes that:

a. EPA expand its current efforts under its Contaminated Sediment Management Strategy so that in addition to assessing the nature and extent of contamination sediments, it focuses on and prioritizes cleanup and restoration of contaminated sediments, and that in the process, EPA attend to disposal issues raised by contaminated sediments that have been removed;

b. EPA conduct robust cleanups and decline to employ "use-restricted" or "risk-based" methods for sites affecting communities of color, low-income communities, tribes, and other indigenous peoples, and that, in any event, EPA refuse to rely on projected or current reductions in fish, shellfish, and aquatic resource consumption and use as a justification for less protective cleanup standards or assumptions;

c. EPA work through every avenue possible to oppose efforts to eliminate funding for CERCLA's "Superfund;" to ensure that, to the extent these efforts are successful, EPA nonetheless continues to place a high priority on cleanup and restoration of those sites contaminated with pollutants likely to bioaccumulate in the fish, aquatic plants, and wildlife consumed or used for subsistence, traditional, cultural or religious purposes; and to ensure that any resulting delay in addressing such sites not be used to justify less protective cleanup standards;

d. EPA work to retain and effectuate the "polluter pays" principle under CERCLA, by, among other things, looking to potentially responsible parties (PRPs) to ensure funding for full restoration of those ecosystems that support fish, shellfish, aquatic plants and wildlife on which affected groups rely; ensure funding for adequate communication with affected tribes and communities and; if appropriate from the perspective of those affected, funding for alternatives that may serve as substitutes for the contaminated resources until such time as the restoration is complete (Please note, however, that such alternatives will NOT be appropriate from the perspectives of some affected groups – the provision of alternative resources, for example, is not endorsed by the Indigenous Peoples Subcommittee);

e. EPA improve cooperation among EPA offices on cleanup and restoration strategies, particularly initiatives targeted at restoring those aquatic ecosystems that are contaminated with pollutants likely to bioaccumulate in the fish, aquatic plants, and wildlife consumed or used for subsistence, traditional, cultural or religious purposes;

f. EPA revise its Principles for the Ecological Restoration of Aquatic Resources to focus not only "on scientific and technical issues"[450] but also on the historical, cultural, legal, and social contexts within which restoration takes place; that EPA revise these Principles to reflect the interrelation between "physical"structures and functions on the one hand and social and cultural structures and functions on the other hand, such that restoring and maintaining "ecological integrity" includes restoring and maintaining cultural integrity; and that EPA work with tribes and other affected groups to undertake "eco-cultural restoration."[451]

5. FCWG also proposes that, with respect to its efforts under the Toxic Substances Control Act (ToSCA), and other statutes regulating new and existing chemical substances, EPA protect highly-exposed populations, including communities of color, low-income communities, tribes, and other indigenous peoples and account for the particular cultural, traditional, religious, historical, economic, and legal contexts in which these affected groups consume and use aquatic resources.

Specifically, FCWG proposes that:

a. EPA's Office of Pesticides, Prevention, and Toxic Substances (OPPTS) flag to its Office of Water (OW) those chemicals that it registers that are expected to be produced or used in high volume and that will potentially affect aquatic ecosystems; OW should then work with OPPTS to secure additional and higher level testing, and where potential contamination of fish and aquatic resources is suspected, to ensure that additional testing and rulemaking are expedited.

6. FCWG also proposes that, with respect to its efforts under other statutory authorities, EPA protect highly-exposed populations, including communities of color, low-income communities, tribes, and other indigenous peoples and account for the particular cultural, traditional, religious, historical, economic, and legal contexts in which these affected groups consume and use aquatic resources.

Specifically, FCWG proposes that:

a. EPA issue a rule regulating coal combustion waste under the Resource Conservation and Recovery Act (RCRA), especially given the presence of arsenic in this waste and the fact that, in many places, this waste is still being disposed of in unlined facilities and leaching into drinking water sources;

b. EPA tighten hazardous waste rules to prohibit toxic wastes, such as dioxins, mercury, lead, cadmium, and other contaminants of concern from being "recycled" into fertilizer, and eliminate the exemption for steel mill waste;[452] and that EPA rewrite its ten-year-old treatment standard for hazardous waste, ensuring that the new rule does not create disincentives (such as those created by permissive provisions regarding recycling) for developing and implementing improved treatment technologies.

7. In undertaking compliance and enforcement efforts affecting the quality of aquatic ecosystems, FCWG proposes EPA to improve its cooperation, coordination, and collaboration with states and tribes, and, in the case of federally recognized tribes, to improve its consultation with tribal governments.

In setting or approving standards and in making other risk management decisions meant to address these contaminants, EPA aims for a level of risk to human health deemed "acceptable" or safe. That is

---

[450]U.S. EPA, Principles for the Ecological Restoration of Aquatic Resources (2000), available at www.epa.gov/owow/wetlands/restore/principles.html.

[451]See, e.g., Jeffrey P. Thomas, Director, Forest Resource Protection Program, Fisheries Department, Puyallup Tribe of Indians, Testimony to the National Environmental Justice Advisory Council, Dec. 4, 2001 (Written Comments) (describing the potential role for the Inter-Tribal Cultural Advisory Group (in Washington) to this end).

[452]Toxic wastes from pulp and paper mills, steel mills, tire incinerators and cement kilns is currently "recycled" into fertilizer and applied to crops, grazing lands and gardens. This waste has been found to contain dioxins, mercury, lead, cadmium, and other contaminants of concern. Although hazardous waste regulations address this practice, (1) they may still permit unacceptable levels of these contaminants, and (2) they contain a loophole that exempts steel mill waste. See, e.g., Washington Toxics Coalition, Visualizing Zero: Eliminating Persistent Pollution in Washington State (2000).

to say, for carcinogens or non-threshold contaminants, EPA in effect determines that it will view the increased incidence of cancer in some number of humans (e.g., 1 out of every 1,000,000 humans) to be "acceptable," and will permit environmental standards to be set accordingly. To the extent that EPA's guidance and standards deem a greater level of cancer risk to be "acceptable" for "more highly exposed subgroups" than for the general population, this is inequitable and deeply troubling as a matter of environmental justice, given that we *know* and EPA *knows* that it is people of color, low-income people, American Indians/Alaska Natives, and other indigenous people that comprise the "more highly exposed subgroups." Moreover, in the view of FCWG, human lives are not expendable. EPA should strive for standards that do not find "acceptable" the increased risk of cancer for *any* humans.

Overarching Proposals

II-6. FCWG proposes that as a general matter, EPA should ensure that the federal environmental laws are implemented and enforced equitably and effectively to protect the health of all people consuming fish, aquatic plants, and wildlife.

II-7. FCWG proposes that substantive environmental standards be set so as to provide equitable levels of protection to all   levels that protect not only the health of the general population, but also the health of people of color, low-income people, American Indians, Alaska Natives, Native Hawaiians and other Pacific Islanders, and other indigenous people located within the jurisdiction of the United States.

II-8. Specifically, FCWG proposes that EPA rescind any guidance setting "acceptable" risk for subsistence and other higher-consuming subgroups at levels greater than the general population (e.g., EPA's revised Ambient Water Quality Criteria Methodology, which defines "acceptable" cancer risk for higher-consuming subgroups as risk that permits up to 1 in 10,000 people to suffer from cancer whereas it defines "acceptable" cancer risk for the general population as risk that permits a fewer number of people to suffer from cancer   between 1 in 100,000 and 1 in 1,000,000, and perhaps as few as 1 in 10,000,000), and to reissue guidance that prevents such a disparity in protection. Moreover, FCWG proposes EPA to reconsider in every relevant context its determination that some greater number of human cancers due to environmental contamination is "acceptable" for more highly exposed subgroups and to strive for standards that do not find "acceptable" the increased risk of cancer for any *humans, i.e., standards that aim for zero risk.*

In setting or approving standards and in making other risk management or regulatory decisions meant to address these contaminants, EPA needs to respect and accommodate the different cultural, traditional, religious, historical, economic, and legal contexts in which affected groups consume, use, and depend on aquatic resources.

Overarching Proposal

II-9. FCWG proposes EPA to work with affected groups better to understand the various different cultural, traditional, religious, historical, economic, and legal contexts in which these groups consume, use, and depend on aquatic resources and to develop methods to incorporate these groups' particular circumstances into the standards EPA sets or approves and into the other risk management and regulatory decisions EPA makes.

Focused Proposals

II-9

> 1. FCWG proposes that EPA use its authority under CWA § 101(e) and elsewhere to encourage states to improve their public participation processes in the development of water quality standards through translation for non-English speaking groups and through greater outreach.
>
> 2. FCWG proposes EPA to work together with affected communities and tribes to explore creative, culturally appropriate ways to inform its prevention and reduction efforts regarding communities' and tribes' actual practices, where these practices expose these groups to contaminants in fish, shellfish, plants, and wildlife within aquatic ecosystems.[453]
>
> 3. FCWG proposes that EPA reconceptualize its role in understanding affected groups' circumstances of exposure, so that it focuses on building longer-term relationships with affected groups. In the context of these relationships, iterative conversations and other on-going processes would then serve to better inform efforts to prevent and reduce contamination in the first place.
>
> 4. EPA's Principles for the Ecological Restoration of Aquatic Resources suggest that restoration efforts "involve the skills and insights of a multi-disciplinary team," and cite among the relevant disciplines "ecology, aquatic biology, hydrology and hydraulics, geomorphology, engineering, planning, communications and social science."[454] FCWG proposes that EPA broaden its understanding of the kinds of expertise relevant to restoration, and include among those it consults elders, anthropologists, ethnobiologists, historians, and others who can provide insight into the "eco-cultural" aspects of restoration.[455]

Prevention, cleanup, and restoration of aquatic ecosystems implicates not only EPA but also numerous other federal departments, agencies and programs (e.g., the Department of Defense, the Department of Energy, the Federal Energy Regulatory Commission, the U.S. Forest Service, the National Marine Fisheries Service, the U.S. Geological Survey, the Bureau of Indian Affairs, the Indian Health Service, the National Institute of Environmental Health Services). Prevention, cleanup, and restoration efforts would be greatly improved and hastened by coordination among these various entities.

Overarching Proposal

II-10. FCWG proposes EPA to take the lead in coordinating the various federal departments, agencies and programs in order to improve prevention, cleanup, and restoration efforts, and to ensure that the results of these efforts, as well as the process for achieving the results, are just.

---

[453]Communities' and tribes' knowledge here simply cannot be replicated by non-members. At the same time, agencies' familiarity with laws, regulations and guidance is crucial. In some cases, affected communities and tribes have already begun to develop relevant processes, e.g., for documenting consumption and use practices and the contexts in which these occur, or to assemble other relevant informational resources. For example, the Tulalip Tribes are gathering "cultural stories" that will help inform their natural resources and environmental management efforts.

[454]U.S. EPA, Principles for the Ecological Restoration of Aquatic Resources (2000), available at www.epa.gov/owow/wetlands/restore/principles.html.

[455]Dennis Martinez, Presentation, Indigenous Ecology and Cultural Restoration Workshop (San Francisco, Sept.21, 1999).

Focused Proposals

II-10

> 1. FCWG proposes EPA to improve cooperation among EPA offices, as well as among federal agencies, on pollution prevention strategies, particularly initiatives targeted at preventing the discharge or release of pollutants likely to bioaccumulate in the aquatic ecosystem and people.

> 2. FCWG proposes that EPA use Interagency Working Group as vehicle for disseminating information on prevention, cleanup and restoration that is attentive to the issue of contamination of aquatic ecosystems and its impact on communities of color, low-income communities, tribes, and other indigenous peoples.

> 3. FCWG proposes EPA to coordinate effectively with other federal agencies to ensure that *sufficient quantities* of water are maintained and protected to support a sustainable and healthy aquatic ecosystem, and to ensure that other actions are undertaken (e.g., under the Endangered Species Act (ESA) to guarantee the health of fish, shellfish, plant, and wildlife species and the habitats on which these species depend.

Tribal governments or EPA are responsible for implementing water quality standards (WQS) within Indian country and on Alaska Native lands. Yet, because only 16 of the 565 federally recognized tribes and Alaska Native villages have EPA approved and/or promulgated water quality standards, there are still considerable gaps in water quality standards coverage in Indian country.

Overarching Proposal

II-11. FCWG proposes that EPA address promptly existing gaps in water quality standards coverage in Indian country and on Alaska Native lands to protect tribal resources and treaty-protected rights as well as the health of American Indian/Alaska Native people who are heavily reliant on subsistence activities and diet. FCWG proposes EPA to make the development, adoption, implementation, and enforcement of water quality standards throughout all of Indian country a high priority. This includes support for tribal WQS in accordance with EPA's Indian Policy and promulgation of enforceable federal core WQS for reservation and other Indian country waters for which tribal WQS are not in effect. FCWG proposes that, consistent with the federal trust responsibility to the tribes, EPA use all available existing authorities under the federal environmental laws to protect tribal resources, treaty-protected rights, and the health of American Indian/Alaska Native people; provided that EPA should cooperate with and support tribal regulatory efforts in those instances where tribes choose to carry out various responsibilities under the federal environmental laws. In the context of Alaska Native lands that are not considered Indian country, FCWG proposes EPA to engage in consultation with Alaska Native tribes and the State of Alaska on the possible revision of WQS better to protect subsistence traditions, such as the adoption of designated uses for subsistence harvesting of fish and wildlife.

Focused Proposals

II-11

> 1. FCWG proposes that EPA, in consultation with tribes, proceed with rulemaking on the Core Federal Water Quality Standards for Indian Country:[456]

---

[456]See U.S. EPA, Office of Water, Federal Water Quality Standards for Indian Country and Other Provisions Regarding Federal Water Quality Standards (unofficial pre-publication copy, Jan. 19, 2001) (available at www.epa.gov/ost/standards/tribal/) [hereinafter "Proposed Core Standards"].

a. The Proposed Core Standards currently call for a four-part hierarchy for selecting a fish consumption rate for use in setting water quality standards in Indian Country. This hierarchy sets up a preference for using "the results of any existing fish consumption surveys of local Indian country watersheds to establish fish intake provisions that are representative of the population being addressed," but in the absence of such data, would look to a default fish consumption rate as low as 17.5 grams/day.[457] In FCWG's view, this default fish consumption rate does not accurately reflect the consumption practices of most tribes. FCWG proposes EPA to employ a default consumption rate that is appropriate for higher-consuming tribes and their members. EPA should select this default rate in consultation with tribes. FCWG further proposes EPA to account for other aspects of tribes' different exposure circumstances, including practices that mean different species are consumed, different parts are used, and/or different preparation methods are employed than those typically assumed by agencies. Again, EPA should consult with tribes to understand the nature and import of these practices. Finally, FCWG commends the fact that the proposed hierarchy sets up a preference for local data, but emphasizes the need for EPA to fund additional, tribally conducted fish consumption surveys in Indian country watersheds. As discussed in Chapter One, currently only a handful of such studies exist;

b. EPA should, in consultation with tribes, develop guidance for EPA permit writers charged with implementing the Proposed Core Standards in order to ensure that permit writers tailor NPDES permits to each individual tribe's circumstances, including their particular cultural practices;

c. EPA should provide adequate funding and technical assistance to enable tribes who wish to do so to develop a plan for adopting their own water quality standards under the Clean Water Act or for developing individualized federal standards together with the relevant Regional Administrator within a reasonable amount of time, as required in order to be excluded from the rule adopting Core Federal Water Quality Standards for Indian Country.[458]

The contamination of aquatic environments and the harmful effects of this contamination are matters of global concern. Pollution, of course, does not respect political boundaries and many of the contaminants of concern persist in the environment and travel great distances, cycling through the air, water, soils, and sediments and affecting people and places far from the source.

Overarching Proposals

II-12. FCWG proposes EPA to be mindful of the interconnected and international nature of contaminated aquatic ecosystems. FCWG proposes that EPA work to ensure the development, ratification, implementation, and enforcement of international law and policy addressing the contaminants of concern.

II-13. Specifically, FCWG proposes EPA to expend every effort to see that the United States ratifies the Convention on Persistent Organic Pollutants (POPs) and to develop, together with affected communities and tribes, an implementation plan for the United States that assures compliance with this treaty.

Chapter Three

Fish and wildlife consumption advisories are one component of a comprehensive health risk control strategy and can serve the useful function of aiding affected communities in determining to what extent they will take the proposed steps to avoid health risks.

---

[457]See Proposed Core Standards at 17.
[458]See id. at 4-6.

Overarching Proposals

III-1. However, FCWG strongly emphasizes that advisories must be coupled with ongoing and aggressive efforts to curb existing and future pollutant sources through stringent implementation and enforcement of water quality and other environmental regulations and cleanup of historic contaminant sources. FCWG proposes EPA to work with affected groups and be proactive in identifying and implementing alternatives that protect the health of disproportionately exposed groups in the meantime, that is, until prevention and cleanup are fully achieved.

Focused Proposals

III-1

1. Fish consumption advisories – which shift the burden to risk-bearers to avoid the risks they have been made to face – should never be allowed to become the primary method by which agencies address risks. Rather, FCWG proposes EPA to require risk-producers to prevent, reduce and cleanup contamination, and to view fish consumption advisories as a short-term, interim strategy to inform and to protect the health of those who consume and use fish, aquatic plants, and wildlife while cleanup is proceeding. To this end:

   a. FCWG proposes EPA to focus, during planning and priority setting, on reducing risk and addressing communities' and tribes' health and safety needs rather than on securing communities' and tribes' "compliance" with fish advisories or other risk avoidance measures;

   b. FCWG emphasizes that EPA needs to couple the use of fish consumption advisories designed to protect people's health "in the meantime" with a real, aggressive push to cleanup, reduce and prevent contamination in the first place;

   c. FCWG proposes a focus in particular on prevention now so that in the future EPA and states will not be faced with having to employ fish consumption advisories.

2. FCWG proposes that EPA develop, and help states and tribes to develop, measures to ensure that reliance on fish consumption advisories is truly a temporary strategy. Given that advisories have been in effect in some places for nearly 30 years (e.g., the Great Lakes), it seems that a renewed commitment is in order. To this end, FCWG proposes EPA to consider a wide variety of measures, including sunset provisions, periodic reevaluation, etc., that would help EPA and other agencies guard against the advisory program taking on a life of its own.

3. FCWG proposes that EPA develop, and help states and tribes to develop, mechanisms to ensure that agency risk communicators coordinate with agency risk managers so that affected groups' responses to fish consumption advisories inform future risk management decisions, including planning and priority-setting. FCWG notes that this coordination is especially important where the affected community or tribe declines to *"comply"* with a fish advisory: to the extent that such a response expresses a protest with current priorities (e.g., reliance on risk avoidance rather than risk reduction), EPA needs to ensure, and help states and tribes to ensure, that this protest gets registered with and taken into account by those setting priorities.

4. FCWG proposes EPA to increase financial and technical support to tribes who wish to determine for themselves what role fish consumption advisories should play in their efforts to protect the health and safety of tribal members and who may wish to fashion tribal consumption guidelines. This would include funding basic research by the tribe into the nature and extent of the contamination of concern, and its health effects for tribal members. FCWG notes that tribes are often the only ones in the position to frame the research questions in a way that reflects their unique knowledge of tribal resources and their sense of what is appropriate for tribal members. Further, FCWG proposes EPA to require states that issue advisories to notify directly all tribes whose land and resources (including resources both on- and off-reservation) are affected by the advisory.

5. FCWG proposes EPA to increase financial and technical support to affected communities to participate in decisions, including decisions at the state and local levels, about what role of fish consumption advisories should play in efforts to protect the health and safety of community members.

6. FCWG proposes that EPA consider how it might meet the immediate needs of communities of color, low-income communities, tribes, and indigenous peoples who are burdened by existing contamination.

Specifically, FCWG proposes that:

    a. EPA work together with affected groups to identify useful alternatives for those who would avail themselves of alternative means of catching or consuming fish or alternative ways of meeting at least some nutritional needs;

    b. EPA consider, *together with those affected*, whether there is a role for providing such things as subsidized construction of alternative fishing ponds; subsidized bus passes or other transportation vouchers to alternative fishing sites; subsidized vouchers for purchasing uncontaminated fish; subsidized vouchers for purchasing alternative sources of protein; subsidized aquaculture; or other measures to meet affected groups' immediate needs. *However, FCWG emphasizes that EPA should proceed cautiously here, working closely with the particular affected group(s) and attending to the possible negative effects of such alternatives* (e.g., government "surplus" foods are notoriously high in fat and sugar and providing such foods could exacerbate existing health conditions – such as diabetes, the incidence of which is much greater among Native American populations and some other affected subgroups). *FCWG implores EPA to recognize that the provision of alternatives will be inappropriate from the perspective of some affected groups.* (The Indigenous Peoples Subcommittee, for example, does not endorse the provision of alternatives or "substitutes" for contaminated aquatic resources.);

    c. EPA make greater use of fines imposed on violators as part of CERCLA enforcement actions that result in settlement to fund studies by and for affected groups, and to otherwise meet affected groups' immediate needs.

7. FCWG proposes that EPA work with state and local environmental and health agencies to ensure that not only is initial testing of fish, shellfish, and aquatic resources undertaken expeditiously but that follow up testing is also conducted, particularly given the importance of fisheries for subsistence and economic needs. Thus, for example, a state may in some cases act to close shellfisheries due to contamination that it has confirmed by testing, but neglect to conduct further testing in order to determine at earliest possible date that the threat from contamination over and it is appropriate to reopen the fishery. FCWG notes that, as a general matter, testing is too episodic at both ends.

While advisories are useful, in order for them to be effective they must be tailored to specific locales and specific communities   there is no one-size-fits-all, and "consistency" across broad regions or population groups may not be useful. The term "affected groups" here includes a large and diverse array of groups, each of which consumes and uses fish, aquatic plants, and wildlife in differing cultural, traditional, religious, historical, economic, and legal contexts. It will be crucial for any risk communication effort to recognize, therefore, the diverse contexts, interests, and needs that characterize affected communities, including but not limited to groups with limited English proficiency; groups with limited or no literacy; low-income communities; immigrant and refuge communities; African-American communities, various Asian and Pacific Islander communities and subcommunities (e.g., Mien, Lao, Khmu, and Thaidum communities within the Laotian community in West Contra Costa, CA); various Hispanic communities and subcommunities (e.g., "Caribbean-American" communities in the Greenpoint/Williamsburg area of Brooklyn, NY); various Native Americans, Native Hawaiians, and Alaskan Natives (including members of tribes and villages, members of non-federally recognized tribes, and urban Native people); and subgroups such as children, pregnant women, or elders within these groups.

Overarching Proposal

III-2. FCWG proposes EPA to learn about and attend to the fact that "affected groups" includes a large and diverse array of groups, each of which consumes and uses fish, aquatic plants, and wildlife in differing cultural, traditional, religious, historical, economic, linguistic and legal contexts. It will be crucial for any risk communication effort to recognize, therefore, the diverse contexts, interests, and needs that characterize affected groups.

Focused Proposals

III-2

1. FCWG proposes that EPA work with each of the large and diverse array of affected groups to determine priorities for defining, gauging, and enhancing advisories' effectiveness *from the perspectives of those affected.* FCWG emphasizes that EPA can better identify the real problems that exist in communities and tribes by listening to and consulting with those affected. FCWG commends EPA's recent efforts, together with the State of Minnesota, to bring together and fund the participation of representatives from communities and tribes in order to discuss some of these issues in the context of its *National Forum on Contaminants in Fish* in May, 2001.

2. FCWG commends the fact that EPA has dedicated resources and staff to be devoted to environmental justice issues and applauds the considerable work that has been done to identify the large and diverse array of affected groups and to attend to the particular cultural, traditional, religious, historical, economic, linguistic, and legal contexts in which these groups consume and use fish and other aquatic resources. FCWG proposes that EPA maintain and expand the resources and staff it devotes to environmental justice, and that EPA encourage states to do the same.

3. FCWG suggests that a focus on national or regional consistency among state and tribal advisory programs is misplaced from the perspective of most communities of color, low-income communities, tribes, and other indigenous peoples, whose concerns tend to be more localized; FCWG proposes, instead, that agency resources be redirected toward preventing, reducing, and cleaning up the contamination that gives rise to advisories.

Affected communities and tribes are integral to relevant, appropriate and effective risk communication. Affected communities and tribes need, therefore, to be involved as "partners" or, in the case of tribal governments, "co-managers" at every stage of the communication process   from identifying needs and priorities, to developing group-appropriate advisory content, language(s), and communication methods, to interpreting community responses and determining their import for agencies' risk assessment and management efforts.

Overarching Proposals

III-3. FCWG proposes EPA to recognize the expertise of members of affected communities and tribes, and to involve them or consult with them throughout the risk communication process. FCWG proposes EPA to follow NEJAC's Model Plan for Public Participation and NEJAC's Guide on Consultation and Collaboration with Indian Tribal Governments and the Public Participation of Indigenous Groups and Tribal Members in Environmental Decision Making.

III-4. Importantly, FCWG proposes EPA to make available additional financial and technical resources to communities and tribes to ensure that they can participate or engage in consultation effectively.

III-5. FCWG emphasizes the importance of capacity-augmentation in communities and tribes, and proposes that EPA recognize and facilitate this as a separate objective of full community and tribal involvement in risk communication.

III-6. To this end, FCWG specifically proposes that EPA, in issuing its advisories and in providing guidance to states and tribes :

(A) Ensure that affected communities and tribes are involved in the identification, design, implementation, and evaluation of culturally appropriate and effective communication of fish advisory information.

(B) Ensure that advisories present information in a form that is culturally appropriate and readily understood by the fisher and fish consumer (i.e. no jargon and in the language(s) of the affected communities, utilizing graphics as appropriate).

(C) Ensure that, where culturally appropriate and practicable, advisories suggest alternative means that would allow for the continued consumption of fish, including alternative fish species or alternative preparation and cooking methods.

(D) Ensure that affected communities and tribes are able to participate in or consult on the development of proposals about alternative or substitute food sources, and alternative preparation and cooking methods.

Focused Proposals

III-3 through III-6

1. FCWG proposes that, depending on the affected group, EPA use the NEJAC's *Model Plan for Public Participation* and/or NEJAC's *Guide on Consultation and Collaboration with Indian Tribal Governments and the Public Participation of Indigenous Groups and Tribal Members in Environmental Decisionmaking* as a guide for informing those affected not only of the fact of contamination and advisories, but also of the nature and extent of the contamination and its impacts on the health and well-being of the affected group. FCWG emphasizes the need to allow adequate time for those affected to digest and discuss the information and then to participate in or consult on relevant decisions.

2. FCWG notes that, in many cases, it will be appropriate for the regional EPA office to take the initiative to organize and collaborate with affected communities and tribes regarding contaminated fish and other aquatic resources. FCWG proposes that the regional EPA office, again using the *Model Plan* and/or the *Guide on Consultation*, as appropriate, assist affected groups to develop and communicate possibilities that would make the group whole. The regional EPA office, together with the affected group, should discuss, evaluate and negotiate which possibilities should be implemented and agree on an implementation plan and timelines; and should then be accountable to the group for "follow through," (e.g., ensuring *and communicating to the group the fact that* the measures identified are in fact implemented.

3. FCWG proposes EPA to set up data bases and other means by which affected groups may access information from and communicate with EPA, working with affected group to identify and meet their needs. FCWG emphasizes the need for EPA to provide financial and technical assistance to communities and tribes that are working to inform themselves in order to participate meaningfully in or consult meaningfully on EPA decisions affecting the aquatic ecosystems on with these groups depend. FCWG notes that this is a matter of capacity augmentation, and proposes EPA to make it a priority.

4. FCWG proposes that EPA, as it works with affected groups, be mindful of the various considerations outlined in Chapter Three, Part D of the Report, and that it encourage state and local agencies to look to the various approaches that have been cited in the Report as successful from the perspectives of those affected as potential models for their current risk communication efforts.

Chapter Four

Although American Indian tribes, Alaska Native villages, and their members share many of the concerns discussed in the preceding chapters, tribes' political and legal status is unique among affected groups and so warrants separate treatment. Tribes are governmental entities, recognized as possessing broad inherent authority over their members, territories, and resources. As sovereigns, federally recognized tribes have a government-to-government relationship with the federal government and its agencies, including the EPA. Tribes' unique legal status includes a trust responsibility on the part of the federal government. For many tribes, it also includes treaty rights (e.g., the rights of the treaty tribes of the Pacific Northwest to take fish "at all usual and accustomed grounds and stations;" or similar rights of treaty tribes elsewhere to fish, hunt and gather). Other laws and executive commitments, too, shape the legal obligations owed to tribes, American Indians and Alaska Natives.

Additionally, due to their special susceptibilities such as poverty, remote location, poor health and extremely high unmet health needs, subsistence-based living, and traditional and cultural uses of natural resources, tribes, American Indians, and Alaska Natives suffer a disproportionate burden of health consequences due to their exposure to pollutants and hazardous substances in the environment.

Overarching Proposals

IV-1. Where tribes and American Indians/Alaska Natives are affected by polluted aquatic ecosystems and contaminated fish, aquatic plants, and wildlife, federal agencies must respond and resolve these threats and environmental and health impacts in ways that fulfill the federal trust responsibility owed to tribes and that are respectful of and consistent with the recognition of tribal sovereignty and tribal rights under federal laws and treaties. In the context of Alaska Natives, federal agencies must respond to and resolve these threats and environmental and health impacts in ways that preserve for Alaska Natives the ability to carry on their traditional practices of providing for their subsistence needs from the lands and waters that they have used historically.

Focused Proposals

IV-1

1. FCWG proposes EPA to support legislative initiatives that will eliminate inequities in federal funding to address the alarmingly high levels of unmet environmental and health needs of AI/ANs, regardless of where they live. Although the EPA leads federal efforts in protecting the environment within Indian country and Alaska Native villages, the Indian Health Service is the principal federal health care provider and health advocate for AI/ANs. The provision of these health-related services arise from the trust responsibility and special government-to-government relationship between the federal government and federally recognized Indian tribes. However, the level of funding for Indian Health Service has long been utterly inadequate to meet the environmental and general health needs of Indian country and Alaska. In 2000, the Indian Health Service was funded and staffed at only 34% of the level of need.

2. FCWG proposes EPA to assert a leadership role among federal agencies in developing new financing mechanisms and leveraging all available resources to fund and implement environmental health-related projects and research in Indian country and Alaska Native villages.

3. FCWG proposes EPA to support regional meetings and a national summit of federal agencies, federally recognized tribes, and concerned tribal organizations to discuss the environmental health needs of AI/AN and design a comprehensive environmental health research agenda to address those needs.

4. FCWG proposes EPA to review available baseline environmental health data for Indian country and Native Alaska villages and take prompt steps to remedy all data insufficiencies, and retain and store environmental and health data on each federally recognized tribal government and provide a means for each tribe to access easily the information applicable to its members and territory. FCWG proposes EPA to request that the Indian Health Service make its annual data on health status readily available to each federally recognized tribe and other federal agencies.

5. FCWG proposes EPA, in consultation with federally recognized tribes and with the involvement of concerned tribal organizations, to conduct environmental research, studies, and monitoring programs to determine the effects on, and ways to mitigate the effects on the health of AI/AN communities due to exposure to environmental hazards, including but not limited to persistent organic pollutants and persistent bioaccumulative and toxic pollutants, nuclear resource development, uranium and other mine tailing deposits, petroleum contamination, and contamination of the water source and/or food chain. *This is critical where the health of such communities is particularly susceptible to environmental harm because they are known to rely on subsistence fishing, hunting, and gathering.*

6. Because federal environmental missions and resources are divided among and in some cases overlap between various agencies, FCWG proposes that EPA take the lead in coordinating and pooling available technical and financial resources to provide environmental health-related services to federally recognized tribes equitably, efficiently, and effectively. Towards this end, the Bureau of Indian Affairs, EPA, Department of Housing and Urban Development, and the Indian Health Service should appraise the usefulness and implementation of a national Memorandum of Understanding (MOU) and take appropriate steps to enhance and better promote interagency coordination and collaboration pertaining to the protection of health and the environment within Indian country and Alaska Native villages. Additionally, interested tribes should be considered appropriate parties to similar regional MOUs addressing the protection of health and the environment on their particular reservations. FCWG proposes EPA, in consultation with federally recognized tribes, to develop a federally-funded, comprehensive, interagency program on environmental health that will address fully the environmental justice needs within Indian country and Alaska Native villages.

7. FCWG proposes EPA to make regulatory decisions and develop federal policies affecting the health of AI/AN communities in consultation with federally recognized tribes. To the greatest extent possible, such decisions should be based not only western notions of what constitutes "science, but also should address and incorporate the traditional knowledge of the AI/AN community. For example, limitations on the consumption of traditional foods such as fish, aquatic plants, and wildlife due to pollution danger may trigger unique social, economic, and health effects within AI/AN communities – effects that are most fully and appropriately understood only in consultation with affected tribes.

8. FCWG proposes EPA to ensure that agency staff and managers have a thorough understanding of federal Indian law and policies, tribal culture, and the unique governmental structure of federally recognized Indian tribes, including Alaska Native villages.

9. FCWG encourages EPA and each office within EPA to develop a strategy for recruitment, retention, and upward mobility of American Indians and Alaska Natives in order to increase the quality of planning and priority setting, standards development, and program implementation. Such diversity in hiring, retention, and promotion at EPA will help to ensure that staff is familiar with and comfortable in affected AI/AN communities.

10. FCWG proposes that EPA focus educational efforts on environmental justice and the cause, effect, and remediation of specific environmental hazards. These efforts also should strive to improve the understanding of these issues among AI/AN communities and health professionals serving these communities, including but not limited to medical, nursing, and public health practitioners.

11. FCWG proposes that EPA acknowledge and learn from the determination, creativity, and expertise possessed by tribes, tribal members, tribal scientists, and other tribal professionals in developing stewardship and restoration programs for the environment and aquatic ecosystems.

12. FCWG proposes EPA to increase the number of professionals specializing in environmental health issues confronting AI/AN communities. Because persons who have been exposed to certain hazardous substances such as lead, mercury, pesticides, TCE, and PCBs are at risk for developing permanent disabilities or diseases such as intelligence and behavioral impairments, endocrine disruptions, and cancer, the Indian Health Service, in particular, should be strongly encouraged to focus on preventing these exposures among AI/ANs, monitoring and educating AI/ANs whose health is at risk due to pollution and hazardous substance exposure, and providing equitable and fair medical treatment and long-term assistance to affected AI/ANs.

13. FCWG proposes EPA to recognize that contamination from past and ongoing mining activities are of particular concern for many AI/ANs. Abandoned mines are a concern for many tribes and Alaska Native villages. Abandoned uranium mines, for example, is a pressing issue in the four corners region and in Santa Fe.

Overarching Proposal

IV-2. Importantly, in order to facilitate tribes' efforts to address contaminated and depleted aquatic ecosystems, FCWG proposes EPA to make available additional financial and technical resources to tribes to conduct their own research, to manage (or co-manage) tribal and culturally-important natural resources whether on- or off-reservation, and to consult on environmental decisions that affect them but that are made at the federal and state levels.

Focused Proposals

IV-2

1. FCWG proposes EPA to promote the federal policy of tribal self-determination and self-sufficiency by building the environmental protection and environmental health capabilities of federally recognized tribes so that they can participate fully and effectively in the protection of the human health and environment of AI/AN communities. Equitable funding for tribal programs is critical.

2. FCWG proposes EPA to promote collaborative efforts to identify the various environmental exposures affecting each AI/AN community as an ongoing task, undertaken in consultation with federally recognized tribes. Specifically, data about the susceptibilities of AI/AN communities to various environmental agents is needed to help these communities understand and ameliorate some of their excess and disproportionate risk of exposure.

3. FCWG emphasizes EPA's obligation to consult with federally recognized tribes and involve members of AI/AN communities in designing, planning, and implementing specific environmental health research that reflects not only the traditional and cultural practices of such communities, but also their needs and concerns. FCWG proposes EPA to ensure that environmental health research data is reported back to tribal governments and AI/AN communities promptly and in an understandable manner.

4. Whenever possible and appropriate, FCWG proposes EPA to include state and local governments in collaborative efforts with tribes:

    a. to address human health and environmental justice issues within Indian country and Alaska Native villages. Because pollution does not respect jurisdictional boundaries, collaborative efforts in the human health and environmental justice arena similarly should eclipse political differences. Additionally, states must be swayed to incorporate environmental justice principles and goals into their laws, policies, and practices;

    b. to collect environmental and health data relevant to Indian country and Alaska Native villages. For example, state environmental protection agencies may have access to monitoring information on off-reservation facilities that may be causing or contributing to adverse health consequences in AI/AN communities, or the aquatic ecosystems used by these communities, located nearby, down-stream, and/or down-wind;

    c. to ensure that state and locally issues fish advisories that may affect tribal treaty fishers or tribal fish resources are communicated to tribal governments.

5. FCWG proposes EPA to be proactive in helping federally recognized tribes identify financial and technical resources throughout the federal government to address their environmental concerns and related health needs. By marshaling all available resources, federal agencies can promote "one-stop" shopping for tribal environmental and health-related programs and transcend traditional agency boundaries.

6. FCWG proposes EPA to consult with tribes on fashioning restoration approaches or remedies appropriate to the specific tribe that will address situations where tribal fisheries or treaty fishing resources have been decimated or impaired.

Overarching Proposals

IV-3. FCWG proposes EPA to respect and accommodate the particular cultural, traditional, spiritual, historical, economic, and legal contexts that characterize the various Alaska Native peoples, and to recognize the ways in which their circumstances may be different than those of American Indian tribes located within the contiguous forty-eight states.

Focused Proposals

III-3

1. Consistent with its Indian policy and the federal trust responsibility, FCWG proposes EPA to work with Alaska Native villages in developing effective and appropriate strategies to address the special circumstances that exist in Alaska and to protect the health of Alaska Natives from environmental threats, particularly those threats associated with their extensive subsistence activities.

2. Consistent with its policy of promoting tribal self-determination and self-sufficiency, FCWG proposes that EPA work with Alaska Native villages to address the hurdles particular to Alaska Natives' efforts to manage (or co-manage) and to access resources that are important for subsistence uses. For example, because the United States Supreme Court has held that only one Indian "reservation" -- the Annette Island Reserve -- exists in Alaska, and because the language of the Clean Water Act recognizes the power of tribes to establish water quality standards throughout their "reservations," Alaska Native villages are unable to assume regulatory authority or to participate in the same manner or to the same extent under the Act as tribes located in the lower forty-eight states. Accordingly, FCWG further proposes EPA to cooperate with the State of Alaska in developing such strategies including, but not limited to the adoption of appropriate designated uses for water bodies that are culturally significant and essential to Alaska Native villages. Similar impediments to the participation of Alaska Native villages may also exist under other federal environmental laws.

3. FCWG proposes EPA to work closely with Alaska Native villages and to assist them in accessing relevant research, data, and studies and in applying for and obtaining grants that support efforts to address the concerns of Alaska Native villages with respect to contaminated aquatic ecosystems and impacts on the health of Alaska Natives. FCWG commends EPA's recent support, together with a host of other state and tribal agencies and groups, for the Aleutian/Probilof Islands Association's research project, *Dietary Benefits and Risks in Alaskan Villages* and proposes EPA to continue to provide and enlarge financial and technical support for this and other initiatives.

4. Because the financial resources of Alaska Native villages are severely limited, FCWG proposes EPA to fund and/or facilitate local forums or to provide other effective means wherein rural Alaska Native villages and communities may express their concerns to EPA on environmental health and environmental justice issues; EPA should contact Alaska Native villages and community groups, and others currently working toward this goal (e.g., the Alaska Native Science Commission; the Manilaq Association; Alaska Community Action on Toxics) to identify appropriate opportunities. A number of Alaska Native village representatives traveled great distances to Seattle, Washington at great expense to participate in the public comment period held during FCWG's December 2001 meeting. This burden should be borne by EPA, not Alaska Native villages. Morever, to further its environmental justice efforts, EPA should strive to ensure that at least one Alaska Native village representative is appointed to participate as member of FCWG or its various subcommittees.

5. FCWG proposes that EPA, in collaboration with other federal agencies, ensure adequate priority funding and technical assistance for the design, construction, and operation of safe drinking water, sanitation, and wastewater facilities to protect Alaska Native communities whose health and aquatic ecosystems are imminently threatened by the absence or inadequacy of such facilities. Because only 40% of Alaska Native families have basic sanitation services such as piped drinking water and flush toilets, and more than half of these systems are rudimentary at best, this effort should be given priority.